Russia's Restless Frontier

RUSSIAN AND EURASIAN BOOKS FROM THE CARNEGIE ENDOWMENT FOR INTERNATIONAL PEACE

Between Dictatorship and Democracy: Russian Post-Communist Political Reform
Michael McFaul, Nikolai Petrov, and Andrei Ryabov

Putin's Russia
Lilia Shevtsova

Ambivalent Neighbors: The EU, NATO and the Price of Membership
Anatol Lieven and Dmitri Trenin, Editors

The End of Eurasia: Russia on the Border between Geopolitics and Globalization
Dmitri Trenin

Kazakhstan: Unfulfilled Promise
Martha Brill Olcott

Russia after the Fall
Andrew C. Kuchins, Editor

Gorbachev, Yeltsin, and Putin: Political Leadership in Russia's Transition
Archie Brown and Lilia Shevtsova, Editors

Belarus at the Crossroads
Sherman W. Garnett and Robert Legvold, Editors

Yeltsin's Russia: Myths and Reality
Lilia Shevtsova

To read excerpts and find more information on these and other publications, visit **www.ceip.org/pubs**.

Russia's Restless Frontier

The Chechnya Factor in Post-Soviet Russia

Dmitri V. Trenin
Aleksei V. Malashenko
with Anatol Lieven

CARNEGIE ENDOWMENT FOR INTERNATIONAL PEACE
Washington, D.C.

Carnegie Endowment for International Peace
1779 Massachusetts Avenue, N.W., Washington, D.C. 20036
202-483-7600, Fax 202-483-1840
www.ceip.org

To order, contact Carnegie's distributor:
The Brookings Institution Press
Department 029, Washington, D.C. 20042-0029, USA
1-800-275-1447 or 1-202-797-6258
Fax 202-797-2960, Email bibooks@brook.edu

Typesetting by Stephen McDougal
Printed by United Book Press
Typefaces: Optima and Palatino

This book, originally titled *The Time of the South: Russia in Chechnya, Chechnya in Russia,* was first published in Russian by the Carnegie Moscow Center.

Library of Congress Cataloging-in-Publication Data

Trenin, Dmitriæi.
    Russia's restless frontier : the Chechnya factor in post-Soviet Russia / Dmitri V. Trenin and Aleksei V. Malashenko ; with Anatol Lieven.
        p. cm.
    ISBN 0-87003-203-8 (pbk.) — ISBN 0-87003-204-6 (cloth)
    1. Chechnëiia (Russia)—History—Civil War, 1994- 2. Russia (Federation)—Relations—Russia (Federation)—Chechnëiia.
3. Chechnëiia (Russia)—Relations—Russia (Federation) 4. Russia (Federation)—Politics and government—1991- I. Malashenko, A. V. (Alekseæi Vsevolodovich) II. Lieven, Anatol. III. Title.
    DK511.C37T74 2003
    947.5'2—dc22   2003026021

---

10 09 08 07 06 05 04   5 4 3 2 1   1st Printing 2004

Contents

Foreword

The conflict in Chechnya, through periods of high and low intensity, has doggedly accompanied Russia's post-Soviet development. In the past decade, the Chechen conflict has been widely covered by the media in Russia and especially in the West. Most authors look primarily for its causes, try to explain its zigzag course, and condemn the brutalities and crimes associated with it. This book is different. While it provides the reader with some of the background of the conflict and is forthright in reporting the crimes committed and the human suffering, its focus lies far beyond the Caucasus battlefield.

Dmitri Trenin, who specializes in Moscow's foreign and security policy, and Aleksei Malashenko, Russia's top expert on Islam, examine the implications of the war in Chechnya in terms of Russia's post-Soviet evolution. Trenin and Malashenko are joined by Anatol Lieven, the author of the widely acclaimed *Chechnya: Tombstone of Russian Power*, who discusses the application of the laws of war to Chechnya and to similar conflicts. Thus, the scope of *Russia's Restless Frontier* is both wider and more important than Chechnya or the Chechen conflict alone.

Consider the following:

- Russia is home to 20 million Muslims who constitute about one-seventh of its population. This number is rising owing to the gap between the Muslim birthrate and that of the Slavs. Chechnya is just one of several national homelands (officially known as republics within the Russian Federation) where Muslims are in the majority.

- Avowedly atheist under Communist rule, Russia is now experiencing a religious revival. As Orthodox Christianity has moved toward an exclusive position as a quasi-state religion, Islam has experienced a complex process of revitalization. Although the war in the Caucasus is not a religious conflict, it certainly affects the emerging religiosity of both Orthodox and Muslim believers in Russia.
- In Russia, the process of creating a new citizenship-based nation is more complex than elsewhere. The end of the Soviet Union resulted in more than its constituent republics going their separate ways. A sense of community among the people, brought together by the imperial policies of the czars and subjected to rigorous unification under Stalin, also disintegrated. Many people have discovered, or rediscovered, their ethnic backgrounds, but no consolidated nations have emerged. The Chechen conflict both reflects and contributes to this harsh reality.
- Since the invasion of Afghanistan a quarter century ago, the Soviet army and later the Russian army have been fighting exclusively, and with few and brief interruptions, against a Muslim adversary that appears under different names: mujahideen, separatists, Islamists, Wahhabis. Historically, the armies have been psychologically and doctrinally configured to fight against an enemy in the West; in practice they have been deployed along Russia's southern flank.
- Putin's celebrated turn to the West, and in particular Russia's rapprochement with the United States after September 11, would probably have been delayed had it not been for the engagement in Chechnya (dubbed by Moscow back in 1999 as an anti-terrorist operation) and growing concerns over the Taliban and the stability of the weak states in Central Asia.

Why should non-Russians care about any of these issues? First and foremost is the potential for the conflict to spill over to other states. Chechnya borders on Georgia, a country undergoing a difficult state-building process. In the past, Russia has threatened to extend its anti-terrorist operation to Georgian territory. Should that happen, the United States, with its military instructors on the ground in Georgia, would face a difficult choice: whether to withdraw the instructors and acquiesce to Russia's viewpoint that Georgia is a terrorist state, or risk its relationship with the Russian Federation by opposing such an intervention.

Second, the continuing engagement in Chechnya erodes the already low morale of the Russian military still further, grossly distorts civil-military relations, and impedes the kind of fundamental restructuring that the Russian military sorely needs. Simply put, for the purposes of opposing Islamic terrorism, political extremism, and the proliferation of weapons of mass destruction, in Eurasia, the United States needs Russia as a security partner. Yet the Russian army that one sees in Chechnya today has virtually no potential to be a U.S. military partner or ally.

Third, the continuing conflict in Chechnya helps to consolidate the forces of political conservatism in Russia proper. It brings forward bureaucrats in uniform; it makes the media more deferential to the government; and it fosters social apathy. All this makes it more difficult for reformers to move Russia to become a modern European country and thus to anchor itself firmly within the international community.

This book was first issued in Russian by the Carnegie Moscow Center in 2002. It was a huge success. The U.S. edition represents a much re-worked and updated text that seeks to explain to Western readers the large stakes for the West, as well as for Russia, in the Chechen conflict.

JESSICA T. MATHEWS
President
Carnegie Endowment for International Peace

Acknowledgments

Russia's Restless Frontier has two principal authors and one contributor, but it owes its realization to a much wider group of people. The idea to write a text on the implications of Chechnya for Russia and its foreign relations was immediately supported by our colleague Robert Nurick, who as the director of the Carnegie Moscow Center (2000–2003) was one of the most thoughtful observers of the fast-changing Russian scene. We were also fortunate to enlist the support of Thomas Carothers, then the vice president of studies at the Carnegie Endowment for International Peace in Washington, D.C. We are especially thankful to Bob's and Tom's successors, Andrew Kuchins and George Perkovich, who took the trouble to read the English translation and made a number of highly valuable suggestions.

As we developed our project, we came to rely on the faithful professional support of Carmen MacDougall, Trish Reynolds, Phyllis Jask, and Natalia Kirpikova, who supervised the publication process in Washington and Moscow, respectively, as well as Carnegie's computer czars Michael O'Brien and Dmitri Basisty. Carnegie Moscow Center junior fellow Sergei Psurtsev provided editorial and other assistance throughout the project, which we greatly appreciate. Copyeditor Lorraine Alexson also provided her invaluable services. Last, but by no means least, we are thankful to our wives, who were not only willing to put up with our writing on evenings and weekends at home, but were fully convinced of the importance of the project we had embarked upon. Whether the result was worth this major effort, only the reader can tell. Needless to say, we bear sole responsibility for any errors and failings of the book.

1

Introduction

Many works have analyzed the Chechen war.[1] This book differs from most other treatments. Its main focus is not so much on the conflict itself, but rather on its wider ramifications. As a prominent Russian politician once despaired, "We've got Chechnya everywhere!" This remark clearly calls for an explanation. Ultimately, Chechnya remains the only example of armed rebellion and large-scale military action in the Russian Federation. However, lawlessness and a propensity to use force are commonplace across the country as a whole.

We proceed from an apparent paradox. Whereas the war is largely peripheral to Russia and is largely perceived that way (except after each new terrorist attack in Moscow), the conditions that have either been created or greatly amplified by Chechnya have spread all across Russia. Those conditions affect Russia's politics, its ethnic environment, the circumstances of its military, and the course and conduct of its foreign relations.

The first war in Chechnya (1994–1996) truly broke the back of Boris Yeltsin's presidency. The second one (1999 to the present) governed the Kremlin's choice of a successor to Yeltsin and provided a political springboard for Vladimir Putin. By the end of his first presidential term, however, the lingering conflict had become a liability that threatened to mar Putin's political legacy.

The conflict has also become a hard test for Russia's territorial integrity within its post-Soviet borders. The authority of the current Russian state was never so weak as in the years of Chechnya's de facto independence, which culminated in the rebels' invasion into Dagestan in the summer of 1999. To many observers, Russia, having ceased to be an

1

empire but not yet a working federation, was on its way to becoming a loose confederacy. Moscow was shifting from a center of power to a place for interregional bargaining.

The first phase of the Chechen war was fought under the slogan of ethnic separatism. That led to the emergence of a new and potentially even more serious challenge to Russia's security. Radical Islam began to spread across the North Caucasus, with links to extremist organizations bent on toppling post-Soviet regimes in Central Asia. Those extremists enjoyed support from the Afghan Taliban and Muslim groups throughout the Middle East. Since the late 1990s, Islamic extremism has developed in Russia parallel to, and often feeding on, the wider Islamic renaissance.

As a result of the war, hundreds of thousands of people (both Chechens *and* ethnic Russians) were internally displaced in Russia. As post-Soviet Russia was struggling to create a nation within its new borders, relations between its dominant but declining Slavic majority and its fast-growing Muslim population—often referred to as people of Caucasian extraction—became progressively tenser.

The conflict in Chechnya has made terrorism a fact of daily life in contemporary Russia. The border provinces in southern Russia between the Caspian and the Black seas have become a restless frontier. Ever since the apartment bombings of 1999, which killed three hundred people, Muscovites have been learning to live with a constant threat. This message of ultimate vulnerability was powerfully reinforced by the hostage crisis in a Moscow theater in 2002.

While the war isolated Russia politically and diplomatically from the West, the events of September 11 enabled Russia to use Chechnya as a stage for achieving rapprochement with the United States and the North Atlantic Treaty Organization (NATO). Without Chechnya, Moscow probably would not have joined the antiterrorist coalition. Yet the issue of Chechnya continues to block Europeans from perceiving Russia as "one of us."

Chechnya, as Anatol Lieven wrote after the first campaign, has become a tombstone of Russian power. That is a powerful symbol of the passing of imperial glory. The Soviet Union was, in a sense, a continuation of the czarist statehood tradition. Although the new Russian Federation has taken several important steps away from that tradition, it is still far from being a truly democratic federation. The problem of Chechnya lies between two models of Russian statehood, and, like a spanner thrown into a machine, it blocks a much-needed transitional phase. When and how Russia can make that transition largely depends on the principles and the timing of the settlement of the Chechen issue.

The conflict in Chechnya is often compared to the French war in Algeria. Algeria had also been an integral part of a metropolitan area rather than an outlying colony. Another oft-cited comparison is with Northern Ireland. Both analogies are seriously flawed. Algeria is separated from France by a wide stretch of water, whereas landlocked Chechnya sits in the center of the Russian North Caucasus. On the one hand, a simple "cut-'em-loose" solution is hardly a feasible option in the case of Chechnya. On the other hand, unlike Grozny, Belfast has never been a target of blanket air and artillery bombings, and the Irish have not been driven to refugee camps in, say, Ireland or Scotland.

The second campaign in Chechnya was waged under the rubric of a counterterrorist operation. After the terrorist attacks in the United States, the Chechen crisis has been increasingly considered in the context of a global antiterrorist campaign. Yet while terrorism is certainly present in the republic (it is sufficient to recall the names of Shamil Basayev and the late Salman Raduyev, men who rose to fame, or infamy, as hostage takers), it is not the dominating element in Chechnya. Rather, terrorism exists alongside separatism and ordinary banditry. Failing to distinguish terrorism from banditry leads to policy distortions and a loss of credibility.

The antiterrorist campaign forms new international alignments. After September 11, a global alliance has formed against terrorism that includes all the major powers, from the United States and the European Union to Russia, India, China, and Japan. This new international lineup, however, has not erased differences in national perspectives. The Russian government had hoped that Chechnya would be subsumed within the global antiterrorist effort. Those hopes have been only partially realized. Whereas criticism in the United States of the methods and behavior of the Russian federal forces has become muted, much of the European public has continued to press Moscow on Chechnya. A postmodern Europe that judges and condemns actions by a modern Russian state over the largely traditional social environment of the North Caucasus illustrates the difference in historical time zones in which countries continue to live, even in an increasingly globalized world.

This book's title refers to Russia's restless border and implies the authors' deep conviction that the most serious security challenges that Russia faces now and in the foreseeable future exist along its southern boundary. More than the smoldering conflict in Chechnya, many problems are in the North Caucasus as a whole, including the long-term development of other Muslim enclaves within the Russian Federation, such as in Tatarstan and Bashkortostan.

Moreover, the importance of Chechnya can be fully understood only in a wider context that there is a similar potential for conflict to develop in nearby oil- and gas-rich regions. Just south of the Russian Federation border, for example, Kazakhstan, with its Muslim-Slav population, is immensely important to Russia. Should relations between the two largest ethnic groups in that new nation deteriorate, Russia would likely be drawn into the gathering conflict. Although Kazakhstan is the only Central Asian country representing a vital interest for Russia, the situation there is immediately influenced by developments in Central Asia, particularly those portions of the Ferghana Valley that lie across the boundaries of Kyrgystan, Tajikistan, and Uzbekistan. The destruction of the Taliban regime in Afghanistan has won Central Asian rulers a reprieve, but it does not guarantee the longer-term stability of the region, for its problems are chiefly domestic. Kyrgyzstan, Turkmenistan, and Uzbekistan all remain essentially vulnerable and potentially unstable. Their territories are more often sources of danger rather than stability.

The choice of a strategy in Moscow's relations with its southern neighbors is critical, not solely in terms of national security and foreign policy. Its strategy will also help to shape the emerging post-Soviet Russian nation. An intelligent choice must be based on a critical assessment of Russia's historical relations with the Muslim world.

The legacy of the Russian Federation on its southern flank (or, strictly speaking, its southern and southeastern flank), is a controversial one. From the storming of Kazan in 1552 by the troops of Ivan the Terrible to the end of the nineteenth century (when the White General Skobelev won the final victory in Turkestan), the Turkic-speaking Muslim south has been steadily subjugated by the Orthodox Christian north. For four hundred years the Russian state expanded from the banks of the Volga and the Oka to the Crimea, the Caspian Sea, the Caucasus, and Turkestan. Entire Muslim khanates (such as Kazan, the Crimea, and Astrakhan) were abolished and replaced by Russian provinces or protectorates (such as Bukhara and Khiva), and local elites were absorbed into the imperial nobility. Still, the people of the annexed regions were neither exterminated nor driven away from their indigenous lands. In spite of sporadic attempts to convert some Muslim peoples to Christianity, religious tolerance by the state and by the general public was a dominating reality in czarist Russia.

During the Soviet period, Moscow's policy toward exporting communism changed repeatedly and drastically. Initially, Moscow encouraged a "class consciousness of the toiling masses of the East" in support of the Bolshevik revolution by assisting the national liberation movement in British India and the nationalist renaissance movements in Turkey, Iran, and Afghanistan. Later, beginning in the mid-1920s, Moscow emphasized a rigid unification of Russia's Muslim borderlands within the framework of the USSR, which resulted in the establishment of proto-state institutions in Soviet border republics. Finally, since the 1970s, it became routine for Moscow to subcontract the day-to-day administration of those republics to local clan-based elites, which were becoming increasingly influential as the power of Moscow waned. Then came the breakup of the Soviet Union.

Beyond Soviet borders, after World War II Muslim Arab countries became Moscow's important resource in its global confrontation with the West.[2] From the 1950s to the 1980s, when the Soviet Union was engaged in bitter competition with the United States for influence in the Arab world, the Caucasus and Central Asia served as both a showcase and logistic springboard for Soviet policy in the region. The main objective of that policy was to turn radical Arab regimes into staunch allies in a confrontation with "world imperialism and its agent in the Middle East, Zionism." That approach is still alive in some parts of the Russian establishment and informs the doctrine of the multipolar world that came into fashion in the mid-1990s.

Stalin's failed attempt to turn Israel into a tool for fighting British colonialism caused Moscow to shift its attention to Israel's defeated Arab neighbors, who were looking for revenge. In 1954 Soviet arms began to flow to the Arab world (initially to Nasser's Egypt). The Suez crisis of 1956 established Moscow as a military ally and political protector of radical Arab regimes. Before the 1990–1991 Gulf War, Moscow had developed close relations with what it called *countries of socialist orientation*, which for much of the period included Algeria, Egypt, Iraq, Libya, Syria, and Yemen.

At the same time, the Soviet Union experienced intense hostility from conservative or pro-Western governments, including NATO member Turkey and U.S. allies Israel, Iran (under the shah), and Pakistan. Saudi Arabia and most of the oil-rich Gulf States did not even have diplomatic relations with the USSR. Even though the Baghdad Pact, and later the Central Treaty Organization (CENTO), never solidified into permanent structures like NATO, the battle lines between the West and the East were clearly drawn in the region to Russia's south. Afghanistan remained the one traditionally neutral area in the entire region.

For the first time since the feudal anti-Soviet opposition (*basmachi*) was defeated in Turkestan, the 1978 Islamic revolution in Iran caused Moscow to pay serious attention to the social and political processes and to the ethnic and religious situations in the Muslim republics of the Soviet Union. Unfortunately, Moscow's analysis was shallow and its conclusions arrogant. To many in the Communist Party Central Committee, it seemed the Soviet Union had gone on a counteroffensive, first by supporting the radical leftist coup in Afghanistan (1978) and then by sending in troops "to defend the revolution" (1979). Although the coup surprised the Soviet leadership and the subsequent invasion of a neighbor was largely a forced step, a rigid communist ideology interpreted the developments in Afghanistan as evidence that the "world revolutionary process" was becoming "broader and deeper." Afghanistan's joining "countries of socialist orientation" contrasted sharply with the fall of the pro-American regime in neighboring Iran—and America's public humiliation during the 444-day-long crisis when U.S. diplomats in Tehran were held hostage by Islamic revolutionaries.

During the Soviet Union's war in Afghanistan, the superpower rivalry was superimposed on a confrontation between two trends within the Muslim world itself: one moderate (traditional and promodern) and one radical (nationalistic and fundamentalist). The United States, guided by the logic of global confrontation and drawing support from the moderate trend, sometimes found it necessary to enter into tactical alliances with fundamentalists in order to contain the spread of Soviet influence. In turn, the Soviet Union, which supported nationalists in their struggle against moderate pro-Western regimes, was becoming an enemy of religious radicals who saw communists above all as militant atheists. In the final days of the Cold War, however, the more farsighted politicians began to realize that Muslim radicalism (fundamentalism) threatened the long-term interests of both Moscow and Washington.

Ironically, the last attempt to support (a genuinely spontaneous) radical leftist coup in a Muslim country—and thus expand Moscow's security zone even farther toward the Persian Gulf—turned out to be the first step in the disintegration of the global Soviet system of alliances and, ultimately, of the Soviet Union itself. Although the Soviets did not suffer a military defeat in Afghanistan, strictly speaking, it took Moscow too long to realize it had driven itself into a deadly trap, and more time and pain than Moscow had were needed to break free from that trap. When it started a pullout in 1988, it was already too late. The Soviet withdrawal from Afghanistan intensified a fundamental change that was already under way. Developments in Eastern Europe and inside the USSR itself unfolded at a breathtaking pace. The Berlin Wall fell within a year, and the Soviet Union ceased to exist only thirty-three months after its undefeated army had finally made a safe comeback from across the Oxus (Amudarya) River.

The war in Afghanistan brought about a deep crisis in Moscow's Middle Eastern policy. Having failed to suppress militarily the armed opposition supported from abroad, the Soviet Union was forced to withdraw from Afghanistan in 1989. The political and military defeat of the Soviet Union, which had failed to protect a client regime in a neighboring country for the first time since 1945, accelerated the erosion and, ultimately, the disintegration of the Soviet presence in the region from Damascus to Aden. The so-called Afghan syndrome—the fear of engaging in a new military conflict with a Muslim enemy—appeared and affected both the ruling elite and society as a whole. That fear had implications for the Soviet Central Asian republics, where ideas of an Islamic renaissance and Muslim solidarity started to spread.

Russia's new leadership viewed the disintegration of the Soviet Union, which soon followed the Soviet war in Afghanistan, as the shedding of an imperial burden and particularly of "the Asian ballast." The process, however, resulted in armed conflicts and in the fragmentation of the former Soviet south. Former Soviet troops, which were already under jurisdiction of the new Russian Federation, became involved in those conflicts. In the early 1990s, the Afghan syndrome demanded that Russia continue its geopolitical retreat northward. At that time, the Kremlin and the Russian Foreign Ministry had a simplistic approach to addressing southern-flank security issues: "Get out of the hot spots." The pro-Moscow Najibullah regime, which held power in Kabul for three years after the Soviet troops were withdrawn, fell after the Russian leadership finally denied it all financial and technical support.

The post-Soviet leadership in Moscow took it easy after it relinquished the Baltic States and withdrew from Transcaucasian and Central Asian republics. Fundamentally important is that by the late 1990s the Russian leadership, elites, and general public were finally reconciled to Ukraine's independence and to Kiev's sovereignty over the Crimea. The significance of that reconciliation as a factor in European security can hardly be underestimated. Equally important is that despite Moscow's official policy of integration with Belarus, the Russian leadership has not been at all enthusiastic about further expansion. While deciding the issue of a state merger, Moscow was careful to look first at the cost and the other practical implications of taking over Belarus. Simple expansion is out of fashion and would represent a historic change in Russia's political stance.

Against this background of a remarkable transition from being a great power to a more "normal" international actor, Russia's policies in its southern provinces stand out as highly traditional. The retreat to the north was never completed, partly for so-called objective reasons, due to logistical problems and financial constraints and partly because of the stubborn resistance of the Russian military, which saw further retrenchment as a threat to national security. Until the first campaign in Chechnya, the Ministry of Defense in Moscow was effectively the only agency ensuring the Russian presence in the southern republics of the former Soviet Union. Embassies were still being created, and the Foreign Ministry was on a desperate search for experts and volunteers. More important, military commanders from the Ministry of Defense and General Staff in Moscow, all the way down to local unit commanders, had effectively become autonomous, if not totally independent, makers of the Russian policy regarding the southern flank.

By the spring of 1992, when the Najibullah regime was overthrown and Kabul fell to the mujahideen, civil war in neighboring Tajikistan had already started and Soviet-Russian troops stationed in the republic had become involved. In the fall of 1992, Moscow made a policy decision to support one of the warring Tajik clans over the others. The resulting suppression of local Islamists by the Russian army started the "Tajik" round of Russia's involvement in Central Asian conflicts.

Meanwhile, inside the Russian Federation itself, the situation grew progressively tenser. In 1991–1992 the standoff between the central government in Moscow and the nationalist government of the Tatarstan republic stopped short of evolving into a full-blown armed conflict in the very center of the country. The balanced and moderate position of the Tatar president, Mintimer Shaymiev, and the federal government's restraint made it possible for the two sides to reach a compromise that gave a serious boost to upgrading the Muslim republics' formal and actual status within the Russian Federation. Tatarstan and neighboring Bashkortostan adopted constitutions proclaiming their sovereignty and entered into special agreements with Moscow. Thus, the very real threat of Russia following the Soviet Union along a path of disintegration was removed, but it was at the price of tolerating confederate elements within the federation.

Moscow, of course, had to deal with the consequences of the breakup of the Soviet Union, but those consequences were largely confined to such peripheral areas as the Caucasus. While the Soviet government, trying to exploit the growing regional tensions in a last-ditch attempt to salvage the Union, had counted on Azerbaijan's conservative leadership to be its main ally in the region, the new Russian authorities, concerned about Turkey's growing influence, placed their bets on Armenia and, covertly, on Armenians in Karabakh. When an armed conflict broke out between Georgia and its separatist province Abkhazia in August 1992, influential Russian political and especially military circles supported the Abkhazians. That fateful choice had important long-term implications. Not only did the Russian government indirectly facilitate a victory of separatist ideas on the Russian Federation's southern border, but it also turned a blind eye to the military and political mobilization of extremist forces in the North Caucasus and their infiltration across the Caucasus's porous borders. It was in Abkhazia that Chechen guerilla leader Shamil Basayev and his fighters first engaged in combat.

From mid-1992, the Russian government had abandoned its policy of retreating northward and tried to consolidate the former Soviet military and political activities under the rubric peacemaking. By then, the products of Soviet and Yugoslav disintegration had already formed an arc of instability from the Adriatic Sea to the Pamir Mountains. Moscow's immediate aim became to ensure a ceasefire across the post-Soviet territories under the Russian army's control. In early 1993, President Boris Yeltsin and Foreign Minister Andrei Kozyrev claimed Russia's special role as the ultimate guarantor of stability within the former Soviet Union's borders. In the same year, peacekeeping forces from the twelve nations comprising the Commonwealth of Independent States (CIS) were deployed in Tajikistan and, in 1994, in Abkhazia. In the summer of 1992 Russian troops marched into the Georgia–South Ossetia conflict area. While doing so, Russia still enjoyed the authority of a country that had managed to avoid armed conflict within her sovereign territory.[3] Georgia joining the CIS in late 1993, a move that had been forced under conditions of civil war and by strong pressure from Moscow, and the simultaneous improvement in Russia-Azeri ties following a coup in Baku in mid-1993, apparently confirmed the efficacy of Moscow's new proactive approach.

Since 1993, the oil factor has contributed significantly to Moscow's increased interest in the Caspian region. Competition with Western (chiefly U.S. and British) oil companies and Turkey for the right to produce and transport Caspian oil became so acute that a ghost of the "Great Game"—the confrontation between the Russian and British empires, between St. Petersburg and London, in the nineteenth century—was almost visible. The clash of ideologies was being replaced by a clash of interests. Moreover, many believed that the new conflict was more fundamental and longer lasting than the opposition between communism and the Free World had been. It seemed that the traditional geopolitics of the nineteenth century had finally triumphed.

In that context, many Russian traditionalists, who liked to call themselves Eurasianists, agreed with Zbigniew Brzezinski, who called the power vacuum the main characteristic of the Caspian region.[4] To be sure, they offered different conclusions. General Andrei Nikolayev, the first director of the Border Service and from 2000–2003 the chair of the Duma Defense Committee, warned that "in the conditions of instability, chaos, and a lack of elementary order," the countries of the region were being "drawn into internal strife and a fight against terrorism" and thus "became vulnerable to external pressures. External forces whose desire is to use an extremely complicated internal situation for their own benefit would always exist."[5] It goes without saying that Brzezinski and his fellow thinkers in Russia had fundamental differences when it came to the qualitative characteristics of "external forces."

In real life, though, the image of the Great Game had little in common with the realities of the twenty-first century. Instead of the sophisticated game that the great powers had played on the regional chessboard, Russia faced a totally different challenge. The problem now was not which of the competing powers would fill the power vacuum and thus win a coveted prize, it was the vacuum's very existence and the fact that it could not simply be filled from without—at least by the traditional means—which created a permanent instability threat. Nation building, rather than old-fashioned imperialism, had to be the answer. Moscow had first faced that challenge even before the Soviet Union broke up, but the Russian leadership failed to understand it and thus chose to ignore it.

Initially, Moscow paid little attention to the international implications of Chechnya's unilateral declaration of independence, made on September 6, 1991. On that very day, the newly created State Council of the crumbling Soviet Union (in fact, the council was its funeral-organizing committee) recognized the independence of the Baltic States. Future relations between Russia and Ukraine topped Moscow's political agenda at the time. After the Russian leadership's half-hearted and failed attempt to suppress the "Dudayev mutiny" in October 1991, Yeltsin's Moscow realized it was helpless in the matter. The good news, however, seemed to be that Chechnya would be a marginal issue. Such thinking allowed the Russian government to recognize de facto Chechen independence. In the spring of 1992, Moscow not only withdrew regular army units from Chechnya, but also transferred to General Johar Dudayev large amounts of military hardware, including tanks, artillery, and aircraft, stationed in the republic. Thus, in terms of sharing the Soviet Union's military legacy, Moscow proved to be much more accommodating in its relations with Grozny than it was with Kiev, Tbilisi, or Baku.

Moreover, Moscow consciously but not altruistically turned a blind eye to the state's becoming an unrecognized internal offshore zone, a channel for large-scale contraband and other illegal economic and financial transactions. Chechnya's, and thus Russia's, borders were open and under neither's control, in either direction. The well-known meter-long private international border (in reality, comprising the whole Grozny airport, which had become an international gateway that the federal authorities could not control) generated huge profits to Chechen leaders and their business partners in Moscow. In general terms, the existence of a de facto independent Chechnya between 1992 and 1994 became tangible evidence of the Russian government's political impotence both at home and abroad. Owing equally to the government's weakness and its corruptibility, Russia failed to respond to the Chechen challenge, thus sending a clear message to neighboring countries and beyond that a power vacuum existed inside Russia from the Caucasus to the Kremlin.

In Central Asia, Russia acted more decisively. During the 1992 civil war in Tajikistan, Russian troops engaged in combating Islamic fighters for the first time on territory that had once been part of the Soviet Union. Soon Islamists were driven from Tajikistan to neighboring Afghanistan, where local military and political groups gave them shelter and support. To prevent the Islamists from re-infiltrating Tajikistan, Russian troops set up a cordon sanitaire along the Pyandzh River. At the same time, lacking long-term objectives or clear-cut guidelines, the Russian policy vis-à-vis Tajikistan succumbed to the interests of the Dushanbe regime (that is, the Kulyab clan led by the Russian army-installed Emomali Rakhmonov).

Even though too little distinction is often made among the countries of the post-Soviet Commonwealth of Independent States, the member countries in the Caucasus and Central Asia stand in stark contrast to Belarus, Moldova, and Ukraine. The collapse of the Soviet Union has led to the emergence of six new Muslim states: Azerbaijan, Kazakhstan, Kyrgyzstan, Tajikistan, Turkmenistan, and Uzbekistan. All are secular, but none is stable. Demographic dynamics have changed the population ratio, to the detriment of Russia's Slavic populations. Today, the 60 million people of the six new states are still dwarfed by Russia's 145 million. Yet, even as Russia's population shrinks, most of its southern neighbors are growing.

Inside the Russian Federation itself ethnic elites in the Muslim republics of the Volga and North Caucasus regions felt resurgent self-awareness as the USSR dissolved. Tatarstan and Bashkortostan declared their sovereignty (although carefully stopping short of outright independence), effectively claiming a confederate status vis-à-vis the rest of Russia. While these claims were downplayed later, they have never been truly forgotten. More important, the power systems in both enclaves largely serve the interests of local Muslim clans.

The Islamic renaissance that has been under way in Russia since the late 1980s has inevitably politicized Islam and spawned nationwide and regional Islamic parties and movements. These parties and movements have become (formally or otherwise) legitimate players in the political process. They are not only instruments of communication among various Muslim enclaves, they also coordinate Islamic activities inside what may be termed the Russian segment of the global Muslim world and are therefore conduits of the interests of Muslim communities.

The Islamic factor influences both Russia's domestic situation in Russia's and Moscow's foreign policy. This trend was amplified by an upsurge of radical Islam at the end of the twentieth century. Chechnya is its prime example but it is not exceptional. In Central Asia, the Caucasus, Afghanistan, the Greater Middle East, and elsewhere across the Umma, conflicts are gestating in which Islam is the prime factor in motivating massive ethnic and social forces.

In their turn, such conflicts affect the policies pursued by neighboring states, including Russia. Over a period of about twenty-five years (at truly short intervals), Soviet, and later Russian, troops have been fighting Islamic forces in Afghanistan (1979–1989), Tajikistan (1992–1993), Chechnya (1994–1996), Dagestan (1999), and Chechnya once again (since 1999). The U.S.-led international coalition against terrorism, of which Russia became a proud member in the fall of 2001, has been targeting terrorists and radicals from the Islamic world. American troops operate inside Afghanistan and in the frontier provinces of Pakistan; U.S. military advisers are training government forces in Georgia and the Philippines to fight local Islamic terrorists; and Iraq has become the target of America's largest military campaign in decades. Even leaving aside Iran, Palestine, Kashmir, and Xinjiang, it has become clear that those who must deal with Islamic separatists, extremists, and terrorists must emphasize, even as they continue to fight, the nonmilitary dimension of their policies in order to prevent isolated conflicts from developing into a clash of civilizations.

Over the years, the seemingly endless war in Chechnya has become an emblem of post-Soviet Russia. Indeed, the Chechen problem came to the fore in the heady months between the August putsch and the formal dissolution of the Soviet Union in December 1991. Former Soviet general Dudayev unilaterally declared Chechnya's unilateral declaration of independence (UDI) in November 1991, with himself as its first president. Yet over the following three years Chechnya remained on the periphery of Russia's political developments. Powerful vested interests in Moscow were using Grozny's UDI for self-enrichment. The first Chechen war, begun in December 1994, initially seemed an absurdity, with military commanders negotiating passage along with local women and old men. This image was abruptly replaced by horror as hundreds of Russian troops were killed in a brutal battle in the streets of Grozny on New Year's Eve 1995. Despite all the horrors of war and war victims' sufferings, however, for many in the Russian capital and beyond, the war in Chechnya remained a distant and unrelated development—at best, a never-ending and gruesome soap opera. It might as well have been waged on the moon. After the Khasavyurt peace accords (1996), which left Chechnya in the hands of Dudayev's successors, many Russians preferred to forget about Chechnya altogether.

Yet the three years of Chechnya's de facto independence brought no peace to Chechnya, the North Caucasus, or Russia as a whole. The Russian government neglected developments in the enclave. The Federal Security Service (ultimately the successor to the KGB) sought to prevent the separatists from consolidating their power, while the military yearned for a rematch. On the other hand, Chechen president Aslan Maskhadov could not establish control over the republic. These trends indicated the trouble to come. The virtually lawless enclave soon became a safe haven for Islamic extremists and terrorists, who often had international connections. A single major provocation was all that was needed to re-ignite the war. In August 1999, forces from Chechnya invaded the Russian republic of Dagestan. The war, on hold for three years, restarted.

At almost exactly the same time, Islamists based in Afghanistan made a far-reaching raid into Central Asia. Both sectors of Russia's southern flank were simultaneously ablaze. Central Asia was back on Moscow's radar screen for the first time since the civil war in Tajikistan, which had reached its peak in 1992. The threat had manifested itself and had to be confronted with force.

As Russia moves into the twenty-first century, it continues to have the Chechnya problem in tow. President Putin denies there is a war. Yet although combat has indeed subsided, bombings, sabotage, and terrorist attacks have not stopped. Rather, these attacks have reached new levels of daring and intensity. As a result, the human toll continues to mount. The conscript army and the practice of sending police officers across the country for tours of duty in Chechnya ensure that the war is anything but an isolated element of the Russian situation. Chechnya has entered Russia.

2

A Chronicle of an Unfinished Conflict

> While a tremendously important role belonged to purely subjective and accidental factors, several in-depth factors made the particular development of the conflict highly probable, if not inevitable.[1]
>
> —*Dmitri Furman, Russian political analyst*

The society and mentality of Chechnya are traditionally based on egalitarianism and the priority of personal freedom. As a result, it was commonly believed the Chechens did not, and indeed, could not, create a sustainable political hierarchy that other peoples, including Chechnya's neighbors, have developed to varying extents. Lacking a structured society, Chechens could not reach a consensus as a people, which made it difficult for them to maintain a dialogue with external actors, including Russia. In the nineteenth century, for example, the fragmented nature of Chechen society prevented a reconciliation with Russia after the Caucasian war. Simply put, there was no one who could speak on behalf of most, let alone all, Chechens.

This same characteristic, however, generated the Chechens' bitter resistance to Russian expansion. By the 1930s, Chechen resistance had not yielded any positive results, but they refused to accept defeat. Thus many Chechens (though not the majority) rebelled against Soviet rule in 1942 when the German Wehrmacht pushed toward the Baku oil fields. The collaborators sincerely believed that siding with the Germans would be merely a continuation of the nineteenth-century struggle for independence, which also had foreign backers. Once the Germans had been repelled, Stalin struck back by deporting the entire Chechen population in February 1944 to Kazakhstan and Central Asia.

This mass deportation became a political time bomb. It prevented the Chechens from forming a consolidated, self-confident Soviet elite that could have peacefully resolved the situation when the Soviet Union started to fall apart. Suffice it to compare Chechnya's case to that of Tatarstan, another Muslim republic, which in 1991 declared its sovereignty. Where Mintime Shaymiev, the president of Tatarstan, was able to cut a deal with Moscow, Dudayev failed.

Chechens are the largest ethnic group in the North Caucasus. The total Chechen population, including those living outside Chechnya, is approximately one million. Moreover, as a result of the Ingush forming their own republic in 1991 (previously, they had been paired with the Chechens in a biethnic union), as well as the exodus of Russians and other ethnic groups, Chechnya was becoming increasingly mono-ethnic. This mono-ethnicity made it exceptional in the North Caucasus and promoted Chechen consolidation in its conflict with Moscow.

The Chechen conflict, which is considered a war, is really a tangle of shady deals and clandestine contacts. What seem to be inexplicable or illogical actions by the nominal antagonists are rooted in selfish individual and group interests and have little, if anything, to do with the interests of either Chechnya or Russia. Throughout the conflict, players on both sides and at different levels have been fighting to gain control over the flow of Chechen oil and money. Many experts have therefore long referred to the Chechen conflict as a commercial war.

The key to understanding why the conflict—and the massive loss of human lives it brought—could not be averted, is to be aware of the players' lack of military and political professionalism. Both parties to the conflict have often sought to compensate for that lack with cruelty. Chechnya's one-time official representative in Moscow, Mayrbek Vachagayev, noted that Chechen problems were being dealt with in Moscow "by cooks and tractor drivers."[2] Similarly, Chechen representatives were often individuals incapable of rational judgment and who lacked a sense of responsibility for the fate of their own people, being those same "tractor drivers" Vachagayev had cited. (Ironically, one of Chechnya's cruelest gang leaders was called *Traktorist*, or tractor driver.)

The Crisis Ripens, 1990–1994

The situation in Chechnya began to deteriorate in November 1990, when the self-proclaimed Chechen National Congress (CNC) set up an independent Chechen state. In the following months, the CNC emerged as an influential political player, despite the refusal of both Moscow and local authorities in Grozny to recognize its legitimacy. In June 1991, the CNC became the National Congress of the Chechen People (NCCP). Its leader, a recently retired Soviet air force general, Johar Dudayev, proclaimed the founding of the independent Chechen Republic.

The developments in Chechnya must be seen as part of the broader process of the Soviet Union's disintegration. On June 12, 1990, the official Supreme Soviet of the Russian republic adopted the Declaration of State Sovereignty of the Russian Federation. Exactly one year later Boris Yeltsin was elected the president of Russia by popular vote. The Moscow elite split. Some switched to Yeltsin and the democrats; others continued to support Mikhail Gorbachev and the USSR. For a brief historical moment, Moscow was the seat of two presidents, each insisting on supremacy. Collision between the two camps appeared inevitable. As the elite was fully engaged in a high-intensity internal strife, a declaration of independence by a tiny exotic republic somewhere in the North Caucasus was barely noticed.

During the August 1991 coup attempt in Moscow, the NCCP, led by Dudayev, supported Yeltsin, while the official authorities in Grozny sided with the putschists. Once the coup had been foiled, Dudayev's supporters launched a vigorous campaign against the local apparatchiks. It came as a surprise to the NCCP, then, that the victorious Yeltsinites continued, ungratefully, to treat the NCCP with suspicion, regarding it as a stronghold of separatism. The Russian parliament refused to recognize the congress and supported instead a body composed mainly of old-guard *nomenklatura*. The following day, October 9, the Chechen congress described this lack of support a provocation "fraught with unpredictable consequences and fratricidal bloodshed." In a violent coup labeled a national revolution, Dudayev and his supporters took power in Grozny. Chechnya's independence was reaffirmed.[3] Moscow responded by introducing a state of emergency across Chechnya effective November 9, 1991. This was a hollow threat because at that very moment the political struggle in Moscow had entered its final stage.

The escalation continued. As Chechnya's first president, Dudayev issued his famous Decree no. 2 in November 1991, in which he called on "all Moscow-based Muslims to turn the city into a disaster area."[4] Preparations were made for an open-armed confrontation with the central government. In particular, Dudayev decreed Chechen citizens had the right to own firearms. In December 1991, the Soviet Union ceased to exist, with Yeltsin succeeding Gorbachev in the Kremlin. Still, Chechnya's confrontation with Moscow gained momentum. February 1992 saw the first armed assaults against Russian military garrisons in Chechnya. The aim of the attackers was to take over military arsenals. Armed struggle in Chechnya became a reality.[5]

Throughout 1992, Dudayev tried hard to normalize life in Chechnya and thus prove his own legitimacy.[6] The principal concern of the Russian government was that the Russian Federation might follow the path of the Soviet Union and disintegrate. To arrest that trend, the federation tried reaching accommodations with regional elites, beginning in Tatarstan. In that context there was nothing particularly special about Chechnya—except the fiery Caucasian temperament. After all, the independence clause in the March 1992 constitution described the Chechen Republic of Ichkeria as "an independent sovereign state" was almost identical to the corresponding clause of the Tatarstan constitution adopted that same year, pronouncing it "a sovereign democratic state."[7]

Yet the Kremlin's attitude to Dudayev as an individual and to his followers remained extremely negative. In November 1992, Vice Premier Sergei Shakhrai, responsible for interethnic and interregional relations, ordered Russian troops on Chechnya's administrative border to go on red alert. The formal pretext for the order was the eruption of ethnic violence between the Ossetians and the Ingush, which represented Russia's first ethnic conflict within its new borders. Still, the Chechens saw this military deployment as directed against them.

For its part, Moscow was fairly relaxed about the possible implications of its tough stance toward the Chechen separatists. A protracted war was not on anyone's mind. Moscow politicians were generally amazed by the actions of the rebels and hoped that Dudayev would finally come to his senses and realize that claims of independence simply had no future. They believed that Chechen separatism was "an infantile disease" of the transition period that would pass as soon as the generic problems of the country's federal system were addressed. No tailor-made solution to the Chechen situation was proposed or believed necessary. The Chechens themselves seemed to have held only vague ideas about building an independent state. Meanwhile, people on both sides were scrambling for economic opportunities offered by the strange situation in Chechnya.

Entrepreneurial individuals, whether in Moscow or in Chechnya, with equally little respect for law, enriched themselves with gusto. Huge fortunes were made virtually overnight. The permanently mudded environment provided an atmosphere in which criminal business could thrive with impunity. One of the most celebrated cases was the Chechen Aviso Scam, the illegal cashing of promissory notes by Chechens. As the authors of the analytical bulletin *Chechen Crisis* delicately put it, the worsening of the situation in and around Chechnya was "provoked by the improper policy of the Russian government toward minority ethnic groups, the prevalence of opportunism over strategic vision, the existence of the considerable personal interests of the participants in the conflict, and a lack of readiness to negotiate."[8] Indeed, any one of these explanations would have sufficed to send Chechen-Russian relations into a risky spiral.

The Kremlin's policy vis-à-vis Dudayev remained one of the carrot and stick. The carrot was proposed talks with the separatists. The stick was rendering support to the anti-Dudayev opposition, which was a diverse group of former Soviet apparatchiks, federation loyalists, and anyone whose vision of independence differed from Dudayev's. That opposition was in a constant state of flux. The new post-Soviet generation of Chechen politicians was supremely ambitious and egocentric. They soon realized that power was a way to get not only glory but also personal wealth. For these people, Dudayev was an irritant. In addition, the Chechen political culture resists in principle granting a monopoly of power to any single individual. Dudayev's authoritarian, if not dictatorial, style was therefore particularly at odds with this tradition of Chechen society.

After the opposition had entered into politics (the first attempted coup against Dudayev took place on March 1, 1992), the Chechen conflict acquired an internal dimension in addition to the external one. Sporadic internal clashes threatened to turn into a full-blown civil war and rendered the situation in Chechnya increasingly precarious. The year 1993 confirmed that Chechen society was divided on many issues, including that of independence. The opposition demanded a referendum on independence, accusing Dudayev of having usurped power and of violating the Chechen constitution. In mid-April 1993, the opposition commenced ongoing street rallies in Grozny, and in May Chechnya's Constitutional Court ruled Dudayev's actions were illegal and even criminal. Dudayev's henchmen retaliated by storming the Grozny mayor's office and declaring the Constitutional Court dissolved.

Another failed attempt to unseat Dudayev took place in October 1993, nearly coinciding with another attempted coup in Moscow by the Supreme Soviet against President Yeltsin. For that reason, Moscow remained somewhat passive about the attempts against Dudayev. The repeated failures of the anti-Dudayev forces must have convinced the Kremlin that the conflict could not be resolved if Moscow continued to rely on internal opposition alone. With the situation at a stalemate, Russian policy makers started looking for military solutions to eradicate separatism. After the adoption in December 1993 of a new Russian constitution that confirmed Russia's sovereignty over Chechnya, Moscow established a provisional council of the Chechen Republic, to be headed by Umar Avturkhanov, one of Dudayev's most consistent opponents. At the same time, Chechnya's boundaries with neighboring Russian regions were declared closed.

In January 1994, the Kremlin decided to use diplomacy, forming a special delegation. Political talks at various levels continued for more than six months yet proved inconclusive.

By the summer of 1994, hard-line tactics returned. Dudayev's opponents, who had never had faith in a negotiated solution, felt considerably strengthened. They also controlled the republic's northern regions. Avturkhanov, Yusuf Soslambekov (the former head of Chechnya's dissolved Supreme Soviet), and Bislan Gantamirov (the ex-mayor of Grozny) joined forces to wrestle the Chechen capital from Dudayev's hands. The opposition was, in fact, acting on orders from a faction in the Russian government favoring strong-arm methods in dealing with Chechen separatism. From then on, Chechnya was plunged into a civil war.

Interestingly but typically, participants in this intra-Chechen struggle for power and for the right to represent all of Chechen society tried hard to follow local traditions. Thus, a disagreement would sometimes arise over which side should open fire first because the one who spills blood first "loses support and prestige."[9] Blood vengeance was also a problem, and close relations often found themselves pitted against one another in a fight. People who participated in the fighting insist that the clashes between Chechens were rarely fierce, with only a few exceptions. Others, however, believe that the developments in Chechnya served to restore a culture of violence that was deemed traditional for the Caucasian people.

The absence of a single central government in Chechnya also resulted in an upsurge of crime. Bandits, both those associated with political rivals and independent outlaws, terrorized the local population, Chechens and Russians alike. The Russians were in an especially vulnerable situation: on the one hand, they did not enjoy clan support; on the other, many people identified them with the hostile central government in Moscow. *Abrechestvo*, a kind of "legitimized banditry"[10] and considerably different from traditional criminal violence, returned and proliferated as the conflict intensified between Moscow and Chechnya.

The First Campaign in Chechnya, 1994–1996

On November 26, 1994, the Chechen opposition supported by the Russian security service (the Federal Counterintelligence Service, then known as FSK, now as FSB) and led by Russian army officers whom the FSK had covertly recruited for the job, attempted to capture Grozny. Poorly prepared and disastrously executed, this was Yeltsin's equivalent of the Bay of Pigs invasion, and its failure presented the Kremlin with a difficult choice between an ignominious retreat and a decisive military intervention by Russian federal forces. On November 29, the Russian air force bombed Grozny for the first time. On December 11, the ground troops marched in, with a mission to "restore constitutional order" in the wayward republic.

Was there a chance for a compromise between Moscow and Dudayev? Was it possible to convince the Chechen general to drop the idea of independence by offering him and his entourage special "sovereign" status for the republic (something like Tatarstan but more,) within the Russian Federation? One thing is clear: radically changing Chechnya's status by recognizing its independence and inviting it to join the CIS at that time would have created a dangerous precedent for the other regions of the Russian Federation.

According to a controversial Russian politician, Alexei Mitrofanov, a longtime lieutenant of nationalist Vladimir Zhirinovsky, the fate of Chechen independence was doomed in mid-1994 when a top Russian government bureaucracy, closely connected with emerging business interests, decided to prevent the financially highly successful Chechens from buying up lucrative assets in the large-scale national privatization campaign, which was just about to start.

Although an opportunity for a compromise might have existed in the plan, the opportunity was missed owing to an important human factor: Boris Yeltsin pointedly refused to meet with Dudayev, who had insisted their meeting be one of equals. Both members of Dudayev's entourage and Moscow-based analysts believe that had such a meeting occurred (in theory, it could have happened right up to the storming of Grozny by federal forces in January 1995), there could have been a mutually satisfactory solution and the struggle for sovereignty might not have degenerated into a war.

The storming of Grozny by Russian troops on New Year's Eve 1995 was the real starting point of the first Chechen campaign, which continued until August 1996. Military operations in Chechnya were accompanied by repeated calls from Moscow for a dialogue as well as a proposal for a unilateral cease fire conditional on Dudayev's relinquishing Chechen independence. From that point, however, the Chechen leader was no longer in a position to accept the proposal. He could only fight until the bitter end. As for Yeltsin, he had even less interest in talking to Dudayev. At his May 9, 1995, meeting with German chancellor Helmut Kohl to mark the fiftieth anniversary of victory in World War II, Yeltsin said that "the classic military campaign was over in Chechnya." That statement became the first in a long series of Kremlin declarations that the military stage of the conflict was over.

Indeed, by the end of spring 1995, federal troops had achieved important military successes by driving Chechen rebels into the mountains. When a terrorist raid led by Shamil Basayev on June 14 took hundreds of hostages at a hospital in Budennovsk, some two hundred kilometers from the Chechen border, it changed the situation radically.

The raid might be seen as a desperate move by separatists who realized they could not possibly win a purely military campaign. It might also be seen as a practical application of a tactic of taking the war into Russian cities, an intention declared by Dudayev in May 1995. Several conspiracy theorists insist that Basayev's actions, and especially his impunity after the raid, was clear evidence that some well-connected quarters in Moscow had a stake in the continuation of the war; the extreme view was that Basayev was acting on orders from Moscow. There is yet another version of what happened in Budennovsk: that the Basayev group was really en route to Abkhazia and that local police stopped the group by chance, which triggered the events that followed. Whatever the truth is, Basayev's actions turned the tide in the war.

Basayev's seizure of the Budennovsk hospital was the threshold beyond which a victorious ending to the "restoration of the constitutional order" was nowhere in sight. Neither the Russian army nor special services were ready for such a war. It became painfully obvious that there were politicians and businessmen within the Russian ruling quarters who had informal ties with Chechen separatists and who were effectively lobbying in Moscow for separatist interests. One of the names most frequently mentioned in this context was Boris Berezovsky, a leading Russian tycoon and member of Yeltsin's inner circle. (In 2000, Berezovsky's vocal opposition to Yeltsin's successor, Vladimir Putin, landed him in a partly self-imposed, partly forced exile in London.)

Ironically, the position of this faction of Russia's political elite was, at least formally, consonant with that of human rights activists, who demanded that Moscow stop the military campaign immediately and begin negotiations with Chechen separatists. The pressure from within the presidential inner circle and from the free media generated a situation whereby the Kremlin could not devise a coordinated conflict-settlement plan. This in turn impaired military operations and prevented the Russian government from taking a clear negotiating position—or, for that matter, from adopting a consistent military strategy.

How Russian power structures (such as the ministries of defense, interior, and the security service) and national leaders behaved during the hostage-taking drama in Budennovsk demonstrated military and political inconsistency, which allowed Basayev to accomplish his mission successfully. It also clearly demonstrated that the government was unable to combat terrorism efficiently. After Basayev had completed the operation without being caught, a wave of accusations and reproaches swept through the Russian political and military elite. Yeltsin was criticized for refusing to cut short his participation in a G–7 summit in Canada to deal with the crisis personally. Prime Minister Viktor Chernomyrdin, who took responsibility for managing the crisis, was denounced for negotiating directly with Basayev by phone in front of television cameras. Accusations of high treason and collaboration with Chechen separatists, which often mentioned the names of top generals and government figures, were freely exchanged. Some people hinted there had been a formal ban on Basayev's persecution and arrest (in light of the events that followed, that assumption might have been true). The resounding political scandal culminated in the resignation of Sergei Stepashin, then the director of the FSK; Viktor Yerin, the interior minister; and Nikolai Yegorov, the minister for nationalities and regional policy. Besides their functional responsibility, the trio was reputed to be hard-liners and were identified by the liberal media as a "party of war."

After the Budennovsk drama, Moscow offered Dudayev a "zero option," where both the general and his opponents at home were to resign voluntarily as a step toward conflict settlement. Naturally, Dudayev refused. He considered himself the victor, and, thanks to his regular contact with "lobbyists" inside the Kremlin, the political and military initiative remained in his hands. While he had to reckon with the ever-growing influence of field commanders from inside Chechnya, he had no serious competitors, least of all from among pro-Moscow Chechens.

Meanwhile, the military operation continued with mixed results. Indeed, the public in Russia as well as in Chechnya was impressed by the victories of the rebels. When Field Commander Salman Raduyev took Chechnya's second largest city, Gudermes, in mid-December 1995, it looked like a brilliant triumph for the separatists. When federal troops took it back ten days later, it looked like a routine military operation.

By the end of 1995 it had become obvious that Moscow's reliance on the anti-Dudayev factions inside Chechnya was wholly and fatally misplaced. Dudayev's most prominent opponents, including Umar Avturkhanov and Salambek Khadzhiyev (the former Soviet oil minister) had resigned, leaving Doku Zavgayev, the former head of the Chechen-Ingush regional Communist Party Committee, who had long since lost any authority in Chechnya, the only challenger to the rebel general. As leading political scientist Lilia Shevtsova commented: "It's difficult to say who picked up Zavgayev or why they did it. Hopelessness may be the only possible explanation."[11]

Failures in Chechnya were casting a dark shadow on the Russian political landscape. During the December 1995 parliamentary elections, the Communist Party won the largest number of seats, just above one-third, in the Duma, leaving the Kremlin Our Home Is Russia Party, led by Premier Chernomyrdin, far behind, with about 12 percent of the seats. While the pro-Kremlin forces failed chiefly for economic reasons, the unhappy course of the Chechen conflict also contributed. Elections in Chechnya took place as part of the national vote, the only difference being that the head of the republic was also elected. Zavgayev was declared the winner, with 93 percent of the republican vote being officially reported. The Chechen elections, notorious for numerous violations, certainly could not be considered a fair expression of the popular will. Instead of demonstrating his authority among Chechens, Zavgayev's victory confirmed that he was merely a puppet. Not only did the election take place under the Russian army's control, but forty thousand troops voted. The separatist leaders had declared from the start that they would not participate in the elections, and they did everything possible to upset the electoral process.

The support that Moscow gave the puppet regime of Zavgayev lent an additional impetus to the consolidation of Chechen society—anti-Russian sentiments. Zavgayev symbolized his position by rarely, if ever, leaving his "office" at the Severny Airport base, which was heavily guarded by Russian troops. The resistance continued under the slogan of *Gazawat,* or holy war. This cemented the unity of Muslim Chechens and generated certain expectations of support from brethren in the faith from outside of Russia. Fighting became increasingly bitter on both sides. Depending on their political affiliation, the Russian mass media reported the atrocities of either Chechen separatists or federal troops (mostly *kontraktninki,* or troops serving under contract rather than on by conscription). The Kremlin in its relations with Dudayev continued its carrot-and-stick policy. In fact, the military believed that the carrot was always used exactly when a determined use of force was in order, as was the case in January 1996.

That month, rebels led by Raduyev again took the war outside Chechnya by seizing about two thousand hostages in the Daghestani city of Kizlyar. The incident seemed to be a repeat of Budennovsk, the exception was that Raduyev's group was attacked just as it was returning to Chechnya. The fighting at Pervomayskoe, during which a number of hostages were killed (although Raduyev and many of his cohorts managed to escape), was another crushing blow to the Russian state's prestige. At the same time, the rebels staged several daredevil attacks in Grozny.

On January 15, 1996, Boris Yeltsin wielded the stick by ordering the Russian army to launch full-scale combat against the rebels. (This order was strange because at the time it was issued, a full-scale war against the separatists had been ongoing in Chechnya for more than a year.) More intensive military operations, however, coincided with a carrot: a new stage of peacemaking activities by a number of Russian politicians, including Yabloko party leader Grigory Yavlinsky, Duma Foreign Affairs Committee chair Vladimir Lukin, and presidential human rights commissioner Sergey Kovalev. In February 1996, the Duma voted to give amnesty to all Chechen rebels held by federal authorities. At the same time, the parliament called on the president to set up a special commission on Chechen settlement.

According to official reports, seven settlement options were discussed simultaneously within Yeltsin's inner circle. There was much hope pinned on the acclaimed diplomatic talents of then prime minister, Chernomyrdin, who in June 1995 had directly negotiated with Basayev by phone.

All these developments unfolded, however, in the context of uninterrupted military operations. The top brass continually promised to put an end to "the Chechen bandits." The belief that the "politicians had stolen victory from soldiers" was becoming increasingly popular both among the military and the public at large. For quite a long time, this argument widely served to explain why the "federals" were suffering defeat after defeat. (Later, at the height of the second Chechen campaign, which started quite successfully in August and concluded in September 1999, the Russian top brass ascribed its achievements to the fact that there was no longer anyone interfering with the conduct of the war. Four years into the war, even with the Kremlin maintaining a policy of noninterference, final victory has not yet been realized.)

The year 1996 became a turning and a termination point of the first campaign in Chechnya. The situation had reached an impasse. The rebels could not build on their earlier successes through surprise attacks, yet with none of the most authoritative field commanders killed or captured, any claim of "victory" seemed paltry. The Russian army could not defeat the largest rebel groups (or at least drive them into the mountains) could not create an impenetrable cordon sanitaire, and could not establish a "pacified" Chechnya on the territory under federal control.

While for the rebels a stalemate equaled victory, for Moscow it undeniably spelled defeat. Boris Yeltsin, preparing for his reelection, could not ignore this fact. His personal involvement with the war in Chechnya often appeared measly and at times even grotesque. During the hostage drama in Kizlyar, for instance, the president appeared before journalists to promise that all the hostages would be freed immediately. He also told media representatives (and through them all Russians) that "thirty-eight snipers were watching the rebels," while demonstrating with uncanny acting skills exactly how the snipers were doing so. This episode sent Yeltsin's popularity rating, already low, into a downward spiral.[12]

Three Years of Independence Degenerating into Anarchy, 1996–2000

On the whole, the Chechen conflict lowered Yeltsin's popularity, a development that threatened to seriously affect the outcome of the 1996 presidential elections. Even Dudayev's killing by a Russian guided missile in April 1996 did not herald victory. In a situation where a military victory was out of the question, Yeltsin and his entourage could only emphasize negotiations. In May, the Russian president made a brief trip to a military camp inside Chechnya and invited Dudayev's successor, Zelimkhan Yandarbiev, to the Kremlin. In June, Russian and Chechen negotiators concluded an agreement in Nazran that had the appearance of a peace plan. The resignation in late June of the so-called war hawks, including Defense Minister Pavel Grachev, Yeltsin's security chief Alexander Korzhakov, the head of domestic security Mikhail Barsukov, and Security Council secretary Oleg Lobov, should have signaled Moscow's more peaceful stance.

Yeltsin also needed to put a new face on his policy. The public was looking for someone capable of cohesive and effective action. Considerable attention was given to General Alexander Lebed, the former commander of Russia's Fourteenth Army in Moldova's Trans-Dniester region.[13] Lebed had repeatedly spoken out in favor of a political settlement, and he enjoyed considerable respect among Chechen politicians. During the first round of presidential elections on June 16, Lebed came in third, with an impressive 14.5 percent of the national vote, with only Yeltsin and Communist Party leader Zyuganov ahead of him. Lebed's electoral success led Yeltsin to offer him the job of Security Council secretary. This move boosted Yeltsin's position as the second round of elections approached. It also enabled him to shift onto Lebed's shoulders the burden of tackling the seemingly hopeless Chechen problem, which, in turn, reduced Yeltsin's own responsibility.

After the election, the Nazran agreement was annulled de facto. Lebed first charged ahead with the military campaign but soon realized the futility of continuing. Yeltsin's political maneuvering had left the army in Chechnya utterly demoralized and deprived of incentives to fight on. Yeltsin himself was secretly recovering from a massive stroke suffered as a result of intense campaigning. The rebels were quick to see their chance and in August, on Yeltsin's inauguration day, they entered Grozny. This formally sealed the final defeat of the federal forces. On August 31, 1996, Lebed and Chechen military commander Aslan Maskhadov signed a cease-fire agreement in the Dagestani town of Khasavyurt. The first Chechen campaign had ended.

Both sides hoped that they would benefit from the cessation of fighting. The separatists were getting ready to reap the fruits of victory. Moscow, which still refused to recognize the independence of the Chechen Republic of Ichkeria, expected that the peaceful intermission would make Chechens turn to Russia for economic support. This, the Russian government hoped, would ultimately tip the balance in its favor. Tackling the solution of the root cause of the conflict—the issue of Chechen sovereignty—was postponed by five years, until December 31, 2001.

Peace lasted for three years, during which Chechen pro-independence politicians tried to reach three equally important objectives:

- Creating a foundation for Chechen statehood and consolidating Chechen society.

- Settling Chechnya's relations with Russia, primarily in order to obtain compensation for war damages.
- Securing international recognition of Chechen independence.

None of the three objectives was ever achieved. The three years of independence revealed that the Chechen elite was unable to get on with building a nation state, consolidate its various social groups and traditional factions, work out an efficient model of government, or make any progress toward modernizing Chechnya's political culture. The Chechen elite also proved to be extremely fragmented. After General Dudayev was killed,[14] it was consistently unable to reach a consensus choosing a new national leader who enjoyed unquestionable authority and could represent Chechen society as a whole.

During 1996–1997, the separatists sought to legitimize their power as they struggled to address social, political, and economic objectives. It was thus necessary to hold elections, first and foremost presidential elections, in order to give the republic a legitimate leader, one who would bring internal stability and engage in a dialogue with Russia. The ideal candidate seemed to be Aslan Maskhadov, a former Soviet army colonel, the chief of staff of the Chechen armed forces in 1994, and the prime minister of the provisional coalition government in October 1996.

Maskhadov had always been known for his moderate political views and readiness for dialogue. Yet he sometimes seemed to find it easier to speak with the federal government than with his own more radical followers. Maskhadov opposed Dudayev's separatist ideas and he had been consistently pessimistic about the idea of Chechnya becoming an Islamic state. During the August 1996 negotiations with Alexander Lebed, Maskhadov agreed to a formula that would have insulted most Chechens: "Russia can live without Chechnya, but Chechnya would not be able to live without Russia."[15] By the time he entered the presidential race, Maskhadov had signed an agreement with Russian Prime Minister Chernomyrdin "on the principles of mutual relations between the federal center and the Chechen Republic." Maskhadov has always blamed both sides equally for the brutality of the conflict.

Although Chechens had mixed feelings toward Maskhadov, his moderate attitudes and ability to sustain a dialogue with Moscow earned him popular support. As for Moscow, it was quite content with Maskhadov's growing influence, and that is precisely why the Kremlin gave barely concealed support to Maskhadov's candidacy during the January 1997 elections in Chechnya. It is also true, though, that Moscow politicians subsequently failed to appreciate Maskhadov's diplomatic approach and readiness for a compromise. Moscow's failure to meet Maskhadov part way seriously undermined Maskhadov's support base in Chechen society.

Maskhadov scored a sweeping victory at the presidential election. He won more than 60 percent of the votes, while his main contenders, Shamil Basayev and Zelimkhan Yandarbiyev, won 20 percent and 10 percent, respectively.[16] The elections demonstrated that most Chechens wanted to avoid a new confrontation with Russia and favored dialogue. On the other hand, the outcome of the election showed that part of Chechen society, primarily young people, was sympathetic to radicalism, including the establishment of an Islamic republic. The 30 percent of the electorate who voted for Maskhadov's rivals soon became the core fighting force of the anti-Maskhadov opposition. This destabilized Chechnya again.

The precarious compromise between Maskhadov and Basayev, who was appointed acting prime minister shortly after the elections, was soon broken. In the middle of 1997, Basayev, no longer content with playing second fiddle to Maskhadov, intensified his criticisms of the president. Basayev effectively declined to abide by presidential orders and he also developed an increasingly close relationship with the Chechen radicals, who the Russian media started to refer to as "Wahhabis." What they meant was not a Saudi connection, which was usually nonexistent, but a rejection of traditional Islam in favor of proactive fundamentalism. Opposition to Maskhadov became well entrenched. In addition to Basayev, it included Zelimkhan Yandarbiyev, who had been acting Chechen president from April 1996 to January 1997, and powerful field commanders and politicians Arbi Barayev, A.-M. Medzhiyev, Islam Khalimov, Movladi Udugov, A. V. Khusainov, and others.

The schism within the Chechen resistance movement was a product of (1) a naked struggle for power, (2) differences over how best to deal with Moscow, and (3) disagreement on the nature of the emerging Chechen state, including the role of Islam.

Religious Disputes

The Islamic factor has always played a dual role in the Chechen conflict. First Dudayev and then Maskhadov consistently advocated a secular state. Both of them realized only too well that only a secular Chechnya had a chance of being admitted into the international community and that, as secular politicians, they would have to step down in favor of Islamic radicals if a religious state were ever to be formed. Finally, these former Soviet military officers, who had received a thoroughly secular (and even atheist) education and training, believed that the proclamation of *Shariah* as the supreme law (the distinctive feature of an Islamic state) would propel the republic back into the Middle Ages.

This secularly minded faction was opposed by Yandarbiyev's group that wanted not merely an independent Chechen state, but an Islamic one. Clearly, Islam was also a tool for them to sideline their secular rivals and consolidate power in their own hands. The traditionally practiced Tarekat Islam, however, was not suited for this purpose. Tarekat, or brotherhoods, of which the *Nakhshbandiya* and *Kadiriya* were the most influential in Chechnya, was characterized by a folksy cult of local Muslim saints, the worship of these saints' graves, and a fairly liberal attitude toward Shariah dogmas. It was only logical that the Yandarbiyev group opted for fundamentalism as a religious trend better suited to building an independent Islamic state in Chechnya.

Opponents of going back to basics have consistently stressed that fundamentalism is alien to the Chechen mentality: fundamentalism limits personal freedom and deprives Chechens of opportunities to follow traditional ways. These opponents also argued that fundamentalism has been artificially spread by foreigners, namely Arabs from Saudi Arabia and the Gulf states, and Afghan Taliban who sought to put the Chechens under its control. Hence both Tarekatists and secularists used the word *Wahhabism* for fundamentalism in order to stress that their religious and political opponents lacked local roots and were in fact agents of foreign interests.

The confrontation between traditional Tarekat Islam and fundamentalist Islam was first manifested during the first Chechen campaign. The 1995 attempt by the fundamentalists to destroy the grave of St. Hedi, the mother of Kunta-Haji, one of the most revered Muslim preachers of the nineteenth century, became one of the most well-known clashes between traditionalists and fundamentalists. It took great effort to quell the conflict. Even then the question of whether Islam should be used for building the nation state already divided Chechen politicians instead of consolidating them.

In the fall of 1996, Yandarbiyev, then acting president, made another attempt to use Islam as an instrument of nation building, when he issued a decree replacing secular courts with Shariah ones. At the same time, a Shariah criminal code, effectively a translation of the 1983 Sudanese criminal code, was enacted in Chechnya. In 1997, the Chechen parliament amended the constitution by proclaiming Islam the state religion. A Supreme Shariah Court was established. These and other measures put the legitimacy of Maskhadov's rule into question, and Basayev and other field commanders were quick to exploit the situation.

Radical fundamentalists seized the initiative. Their main opponents, Maskhadov and scholars of Muslim law, the Mufti of Chechnya, Ahmad-Haji Kadyrov, did not dare to openly oppose the idea of an Islamic state. Instead, they confined themselves to criticizing fundamentalists over the premature introduction of Shariah law and the low professional level of Shariah courts. Most important, they branded Wahhabism an ideology of terrorism. At the same time, Maskhadov was taking steps to prevent the radicals from monopolizing Islam as a political instrument. In February 1999, he issued a decree introducing "full Shariah rule" in Chechnya and forming a presidential *Shura* (an Islamic Council). These measures had mixed success.

There are several aspects to the re-Islamization of Chechnya. First, it can be seen in the context of the religious renaissance that has been sweeping across post-Soviet Russia. Second, it is characterized by the open use of Islam as an instrument of political struggle. Third, the development of a radical Islamic trend, which culminated in an attempt to create an Islamic state, put Chechnya into the worldwide context of Islamic radicalization aimed at replacing secular regimes with a religion-based political system. In other words, Chechnya represents another attempt to implement a fundamentalist Islamic project. (This problem is considered more fully in chapter 3.)

Meanwhile, the internal political confrontation in Chechnya had degenerated into a series of bloody clashes. In the summer of 1998, a tent camp of Islamist protesters led by Dudayev's nephew Salman Raduyev, was dispersed on Maskhadov's orders. In response, the radicals assassinated Lecha Khultygov, the head of Chechnya's National Security Service. Shortly thereafter, in Gudermes, an armed clash occurred between fundamentalists and National Guard troops, followed by an attempt to assassinate Maskhadov, which could be seen as the fundamentalists' attempt at a coup d'état. At the end of 1998, Basayev, Israpilov, and Raduyev appealed to the Chechen Parliament and Shariah court, demanding that Maskhadov be impeached. In criticizing Maskhadov, his opponents insisted that "Chechens had traded freedom for cabbage soup from Moscow."[17]

All these events made the unity of the Islamic and secular factions within the separatist movement even more ethereal. The schism inside the Chechen resistance movement has become a permanent factor. While weakening the Chechen resistance, this trend has also made life more difficult for Moscow, and more specifically, for the Moscow-based politicians had advocated negotiating with the separatists. The problem was that these politicians had extremely vague ideas of whom specifically they wanted to negotiate with, and had uncertainities about whether such negotiations could be efficient if the other side were represented by Maskhadov alone.

As for Maskhadov, he was still behaving as though he were the only person in control over Chechnya. He bluntly dismissed his opponents' actions as illegal. In turn, the president's opponents, to underscore their own legitimacy, similarly claimed to represent the interests of the Chechen state. What resulted was that Chechnya became a dyarchy, which complicated contact with Moscow and often rendered negotiations meaningless.

Chechnya and Dagestan: The Conflict Spills Over

Maskhadov, Basayev, Yandarbiyev, and other Chechen leaders took parallel measures to affirm their influence in the North Caucasus by canvassing a broad range of interests, from government bodies to opposition factions. As the legitimate president, Maskhadov appreciated that the leaders of other North Caucasian republics condemned separatism and yet recognized him as the only person to represent the Chechen people. He expected that these leaders would understand him and thus bolster his position, both vis-à-vis his Chechen opponents and Moscow.

As for Basayev, Yandarbiyev, and their followers, they preferred to bypass Maskhadov, emphasizing contacts with local opposition forces. While Maskhadov called for solidarity with the Chechen people, expecting that his authority in the North Caucasus would help his negotiations with Moscow, more radical Chechen politicians advocated the Islamic integration of the North Caucasus and a rejection of talks with Russian authorities. They pinned their strongest hopes on neighboring Dagestan, where in the late 1990s several fundamentalist enclaves, sympathetic to the idea of an Islamic state, were formed. Indeed, they tried to put that idea into practice (in, for instance, the so-called Kadar area, which included the villages of Karamakhi, Chabanmakhi, and Kadar).

In 1997, Yandarbiyev invited Bagauddin Muhammad, easily the most prominent fundamentalist preacher in Dagestan if not in all the North Caucasus, to move to Chechnya. In 1999, Muhammad and his followers made the *Hejira* (resettlement) to Chechnya, where the fundamentalist leader took an active part in creating Islamic government bodies. In June 1998, Shamil Basayev convened a permanent "Congress of the Peoples of Chechnya and Dagestan." With Basayev as chair, this body institutionalized the idea of the unification of Chechnya and Dagestan into a single Islamic imamate (a theocratic state). This idea recalled the imamate that had existed in the region from the 1830s to the 1860s. Its leader, Imam Shamil, led a long and bloody war against Russian forces that ended with his surrender in 1864.

By late 1998 and early 1999, Basayev and his followers had effectively lost all remaining interest in sustaining even minimal stability in Chechnya, had withdrawn from all economic rehabilitation activities, and had stopped discussing economic reconstruction with Moscow. The Islamic radicals' main objective was no longer to secure Chechen independence, but to prepare a political and ideological expansion into neighboring North Caucasian republics, primarily Dagestan and Ingushetia.

By the middle of 1999, Maskhadov had lost control over most of his combat-ready armed groups. Yet Basayev and his followers could not yet afford to break away definitively from the legitimately elected president, let alone openly seek his ouster, a move that would have led to an open civil war the radicals could not hope to win.

Instead, the way that Basayev chose to consolidate his influence in Chechnya was a logical, albeit risky one. He tried to achieve a strategic success outside the republic, in Dagestan. A victorious return to Chechnya after a successful raid might make it possible for Basayev to ditch Maskhadov and become the lone national leader. Recall that it had been the terrorist attack at Budennovsk in 1995 that had saved the rebels from defeat and turned Basayev into a war hero. The plan seemed logical enough, provided one forgets the impossibility of becoming an autocratic leader of Chechnya, given the anarchic traditions of Chechen society.

Basayev's invasion of Dagestan in August 1999 has yet to be scrutinized by historians. The information available about the invasion, including official documents, media reports, and participant and eyewitness accounts, is often contradictory. Yet the general nature of the military actions, which ultimately resulted in Basayev's defeat, suggests that Russian intelligence knew about the raid well in advance. Interestingly, information about the planned raid spread across the North Caucasus like wildfire. According to the founder of the Islamic Democratic Party, Abdrashid Saidov, "Anyone who traded on the Grozny market in May–June 1999 was taking account of the imminent war in Dagestan."[18]

The Results of the Counterterrorist Operation

Basayev's adventure in Dagestan, which led to Russian troops rolling into Chechnya on October 1, 1999, became a crucial turning point in the conflict between Moscow and Grozny. By spring 2000, the counterterrorist operation had resulted in Russian troops controlling about 80 percent of Chechen territory, although they have not yet been able to gain complete control.

Vladimir Putin's skyrocket accession to the presidency was the main result of the second campaign in Chechnya. On August 7, 1999, right after Basayev entered Dagestan, Yeltsin appointed Putin (then the head of the FSB and the National Security Council secretary) prime minister. On December 31, 1999, Yeltsin suddenly abdicated, six months before the end of his term, and Premier Putin became acting president, in accordance with the constitution. On March 26, 2000, Putin was elected the second president of the Russian Federation. The phenomenal success of the hastily organized political movement *Yedinstvo* (Unity) during the December 1999 parliamentary elections depended on nothing more than Putin's war popularity. Yet that success upset the seemingly unstoppable drive of Yevgeni Primakov and Moscow mayor Yuri Luzhkov to end the domination of Yeltsin's relatives and cronies.

Mainstream analysts believe that the Kremlin planners of presidential succession skillfully exploited a developing situation. Those who disagree grimly insist that Basayev's incursion into Dagestan was paid for by people in Moscow and even that it was a "special operation" orchestrated by the Kremlin. The bombing of apartment houses in Moscow and two other towns in September 1999 claimed some three hundred lives. These attacks also gave the second campaign against Chechnya both popular support and the unmistakable tenor of a campaign against terrorism. Moreover, the bombings were blamed on the same "dark forces" whose overriding interest was to engineer Yeltsin's succession so as to maintain their power, wealth, and freedom.

One thing is certain, however. Moscow's tactical success at the beginning of the second campaign in Chechnya was, above all, a political instrument to create a springboard for Putin's leap to the presidency and then boost the new Russian leader's authority in society. Chechnya made Putin Russia's president.

In Chechnya itself, Russian authorities, while utterly and deliberately ignoring the issue of possible Chechen independence, soon took decisive steps to install a civilian administration. In June 2000, President Putin appointed Mufti Akhmad-Khadzhi Kadyrov to head the administration of the Chechen Republic. The appointment of the man Aslan Maskhadov had declared "an enemy of the Chechen people" and for whose head Basayev had promised $100,000, clearly demonstrated that Moscow had no intention of talking with the radical separatists.

The appointment of Kadyrov generated mixed feelings in Chechnya. M. Yusupov, a prominent expert on North Caucasian affairs, believes that it "came as a surprise to the Chechen public" and was moreover "an insult to the pro-Russian [Chechen] bureaucracy."[19] The Chechen bureaucracy's discontent was understandable, because instead of choosing someone who had supported the Kremlin throughout those troubled years, President Putin picked its former enemy, someone who had declared a holy war against Russia. It suddenly turned out that steadfast loyalty to Moscow could have adverse career implications. Kadyrov's appointment can be seen as a step toward splitting the opposition and creating opportunities for wooing influential opposition leaders into the Moscow camp. Interestingly, at that time the Russian media, which had talked a lot about Kadyrov, now often avoided mentioning his recent separatist past.

Many observers believed that the appointment of Kadyrov (who gave up his clerical status shortly thereafter) was a strong and efficient move by Moscow. The main objective of the new administration was to begin to bring life in Chechnya back to normal. Whether that objective could be achieved had been in question from the start. First, Kadyrov's influence was limited to Chechnya's northern and northeastern regions, where separatist sentiments had been traditionally weaker and federal controls tighter. Second, Kadyrov had never been supported by the majority, let alone all, of Chechen society. Third, the new administration was only nominally autonomous because it depended on Russian ministries that ultimately ensured its very existence. Fourth, shortly after he had been appointed, Kadyrov entered into a conflict with Bislan Gantamirov, Grozny's former mayor, who the federal government had released from prison and appointed (without Kadyrov's consent) to be the deputy head of administration and also the commander of the Chechen police force. The situation was exacerbated by Kadyrov's support by Viktor Kazantsev, the presidential representative in the south of Russia, while Gantamirov was widely seen as an associate of Anatoli Kvashnin, the chief of the Russian General Staff, and backed further by the federal Ministry of Internal Affairs. Fifth, many influential figures in the Chechen diaspora refused to recognize or accept Kadyrov.

The most sensitive issue was ultimately who would control the funds that Moscow had once again allocated for the reconstruction of Chechnya and the neighboring war-torn regions of Dagestan. Funds had been widely known to disappear on their way to, or stolen from, Chechnya. Innumerable stories circulated about how money had been misappropriated. People would claim, for example, that the money had indeed been spent to rebuild some facility, but that the facility had been destroyed in the course of subsequent fighting or blown up by rebels. Stories were also told of reconstruction funds diverted for purposes other than those intended, and of hugely inflated electric bills, allegedly for such things as electrical supplies for buildings and blocks that no longer existed.

In this connection, during a 1997 meeting he held with Aslan Maskhadov, Yeltsin complained about receiving inconsistent information about the amount of reconstruction resources allocated to Chechnya. For instance, while Moscow had sent 800 million rubles (then about $130 million) to Chechnya, the Chechen National Bank reported that it had received only 129 million ($20 million). Incredulous, the Russian president protested many times: "The blasted money is draining somewhere!"[20] (Later, in 1999, he used the same words when he was informed about a leak of funds intended for the reconstruction of the Botlikh district of Dagestan.)

In 1995, Arkady Volsky, an influential politician and business lobbyist, insisted that a quarter of the funds allocated to Chechnya for reconstruction had been stolen.[21] Other, although probably exaggerated, numbers were cited as well: Prominent Duma member Aleksey Arbatov said that $1 billion had been stolen during the first Chechen war;[22] the political and economic weekly *Profil* insisted that $2 billion of reconstruction resources had "vanished without trace" in 1995–1996 alone.[23] For Chechnya, these are enormous sums of money. According to diaspora figures, the economy of Chechnya could be revitalized with $700 million would have been enough in 1995–1996.

After 1999, both military and civilian authorities, each trying to convince Moscow that the money would be safe in its hands, competed for the control of "Chechnya" funds. In January 2001, the Russian government adopted a social and economic reconstruction program for Chechnya worth 14.7 billion rubles (about $500 million). At the end of the spring of that year, Vladimir Kalamanov, President Putin's special envoy for human rights in Chechnya, declared indignantly that only 10 percent of that amount had been used for reconstruction and that "no one knew where the rest of the money was."[24] It was estimated the total amount required to rebuild the Chechen economy in 2002–2003 (that is, after the second military campaign) was 40 billion rubles ($1.4 billion), a burden that the Russian economy can hardly bear. Meanwhile, misappropriation and the blatant stealing of funds continues unabated. In November 2002, FSB director Nikolai Patrushev reported that 700 million rubles ($22 million) had been "misused." That figure is probably just the tip of the iceberg. Indeed, who can be trusted to ensure that the money allocated for reconstruction will be used productively and to benefit of the people of Chechnya? We will know the answer only after the fact. Meanwhile, reconstruction will proceed in the context continuing armed conflict.

Separatist Opposition

The main problem for Kadyrov and his administration was how to deal with the separatist opposition. On the one hand, Kadyrov stayed committed to the destruction of opponents who were irreconcilable. On the other hand, he realized that the very survival of his administration depended on contacts with those field commanders who were ready to compromise. In that respect, Kadyrov's position was consonant with Moscow's, which had tirelessly tried to divide the opposition and woo the moderate mujahideen. In late 2000, Kadyrov repeatedly attempted to establish contacts with Ruslan Gelayev, a ruthless field commander. Kadyrov insisted that he "had never lost touch with these people"; considered them "rebels rather than bandits, for there was no criminal blood on their hands"; and believed "they would be useful members of society during peacetime."[25]

These efforts notwithstanding, no radical change in relations with the rebels ever took place. First, the rebels considered Kadyrov a collaborationist and preferred to speak directly with Moscow rather than depend on his good will. Second, the moderates always felt their more radical colleagues were scheming behind their backs. Third, neither moderately minded rebels in Chechnya nor their counterparts in Moscow had any idea how former field commanders and their troops could possibly be integrated into Chechnya during peacetime or whether the different factions would subsequently settle old scores.

Likewise, no radical changes have occurred to restore peace and normalcy in Chechnya. In the winter of 2000–2001, separatists began killing representatives of the Kadyrov administration. Moreover, some of those invited to join the administration or the Chechen police force were known to have asked Basayev for permission. By the end of 2003, not even a semblance of a peacetime economy has been created in the republic. At this writing, only a few companies are back in operation. Many children are denied the opportunity to attend school, resulting in ever-increasing rates of illiteracy, and unemployment has grown drastically because employment opportunities do not exist in Chechnya.

The Russian authorities, including President Putin, had hoped that Kadyrov and his entourage would be just the people to establish a basis for peace in Chechnya. The new Chechen administration, however, has proved to be nothing more than another political interest group, unable either to consolidate society or to initiate a full-scale reconstruction of the Chechen economy. In that respect, the administration is not unlike pro-Moscow groups that attempted in vain to oppose General Dudayev.

At the same time, the Kadyrov administration has its own distinctive features. First, it operates in a situation where the separatist idea has proved untenable and the war for independence has become a struggle for survival. The new collaborators, as former proponents of independence, have had to concede therefore, that independence is unobtainable at any price. Their objectives now are to save Chechen society and to prevent genocide. Consequently, their cooperation with Moscow reveals political flexibility and not capitulation. Second, since many Kadyrovites fought federal forces, they cannot be accused of cowardice. Finally, after appointing Kadyrov to head the Chechen administration, the Kremlin has kept him in office despite a lack of firm support from some highly placed civil servants and generals. The Kremlin hopes to demonstrate that the course toward Chechnya's reconstruction will be a strategic and not tactical move. Unlike Yeltsin, who changed his Chechen protégés frequently, Putin has recognized Kadyrov and his followers as permanent partners of Moscow.

Difficulties in Governing

Meanwhile, the federal center has consistently failed to create a comprehensive governance model for Chechnya that fits the new conditions. The problem is that, while political necessity requires some evidence of progressive normalization, reality requires that Moscow maintain all options, including military ones, at all times. In 2001, general responsibility for Chechnya was transferred from the armed forces to the security service. In 2003, the FSB handed that responsibility to the Interior Ministry. In conjunction with these moves, in 2000 Putin appointed a head of Chechen administration and endowed him with a government. Three years later, Putin blessed a referendum on a new Chechen constitution, followed by presidential and parliamentary elections. In practice, each federal ministry retains its virtually independent fiefdom in Chechnya, and is usually scornful of Kadyrov's administration. Kadyrov, on the other hand, can rely only on his own clan, whose domination is resented by other Chechens.

The Chechen government has had a difficult relationship with the federal cabinet in Moscow. In January 2001, for example, Vladimir Yelagin, formerly the governor of Orenburg, was appointed to the new post of federal minister in charge of Chechen affairs. In February of the same year, Stanislav Ilyasov, who previously had chaired the Stavropol government, was appointed the head of the new government of the Chechen Republic and became the minister for Chechnya in the fall of 2002.[26] The new Chechen government was composed of thirty-four ministries overseen by seven Ilyasov deputies. Earlier, Kadyrov had taken until mid-2001 to transfer his office from Gudermes to Grozny, which federal troops had formally claimed to have under their control. It is still difficult to say how and with whom the thirty-odd ministries will function. For some time Chechnya's new leadership prided itself on having a multinational government, comprising the representatives of five ethnic and cultural groups: Chechen, Russian, Korean, Ukrainian, and a Jew. This multicultural structure of the new government neither encourages professionalism nor decreases its level of corruption.

The mushrooming of government bureaucracies and the appointment of so-called commanders without armies failed to promote restoration of normalcy in the Chechen Republic. The federal power structures still enjoyed the most influence. They were unhappy with the ever-increasing number of incompetent civilian administrators, who were always asking for support, and incapable of taking a single step without military backing. This dependency put military commanders in an ambiguous situation. On the one hand, they were carrying out their professional duty of fighting an armed opposition; on the other hand, they had to interfere in problem areas that would normally be addressed by a civilian authority.

The continuous instability of governance added to the colossal chaos generated by the hostilities. The conflict continued, and the central government in Moscow lacked a clear view of how to resolve it. Meanwhile, Russian troops were regularly being ambushed and attacked by the rebels, and in turn, these poorly paid, often undisciplined troops harassed the local population. By February 2001, with the military phase of the operation declared over, about seven hundred criminal charges were brought against federal servicemen accused of marauding and of the unauthorized use of firearms.[27] While soldiers engaged in looting, many among the top brass formed networks of corruption. As a result, ordinary Chechens found themselves helpless, caught between the hammer of the federals and the anvil of the rebels and common criminals. This gave the Kremlin's opponents additional arguments for claiming that "Moscow was waging a war against the Chechen people."

Massive human rights violations by both sides characterized the confrontation. It became routine to take and release hostages in exchange for hefty sums. Politicians, journalists, the staff members of international organizations, Russian servicemen, and both Russian and Chechen civilians were the easy targets of hostage takers. Each side has of course insisted that its opponent is guilty of these outrages.

One reason for growing Chechen bitterness has been the lingering feeling of helplessness before a central government in Moscow that had once before (in 1944) resolved the Chechen question by sending the whole nation into exile. The memory of that deportation is a constant stimulus for continued resistance.

Escalating brutality has demonstrated that there has been no military solution to the conflict; the direct armed confrontation has exhausted itself. The federal troops have indeed achieved some success by liquidating, or more accurately, *dispersing,* large groups of the armed Chechen opposition. At the same time, the federals have proved incapable of staging effective counterinsurgency operations. Victorious in broad daylight, the federal troops have lost the initiative to the rebels at night. In fact, after Moscow had formally taken control of the lowlands of Chechnya and the rebels had been confined to the forested mountainous hideouts, the conflict became one between an elephant and a whale, each invincible in its own medium. Tellingly, the most wanted Chechen separatists and terrorists were still running free.[28]

In this situation, in the winter of 2001 the Kremlin made a surprise decision to shift authority for the Chechen operation from the Ministry of Defense to the Federal Security Service. By doing so, the central government sought to convince the public in Russia, and the international community (and, indeed, itself) that the "big war" had been won. There was something to show for it. Several notorious figures, such as Khattab and Arbi Barayev, were killed in 2001–2002. Yet the psychological comfort that this news produced was deceptive.

The decision to put FSB director Nickolai Patrushev in charge of the operation in Chechnya meant that the military contingent there would be reduced and that "excessive" troops would be pulled out (in total, 70,000–80,000 troops were in Chechnya, of which about 60,000 were immediately under federal control). There were proposals to reduce the Chechnya contingent by at least 40 percent, and pro-Moscow Chechen authorities believed that such reductions were appropriate and realistic in order to preserve stability in the republic. Kadyrov himself insisted that the federal contingent could easily be reduced to 15,000 men.[29] Prominent Chechen politician and Russian Duma deputy (and police general) Aslambek Aslakhanov suggested reducing the federal contingent to between 22,000–24,000 men. At the same time, General Valery Manilov, then the first deputy chief of the General Staff, believed that at least 50,000 federal troops should remain in Chechnya following all reductions.[30]

Military experts doubted the expediency of a troop pullout. To begin with, they insisted that the army's Forty-second Motorized Infantry Division and an interior troop brigade, each capable of carrying out large-scale combat operations, should remain in the rebel republic "on a permanent basis." Moreover, they suggested creating a network of strongholds, or small garrisons, based in at least 162 Chechen villages and towns. That plan, proposed by the Russian General Staff, effectively replicated the creation in the nineteenth-century of a network of small fortresses across the North Caucasus to enable administrative control over the newly conquered territories. Yet such a strategy seemed precarious under contemporary conditions. The primary objective of the new garrisons would be to defend their position while remaining combat-ready in a hostile environment. This plan raised questions of logistics, technical maintenance, and supplying food to the augmented checkpoints. It would also have been necessary to establish secure communication channels and to ensure close operational coordination between the garrisons. Had the plan been implemented, it might well have worsened instead of alleviating the problems encountered by Russian troops.

Moscow's military plans were uncertain in part because no coherent political plan had been devised to manage and settle the Chechen conflict. After Vladimir Putin's rise to power, only one fundamental question—whether Chechnya could ever be granted independence—was answered, in the negative. The periodic vacillations of the Yeltsin administration were replaced by the axiom that Chechnya was to remain part of the federation. Whatever one might feel about this policy, it certainly introduced clarity into the positions of the conflicting parties. Equally important, it enabled Moscow to be more consistent in its relations with international organizations.

Yet refusing to grant independence to Chechnya does not address how a compromise could be reached with the advocates of an independent

Chechnya. It is absolutely unclear how such a compromise could be legally formalized. In the early 1990s, various policy makers discussed an agreement to delineate power, modeled on the Moscow-Tatarstan agreement, and then also discussed delegating even broader powers to Chechnya. Since 2000, however, when President Putin made strengthening "vertical power"(that is, a top-down hierarchy) his policy priority, the concept of sovereignty within a federation has ceased to be a workable policy option.

Various Russian politicians devised their own plans to bring normality temporarily to Chechnya and to pacify its people. The options they proposed included turning Chechnya into an Eighth Federal District (in addition to the seven federal districts established in the spring of 2000); splitting Chechnya into "lowland" and "highland" components as a start to bringing normalcy to the pacified areas of the plains; and proceeding with the military campaign to uproot rebels in the republic's mountainous areas. Discussions continued on whether a single federal authority should be in charge of Chechen affairs or whether that responsibility should be dispersed among various government agencies. After all this discussion, it remains unclear which body or agency is ultimately responsible for Chechnya or who (besides, of course, the president) has the final word when making decisions about Chechnya.

As the year 2001 drew to a close, the American war against terrorism in Afghanistan laid the foundation for the negotiations initiated by the Chechen side between the federal government and Maskhadov's representatives. The public showed little interest in these discussions, which took place between Maskhadov's envoy, Ahmed Zakayev, and Putin's representative in the Southern Federal District, Viktor Kazantsev. These discussions were overshadowed in the media by developments in Afghanistan. Many politicians were quick to recall that the Chechens had initiated such contacts every fall because winter in the mountains is not a time for fighting. When spring brings back the foliage, the rebels' most reliable cover, Chechen calls for negotiations end. The official attitude to the negotiations remained reserved, especially because all pro-Moscow Chechen politicians, primarily Ahmad Kadyrov, firmly opposed any such contact. In the wake of the October 2002 hostage-taking drama in Moscow, the Kremlin not only refused to talk to Maskhadov again, but also insisted (to date, unsuccessfully) on Zakayev's arrest in Europe and his extradition to Russia.

The quick military success of the United States in Afghanistan (which, however, did not and could not immediately or fully stabilize that country) came in sharp contrast to the Russian army's military impotence in Chechnya. On the one hand, this impotence was conducive to yet another downward spiral in the negotiating process; on the other hand, it stimulated the military's stronger claims for increased financing and firmer state support. Russia, meanwhile, was afforded another opportunity to compare the tactics and true might of the U.S. and Russian armies. Where they had been equally powerful a short time before, one now lagged hopelessly behind the other.

The U.S. operation in Afghanistan also provided an example of a different approach to settling a conflict such as Chechnya is. Seeking to reduce its military losses as much as possible, the United States had paid tens, if not hundreds, of millions of dollars to Taliban leaders, primarily to field commanders (as much as $600 million has been cited). Why could Russia not pay a "ransom" to the Chechen separatists instead of sacrificing Russian soldiers? That idea is debatable, of course, but it is not so absurd if one recalls that at the end of Yeltsin's presidency, Moscow spent millions of dollars in exchange for Chechen-held hostages.

The routine nature of the Chechen war was not affected by the dramatic hostage taking in the nation's capital. In October 2002, a group of Chechen terrorists took over a musical theater in Moscow and held about eight hundred spectators hostage for two and a half days. The authorities entered into talks with the terrorists, but from the very beginning the terrorists knew they could not afford to free the hostages. Putin's position as president was at stake. During the storming of the theater, Russia's special operation forces used a powerful concentration of anesthetic gas that incapacitated the captors but resulted in the deaths of more than 130 hostages. Public opinion, while blaming the authorities for having allowed three dozen armed terrorists to appear in central Moscow and for failing to provide the antidote to the hostages quickly enough, expressed absolutely no sympathy for the terrorists' avowed cause, the liberation of Chechnya.

Putin and his men emerged from the agonizing crisis as victors. Patrushev, among others, was awarded the title of Hero of Russia (similar to Hero of the Soviet Union). It was not clear what to do with such success. Ironically, immediately after the end of the crisis, the Kremlin had an opportunity to launch a constitutional referendum in Chechnya, which in March 2003 resulted in overwhelming support for a document based on Chechnya's being an autonomous part of the Russian Federation. The referendum and ensuing elections of the Chechen president and parliament, however, have failed to provide a context or a substitute for a more imaginative plan of political consultation, thus undercutting the significance and durability of the Kremlin's project. A series of terrorist bombings in Chechnya in the winter of 2002 and the spring of 2003, resulting in hundreds of casualties, testifies to the widespread fragility of the situation there.

In the wake of the Moscow hostage drama, there were some people across Russia who were satisfied that finally "affluent and carefree" Muscovites had experienced pain, reflected in the sentiments expressed by some 7 percent of Russians in the wake of September 11: "It serves them right." More broadly, the Russian population has been losing interest in Chechnya. They have become indeed war-weary. Not only do they not demand that the war end, they do not even want to hear about it. Those who can afford to are fully prepared to ensure that their sons will not serve in the North Caucasus. In the 2003–2004 election cycle, Chechnya will hardly be an issue.

Preliminary Conclusions

Although the conflict in Chechnya is far from over, there is sufficient evidence on which to base preliminary conclusions that have potential implications beyond Chechnya and the Caucasus as a whole. These are as follows:

1. The Chechen conflict does not represent "an attack of international terrorism against Russia." While terrorism against civilian targets and, more often, sabotage against military targets occurs widely, these are but methods. At the root of the Chechen problem lies ethnic separatism.
2. While ethnic separatism is a threat to the stability of Russia—which even after the breakup of the USSR remains a multiethnic state—it does not currently pose the kind of danger it did in the

early 1990s. Here, the example of Chechnya has been of crucial importance. A region committed to and historically prepared for secession has failed to reach that objective. The Russian state, historically in one of its weakest moments, has managed to oppose the separatist bid. Russia has taken heavy losses, but the price that Chechen society has paid and continues to pay for its attempt at secession is horrendous. None of Russia's other ethnic republics will want to follow Chechnya down that road.

3. The idea of a loose federation or a confederation (a "Russia of the regions"), popular among regional elites in the late 1990s, was buried in the rubble of the second campaign in Chechnya. The reintegration of Russia became Putin's first priority upon assuming the presidency in 2000. By 2001, a provision in the constitution of Tuva that provided for Tuva, a once-independent republic on the Mongolian border, to withdraw from the Russian Federation, seemed an alien and meaningless relic of an earlier period when a parade of states was seeking sovereignty. Then it was quietly repealed. Thus, the specter of Russia's disintegration is now no more than a myth. Russia survived the breakup of the Soviet Union as a state with stable borders. The Chechen independence movement has become a vaccine against separatism.

4. Chechen separatists have failed to obtain the broad-based support of Russia's Islamic community. Apart from isolated manifestations of sympathy for the Chechen cause and psychological support—as when a Chechen singer performing elsewhere in the North Caucasus is given a standing ovation by an audience consisting of representatives of all Caucasian peoples—there has been no organized movement of Russian Muslims in support of the Chechens. Moreover, separatist sentiments have become anathema to Caucasus Muslims, particularly to the Dagestanis, on whom Chechen separatist leaders had placed very special hopes. Chechnya has failed in its attempt to trigger a separatist movement across the whole North Caucasus. Contrary to early fears, there has been no new Caucasus war, only a Chechen one.

5. The continuation of the Chechen war into a second decade is a clear sign that the Russian state remains weak and disorganized.

The smoldering conflict is a factor that undermines the authority of Russia's second president and the regime he heads. The apathy with which most Russians view the developments in Chechnya can quickly turn to anger and despair, however, when the war strikes closer to home, as it occasionally does in the streets of Moscow. Politically, Chechnya is a wild card.

6. Russia's preoccupation with the developments in Chechnya has turned the attention of the elites and the public southward, from the Caucasus to Central Asia and more broadly, to the Greater Middle East. A decade after the start of the first Chechen campaign, it is this broader "South" that dominates the security discourse. From suicide bombers to illegal migrants, and from drug smugglers to Qur'an-and-Kalashnikov-wielding militant Islamists, this "new face of the south" has rocked Russian society.

3

The Chechen War and the Russian World

How has the war in Chechnya influenced Russian society? What imprint has it left on Russia's emerging national identity, self-image, and attitudes to state power and to the supremacy of a central government? In what way has the war changed the political affiliations of Russian citizens? What will be the long-term consequences of the war for Russian society? Will it be remembered as an episode, or as an important and enduring factor?

These questions have no simple answers. The conflict, after all, is far from over. Although the military phase of the counterterrorist operation was officially declared at an end in late spring 2001, not a single independent expert, civilian or military, with any claim to objectivity, will predict when the military confrontation in Chechnya might truly be over. Russian officers and enlisted men openly face television cameras and say that a real war continues to be fought in Chechnya. Each week brings new casualties, usually in double digits. Major disasters sporadically occur, like the downing of the Mi-26 military transport helicopter in August 2002 that killed 120 people—as many as died in the *Kursk* submarine—or in the October 2002 music theater hostage crisis in Moscow.

War and Public Conscience

Public opinion in Russia on the Chechen war has fluctuated, reflecting developments on the battlefield. Thus, at the end of 1995, after the federal forces had failed to tilt the military situation radically in its favor, only 3.2 percent of the Russian public advocated continued military action, while 51.1 percent demanded troop withdrawal. Four years later, in November 1999, after Russian troops had crushed Basayev's invasion of Dagestan, moved into Chechnya, and achieved a certain military success with low casualties, 62.5 percent wanted the war to go on "to final victory," and only 13.2 percent wanted to end the operation and bring the troops home.[1]

Similar data were presented by the Moscow-based Russian Independent Institute of Social and Ethnic Studies, working for Germany's Friedrich Ebert Foundation. The survey "Russians on Russia's Destiny in the Century and Hopes for the Twenty-first Century" showed that whereas an absolute majority of those polled called the first campaign in Chechnya (1994–1996) "a tragic event," 70 percent of respondents approved of the second campaign, which began in 1999.[2] Participation in both polls, it is interesting to note, was limited to religious believers.

The broad political context of the war has played a key role. In 1995, most Russians were hard on President Yeltsin, who was blamed for both economic and political failures. He was likewise held responsible for the conflict in Chechnya. The poor performance of federal forces during the first Chechen campaign reflected poorly on the popularity of the commander-in-chief and his generals. Chechnya was seen as Boris Yeltsin's war, and the public wanted to get rid of both its hapless president and his Caucasian "adventure."

The popular mood changed, however, when Putin was an energetic leader on his way to power in 1999. He was seen as bold enough to assume full responsibility for the war's prosecution. He also proved capable of ending the precarious stalemate that existed with the separatists. The euphoria to which the greater part of Russian society succumbed in the fall of 1999, made the public more confident that the war in Chechnya could be won. Whereas the public wanted to cut the country's losses at the end of the first campaign, at the beginning of the second campaign the public would settle for nothing short of total victory.

Although opinion polls have made it possible to capture general trends in the public's attitude to the conflict in Chechnya, such findings can hardly be used as a basis for judging the conflict's impact on the popular state of mind in Russia. An unavoidable difficulty in this regard is the temptation to present the Chechnya factor either as a major, if not main, development of the 1990s or to downplay its importance, reducing it to an event of local and peripheral significance similar the Caucasian war of the nineteenth century.

The first extreme is illustrated by the numerous prophesies made by politicians and journalists that Chechnya would trigger Russia's disintegration, that Chechnya would cause the North Caucasus and the south of Russia to blow up, and that the crisis would ultimately bring the country to collapse. In 1995, the authors of a project ambitiously called "Russia in the Third Millennium" believed that "the conflict in Chechnya had aggravated the social and political situation in Russia, and if the conflict goes on for too long, it can spill over to the whole of the country."[3] In an interview with the leading national daily *Izvestia*, Boris Fedorov, a prominent liberal politician, businessman, and former minister of finance, issued a melancholy warning: "If Russia fails to find a dignified solution to the Chechen problem, the fate of Russia will be a sad one." The Fedorov interview was published under a pretentiously gloomy headline "Chechnya and the Collapse of the Russian State."[4]

Such statements were consonant with predictions that so-called dark forces in the Kremlin might use the Chechen conflict to put an end to democracy and to install a new dictatorship. In 1995 and once again in 1999, people close to Russian policy makers often speculated about the coming of a Russian Pinochet or even a Napoleon. (*Nezavisimaya gazeta* published a cartoon depicting President Putin as the first consul and French emperor-to-be.) Although the conflict in Chechnya did not develop (and, we believe, could not have developed) into a crisis involving the entire Russian Federation, in the fall of 1999 it was skillfully exploited as an instrument for establishing a much tougher political regime in Russia. The new regime succeeded in imposing its interpretation of the Chechen situation on all of Russian society. In 2000, three-fourths of the Russian population believed that the federal troops were fighting bandits in the North Caucasus, and about 50 percent of those polled said that the war in Chechnya was a war to stave off the breakup of Russia.[5]

Those few who held the opposing view insisted that the Chechen conflict was merely part of routine Russian politics and had little impact on Russian life and thinking. It could hardly bring about a national collapse. For most of those not immediately affected by the war or who were concerned chiefly with physical survival (especially in 1995–1996), Chechnya existed in another world and had no direct connection to their world. Such sentiments, however, never made their way into the Russian press. Public figures and experts were generally expected to issue rousing statements and to supply all the terrible details of the war. Not infrequently, people who made apocalyptic statements on television privately insisted that the Chechen conflict had only limited significance.

Regional and Group Differences

To date, Russia has not been able to produce an objective general assessment of the social impact of the Chechen conflict on Russia. Nor is there consensus on how to resolve the conflict. In the previous chapter we discussed how all of Russian society viewed the options for conflict resolution during the first and second campaigns of the Chechen conflict. Yet different regions and different groups hold different preferences.

A general rule is the farther you travel from the Caucasus, the less public interest there is in the conflict. Likewise, the fewer local people there are in an area who take part in the fighting or the policing of Chechnya, the less their neighbors care. This latter factor is of special importance because attitudes to Chechnya are more sensitive in those regions and cities where there have been the most casualties and where Chechen war participants have established their own organizations or have joined forces with the influential associations of Afghan war veterans.

The people of Russia's southern regions—Astrakhan, Krasnodar, Rostov, Stavropol, and Volgograd, which are either adjacent to or near the area of conflict—are generally more sensitive about it. In these regions, public opinion tends to gravitate to extremes, from support for fighting the war to a victorious end, to shutting down the borders with Chechnya, and thus totally isolating the rebel republic from Russia. A good example is the opinion of Duma deputy and prominent film director Stanislav Govorukhin, which was widely published in Stavropol and Krasnodar newspapers during Shamil Basayev's raid on Budennovsk in 1995. While local and federal authorities were experiencing loss, if not panic, Govorukhin called for a return to the practice where borders are "guarded by a chain of villagers, in which the cooperation of neighbors and even family provided better security than any amount of barbed wire and border fortifications."[6] Moreover, many Cossack organizations have called for the defense of "Russian borders against Chechnya." Although Cossacks in general are believed to have a negative attitude toward people of Caucasian extraction,[7] there have been frequent calls in the Stavropol *krai* (territory) to change the region's borders and incorporate the neighboring Chechen *rayons* (administrative districts) of Naursky and Shelkovskoy together with their predominantly Russian population. Such sentiments have been published in the same newspapers and on the same page as have Govorukhin's calls to "put an end to Chechen separatism" and to exterminate all rebels. Opposites are known to attract. Separating Chechnya from Russia with an ethnic fence has proved to be as unfeasible as annihilating all those committed to Chechen independence.[8]

In the mid-1990s, Alexander Solzhenitsyn, who believed that "Russians must withdraw from the Caucasus," sounded naive. (Later, Solzhenitsyn called for the reintroduction of capital punishment for rebels, a statement that General Johar Dudayev's widow, Alla Dudayev, cited as grounds for stripping Solzhenitsyn of his Nobel prize.) Solzhenitsyn's words reflect the opinion of a certain segment of Russian society that is convinced that Russia would benefit from expelling non-Russian ethnic and religious groups, who constitute a permanent source of instability. Those who have advocated expelling Chechnya from Russia were never confused by the fact that drawing clear and acceptable borders between Slavic populations and their neighbors would be extremely difficult, if not impossible.

In arguing with Solzhenitsyn, Orthodox cleric Metropolitan Gedeon of Stavropol and Baku, who is known for his nationalist tendencies, asked a rhetorical question: "Where should Russians go, abandoning their temples and ancestral graves, abandoning the land of their birth? To whom should they flee? Who awaits them?"

In a sense, the isolationist approach to Chechnya has not been unlike the popular attitudes about post-Soviet Central Asian and (to a lesser extent) the Caucasian republics that existed in the early 1990s shortly after the breakup of the Soviet Union. At that time, two polar yet essentially close viewpoints were dominant. One held Russia needed to shed these republics because they were a drag on development and reform efforts; the other maintained Chechnya could not ultimately do without Russia: "They would crawl on their knees begging to be allowed to return." Both approaches have proved impractical, unacceptable, and harmful to Russia.

The calls for getting rid of Chechnya were sometimes more pragmatic. For instance, Nikolai Gonchar, a moderate nationalist politician who commanded a certain amount of authority in the mid-1990s, believed that Chechnya "should be made independent of the Russian budget."[9] This opinion was shared by Alexander Lebed, at that time a rising star on Russia's political horizon. Effectively, this approach implied that the Chechen crisis should be overcome by financial and economic, rather than by military, methods. Although certainly attractive, this option was not practicable either, at least because Chechnya remained a constituent state of the Russian Federation, and many influential politicians and "businessmen" in Moscow were cashing in aggressively on their financial ties to the rebel republic.

The Reactions of Chechnya's Neighbors

Late in 1994, it finally became obvious that the Chechen problem had become a central issue of Russia's political life and that a real war was about to begin in the North Caucasus. Regional leaders could no longer afford to either ignore the conflict or consider it only Moscow's concern. Most regional barons reacted cautiously, which was understandable because few of them would risk jeopardizing their relations with the Kremlin. The governors preferred to keep silent, and in some regions local legislatures adopted empty resolutions calling for a peaceful settlement to the conflict.

Unlike the governors of predominantly Russian oblasts, the leaders of ethnic republics were more critical of Moscow's actions. The most prominent critics included the president of Tatarstan, a republic that had long insisted on special status within the federation, and the leaders of Bashkortostan, Buryatia, Kalmykia, Tuva, Chuvashia, and Yakutia. In these regions, the prevailing attitude to the Chechens was similar to that in the rest of the Russian Federation. Local ethnonationalist elites, however, saw the Chechen situation as an excuse to press Moscow for more autonomy and to use their loyalty to the federation over Chechnya a bargaining chip in negotiations with Moscow. Needless to say, none of Moscow's critics ever dared to challenge the central government's authority as the Chechens had.

Although the conflict between Moscow and Chechnya made relations worse between the federation and its constituent entities, it never compromised the integrity of the Russian Federation. Regional leaders, including those in the ethnic republics, considered Chechnya an exceptional region whose rebellious experience might cause the federal government to be more inclined to compromise. This dual position of republic leaders irritated the Kremlin, which has been forced into making concessions in its relations with the regions. Between 1994–1997, the Russian Federation and a number of regions signed a series of bilateral agreements on the delineation of powers. Tatarstan obtained particularly broad rights, a development that made it possible for Kazan leaders to speak of "confederate" relations between Tatarstan and Russia.

Yet the refusal by ethnic republic leaders to embrace Chechen independence gave Moscow the freedom to ignore Islamic and Turkic solidarity, both of which were, in fact, rather limited. Nevertheless, in some republics the Chechen conflict gave a boost to nationalist and religious opposition activities. This phenomenon was most visible in Tatarstan, where especially brazen opposition leaders like Fauziya Bayramova of the radical *Ittifaq* movement, called for Chechen-style "resolute" action. In 1995, a leader of the Tatar opposition youth organization *Azatlyk,* following a diplomatic and politically correct discussion, declared: "If we Tatars had the Chechen mountains and spirit, we too would give Russia a trouncing!"

While Dudayev was alive, various leaders from ethnic republics occasionally felt free to contact him through their representatives, allegedly to convince Chechen president of the need to negotiate. Thus in 1995, Nikolai Fedorov, president of Chuvash Republic (and a former Russian minister of justice) sent envoys to Dudayev. Instead of talking the Chechen leader into accepting peaceful options, however, the Chuvash delegation confined itself to praising Dudayev.

Ingush president Ruslan Aushev has long been a mediator. His contacts with separatists have created the illusion of never-ending negotiation. Aushev's role was as a confidant to both the Russian leadership and those Chechens who sought to add diplomacy to their military action against the Russians. He developed informal relations with Aslan Maskhadov, who visited Ingushetia from time to time, and then lived there openly, even attempting to perform his presidential functions. The

Kremlin was vigilantly watching Aushev's contacts with Chechens, which Moscow considered too intimate. Finally, when Moscow decided it no longer needed Aushev's cooperation, the intimacy of his Chechen contacts was one of the reasons for why he had to "voluntarily" step down as president in December 2001. Despite Aushev's contacts, the idea of mediation was never seriously given a chance. In 1996, Tatarstan president Mintimer Shaymiev considered mediating between Moscow and the Chechen separatists. Several Tatar politicians had frequently met with Chechen representatives, and Shaymiev had been perfectly aware of those meetings. Johar Dudayev, who favored any possible mediation in Moscow-Chechen contacts, welcomed the Tatarstan president's position. In addition to Shaymiev, he named the then Turkish president Suleyman Demirel and Kazakhstan president Nursultan Nazarbayev as possible intermediaries in such contacts. This arrangement, therefore, placed Shaymiev in the company of international Muslim leaders.

With the start of the second Chechen war, when President Putin had already built a hierarchy of power (with the executive office at the head) and hopes for Chechnya's broad autonomy within the federation had withered, Shaymiev rejected the idea of mediation altogether, saying that "the Russian government has sufficient ways and means to address this problem through its official representatives, and additional intermediaries are no longer needed."[10] The fact that after 1999 Moscow lost all interest in Aushev's involvement in the negotiating process confirms that Shaymiev was right in so saying. The issue was dead.

Despite all the differences in regional and social attitudes to the conflict in Chechnya, the war at the beginning of the second campaign probably did more to consolidate Russia than to tear it apart. Two principal factors were primarily responsible. First, the virtual destruction of Chechnya in the first campaign delivered the message to would-be seekers of independence that armed separatism carries a horrendous price, and it was a major lesson for non-Russian elites. Second, with the "external threat" of international terrorism, and Chechnya came to be considered part of it. Most Russians learned about international terrorism at close hand from the second Chechen campaign. When Putin talked about the plans of Islamist extremists to establish "caliphates" in the North Caucasus, Central Asia, and even the Volga region, these warnings resonated loudly with the electorate.

A Strange War

The Russian leadership initially tried to present the Chechen conflict as a bizarre development that could be easily addressed by parachuting several hundred troops into Grozny. In a society still convinced of the invincibility of its armed forces, this plan sounded plausible. In that sense, Defense Minister Pavel Grachev's rash promise at the end of 1994 to end Dudayev's regime by using no more than a single airborne regiment faithfully reflected that society's attitude on dealing with Chechen separatism. (The minister, of course, should have known better.)

Until the New Year's Day disaster of 1995, neither the authorities nor the general public had any idea of the implications of a strike against the rebellious Chechens. The intricate start of the first Chechen campaign, which soon led to a bloody massacre, put Russian society in a trance. Few people truly understood the meaning of what was happening; everyone had expected a quick resolution.

The Kremlin viewed Dudayev as nothing more than an unruly adventurer whose brazen behavior had forced the authorities to resort to extreme measures. No one in the country's top leadership ever doubted the success of a blitzkrieg tactic. (A few academic experts had warned a quagmire loomed but their opinion was ignored.) Thus, no one thought to prepare the public for a protracted and painful conflict on Russia's constitutional territory. When the battlefield situation turned sour, government propaganda, still using Soviet-era techniques, was unable to marshal popular support for the war.

The Russian elite, however, learned to use the war for its own purposes. President Yeltsin turned his first and only visit to Chechnya, in May 1996, which lasted a few hours on a military base, into an election campaign platform. He pompously proclaimed Russian soldiers to be "winners" and leaned against a tank to sign a decree abolishing conscription and ordering the introduction of contract-based armed forces by 2000. After Gen. Alexander Lebed was taken on board by the Kremlin team to secure Yeltsin's victory in the second round of elections, he was immediately assigned to oversee Chechnya-related affairs—a poisoned chalice that should have politically killed Yeltsin's former rival and would-be successor. In August 1996, Yeltsin authorized Lebed to sign the Khasavyurt peace accords with Chechnya, thus seemingly killing two birds with one stone: ending the war that had been sapping Yeltsin's presidency, and stigmatizing the popular and dynamic general as a defeatist.

Toward the end of Yeltsin's reign two or three years later when the mood in the country had changed, the president's communist and nationalist opponents blamed him for ending the war as much as for starting it; all those who still feared Lebed (now a governor in Krasnoyarsk) as a potential contender for the Kremlin branded the retired general as a traitor to the nation.

The actual transfer of power in Russia in 1999–2000 had much to do with Chechnya. Faced with a serious challenge, not from the communists but from a faction of the party in power—led by such political heavyweights as former prime minister Yeugeni Primakov and Moscow mayor Yuri Luzhkov, and supported by regional leaders including Tatarstan president Shaymiev and St. Petersburg governor Vladimir Yakovlev—the Kremlin clique (often referred to as Yeltsin's "family") sought a candidate who could guarantee its power and privilege and who could also win a national election.

The Kremlin's eventual choice of Vladimir Putin as the potential successor to Yeltsin still had to be validated by Russian voters. Whether that validation would have come at all, and at what cost, without a successful military campaign, is anybody's guess. Vladimir Putin, who was mainly involved in the prosecution of the war during his brief tenure as prime minister (August–December 1999), demonstrated exactly the qualities the average voter wanted to see in a head of state and despaired of finding in Putin's competitors: energy, resolve, and old-fashioned patriotism. It was not just Putin's notorious promise "to lay waste terrorists in an outhouse" that produced the right effect on the average Russian at the right time. Such significant factors as small-scale but real military victories renewed confidence in the army, whose prestige had fallen during Yeltsin's presidency.

The shock of the bombing of apartment houses in Moscow precipitated the order to send federal forces into Chechnya proper, a momentous decision made by Putin and ratified by Yeltsin. Public opinion was demanding swift revenge, and war accomplished what all attempts at reform had failed to do. National solidarity prompted by anger now appeared to be within reach. The goal was victory. Putin, who most people had not heard of a year before, emerged as a wartime leader. Few people asked him about his future agenda or questioned his KGB past, which a decade earlier would have been unimaginable in a Russian president. Yet by the late 1990s the yearning for security was stronger than the passion for reform. Although he was selected by a clique believed to be totally self-serving and corrupt, Putin himself seemed fresh and so different from his early patrons that he was credited with the capability to put things right.

Putin's preference for an election block masterminded by vilified tycoon Boris Berezovsky and composed of essentially faceless and nameless people (those of the "Unity" party, *Yedinstvo*) enabled that block to surge to victory in the parliamentary elections of December 1999. Admittedly, large infusions of money and dirty propaganda against the opponents (notably Primakov and Luzhkov) played a major role. Yet the vote for Putin's adopted friends was not a protest vote. It was a vote of confidence for someone who did not run himself: Vladimir Putin. The Duma campaign was in fact a dress rehearsal for the presidential election. Unity's strong showing gave Yeltsin the confidence to proceed with the transfer of power, and it happened quickly. In a dramatic surprise move, Russia's first president abdicated a few hours before midnight on December 31, 1999, and, in accordance with the constitution, Putin became the acting president. Three months later he won in the first round of the presidential election. Symbolically, Putin's first move within hours of appointment as acting head of state was to welcome the new year of 2000 by sending troops into Chechnya.

During the presidential campaign Putin had stunned everyone by flying an air force fighter plane into Chechnya. After the transfer of power, however, the Chechen factor was used less often as an instrument for sustaining the Kremlin's positive image. Once victorious, Putin no longer needed to have his popularity rating boosted every day by military successes in Chechnya; indeed, such successes became less and less frequent. Once again, it was becoming obvious that the Chechen conflict could not possibly be resolved in a month or even six months. There was a growing realization that conflict resolution required purposeful and sustained economic, social, and diplomatic efforts. Clearly, no popularity, let alone glory, could be earned in such a war. The war ceased to be a tool for creating national solidarity as soon as the sophisticated, intricate, and brilliantly directed "transfer of power at the Kremlin and its subsequent legitimization" was over.

Caucasophobia and Islamophobia

It was the Chechen war that seemed to give credence to the arguments of many Russian politicians, journalists, and military figures who pointed to the "Islamic threat" and who called for national solidarity within mother Russia in response. Yet, solidarity was as elusive as ever. Instead, those who sought to portray Islam as the new enemy were dividing society even more. They were rousing what had been only vague sentiments during Soviet times, namely Caucasophobia and Islamophobia. Not that ethnic phobias were alien to the Soviet citizen: recall the widespread anti-Semitism of those times. Previously, however, Muslims had not been particular targets. As for Armenians and Georgians, they had been pretty well integrated into the "Soviet community." As for religious phobias, they did not exist in the Soviet Union for the simple reason that the avowedly atheist state had surpressed all religious expression, thus leaving believers no room for settling interreligious disputes. It is fair to say any marginalizing of ethnic-based phobias that went on during the years of the Soviet Union was partially compensated for by state-sponsored xenophobia and class-based phobias (the latter survives even to this day).

In post-Soviet Russia, the new target of ethnic phobia has become "persons of Caucasian extraction," as they are popularly known. This derogatory phrase, which probably originated as police jargon, is loosely applied to anyone having olive skin and dark curly hair. Having these characteristics are often sufficient grounds for Russian police to detain someone on sight. Especially in major Russian cities, therefore, the police effectively employ profiling, discriminating against anyone who does not look Slavic.

Caucasophobia

Caucasophobia preceded the first Chechen campaign. Professor Viktor Dyatlov, from Irkutsk in Eastern Siberia, argued that "relatively small groups of people from the Caucasus, scattered all across the country, are the most important source of tension in today's Russia."[11] The average Russian's fear of Caucasians has been well documented, and these suspicions and hostilities have become mutual, with long parallel lists of grievances, real or imagined. The Chechen conflict richly adds to that atmosphere. The average Russian envies prosperous Azeri and Dagestani market vendors and are annoyed with their emotional behavior in daily life, which contrasts sharply with quieter Russian ways. They are enraged when they hear about Caucasians' allegedly scornful attitude toward Russian women. Many Russians have come to believe that all Caucasians are their enemies, either openly or covertly, and that Caucasians "down south" are killing "our boys," with the goal of breaking up Russia.

The war, however, is fully responsible for some Russians treating Caucasians not so much as annoying "domestic aliens," but as external enemies. Valery Tishkov, a leading scholar of ethnicity, cites an episode in which he witnessed two boys play a war game in Moscow: "You'll be a Chechen, and I'll be a Russian,"[12] one boy said to the other. A typical experience: a five-year-old boy (actually the son of one of the authors) rushes around the house with a plastic rifle. When asked whom he is firing at, these days the child is likely to reply "Chechens." Nothing like that has happened since the 1950s and the early 1960s, when Moscow boys played Russians against Germans. (Russian courtyards were never the sites of boys playing Soviets against Americans.)

Normally, of course, the average Russian would not be able to distinguish between Georgians, Avars, Ossetians, Chechens, or others in the Caucasus: first because Caucasians cannot be distinguished by physical appearance, and second because the conventional Russian attitude is that Caucasians are all of the same stripe and that there's not much difference between them." Further, people become convinced from television, radio, and popular newspapers that everyone in the Caucasus is a "partner in crime."

This opinion has been bolstered by reports suggesting that since the breakup of the Soviet Union, the living conditions of Russians in the North Caucasus have deteriorated considerably because representatives of the indigenous nationalities have occupied all the key government positions and local Russians have lost the opportunity to live in peace and stability. Tishkov dubs this Caucasian nationalism "peripheral [non-Russian] nationalism."[13] To many Russians living there, the North Caucasus has indeed become something of an "inner abroad." The Russian situation in the North Caucasus had become similar to Russian diasporas elsewhere in the Caucasus and in Central Asia.

Shortly before the first Chechen campaign began, there was a flood of information about the mistreatment of ethnic Russians living in Chechnya or how they were being forced to leave the land they considered home.[14] Later, various media frequently carried similar reports, yet their sources were never questioned. The media reporting of the Russians' plight in Chechnya became as an additional catalyst for the spread of anti-Caucasian sentiment across the rest of Russia.

Remarkably, some media have started to call Caucasophobia "the Chechnya syndrome."[15] Actually, the term was more often used with reference to the problem of psychological rehabilitation of soldiers returning from Chechnya (akin to the Vietnam syndrome, or, more aptly, the more recent Afghan syndrome). The return of veterans of the Chechnya wars to normal life has proved to be complicated, and the failure of many to make the transition has resulted in a rise of violence and organized crime.[16]

Islamophobia

Caucasophobia is intimately linked to Islamophobia. Again, the Chechen conflict is not wholly to blame. Russian society has always had mixed feelings about Islam, ranging from indifference to rejection and hostility. During the Soviet era, the country's Slavic majority perceived Islamic peoples primarily as representatives of certain ethnic groups rather than of religions. This was especially true in light of the fact that Soviet citizens, including Muslims, were not permitted to display their religious affiliations publicly.

Russia's Islamophobia is an unavoidable side effect of the post-Soviet religious renaissance. After the collapse of the official surrogate religion, communism, Russians rediscovered various religions as well as religious differences. The Islamic renaissance in Russia was a much more dynamic and bottom-up process than the revival of Orthodox Christianity.

The negative attitude toward Islam in Russia was strengthened by the use of Islam for political ends; the spillover into the Russian Federation of radical fundamentalist ideas from the Middle East; and the activities of Islamic radicals inside Russia. Finally, this attitude was promoted by provocative publications in the Russian mass media, which effectively equated Islam as a religious and cultural tradition with its most radical segment. A large number of Russians quickly became accustomed to the cliché of equating Islam with fundamentalism.

In conjunction with the existence of Islamophobia, Russia's Muslim minority may be similarly intolerant of Christianity: a potentially serious problem. Contributing factors are such acts as Russian troops painting "Merry Christmas" on artillery shells about to be fired at Chechen targets on Christmas eve and Orthodox priests participating in combat and blessing tanks, which provided the Chechen propaganda machine with ample ammunition. A number of Muslims consider the Chechen conflict to have a religious dimension.

Some Russian journalists and politicians have interpreted the developments in Chechnya according to Samuel Huntington's concept of the clash of civilizations, that is, as a war of "Orthodox soldiers of Christ" against "aggressive Muslim fanatics and separatists." This view threatens to entrench Islamophobia in the public conscience. In the eyes of the ordinary Russian citizen, the image of Islam is an "evil Chechen" (phrase that dates back to the nineteenth-century Caucasian war). In a remarkable book on the Yeltsin presidency written by former Kremlin advisers, foreign Islamic fundamentalists—alongside criminal groups and terrorist centers—were identified as those who "took control of Chechnya."[17] Note that this is a view held by the most well-informed and self-avowedly liberal members of the Russian political elite.

Since September 11, 2001, Islamophobia has become even more pronounced in Russia. The official Russian propaganda went out of its way to present Islamic terrorism and Chechen separatism as a single phenomenon, or at least as equally important and interconnected phenomena. Russian leaders tried hard to convince their counterparts in Europe and the United States that a successful action by Russian federal troops against Chechen insurgents was tied to the international fight against terrorism. On September 24, 2001, President Putin issued a special statement linking international terrorism to the conflict in Chechnya, and he effectively warned Chechens that Russia's contribution to the American-led retaliation action against the Taliban in Afghanistan would take the form of a massive attack against rebellious Chechnya.

The terrorist attacks in New York and Washington, D.C., provided Russian authorities with an additional justification for their campaign in Chechnya.

Shortly before September 2001, two countervailing trends had become extremely pronounced in Russian society: anti-American sentiment (45 percent of Russians believed that terrorist attacks against the United States had been generated by hatred for America, and that the United States "deserved to be attacked" for its inflated geopolitical claims); and anti-Islamic sentiment ("You can't treat Muslims nicely. The only thing they respect is brutal force"[18]). After September 11, the first trend weakened and the second grew much stronger. The apartment bombings in Moscow in September 1999 were finally linked to the war in the North Caucasus, and the theory that certain "dark forces" had organized the bombings in order to consolidate the nation around Putin as Yeltsin's anointed successor, gradually faded. The trial of the alleged perpetrators of the Moscow bomb attacks, which began in 2001 but was later suspended, also contributed to the almost complete rejection of that theory.

Finally, many of the hundreds of thousands of officers and enlisted men who have fought in Chechnya have been more influenced by the anti-Chechen, and in a broader sense anti-Caucasian, sentiment than has the rest of Russian society. (The issue of the Russian military's special Caucasophobic and Islamopohobic attitudes are explored in greater detail in chapter 4.)

Russian Literary Classics and Present-Day Realities

Anyone analyzing the Chechen conflict's influence on the state of mind of contemporary Russian society cannot help but to note striking similarities in the general public's attitudes about the Caucasian war of the nineteenth century. Yakov Gordin, a historian, writer, and the author of one of the most interesting studies of the issue, has been particularly interested in how the attitude of contemporary Russian society to the Caucasian war was influenced by the views of the great figures of Russian literature: poet Mikhail Lermontov, novelist Leo Tolstoy (who had fought in the war), poet Alexander Pushkin, and playwright Alexander Griboyedov.

In the 1990s, Russian society gradually embraced the quintessential image of the nineteenth-century Russian soldier, the noble conqueror of the Caucasus who sympathized with the locals and only fought them against his will. This unrealistic image contrasts sharply with that of a thoughtless, greedy, and bloodthirsty federal soldier, an image that was especially widespread during the first Chechen campaign.

To support the image of the noble Russian conqueror of old, contemporary authors often cite both the memoirs of Russian generals and the classics of Russian literature. Sometimes they refer to Tolstoy's famous statements (which were one reason for his excommunication) that for him "there could be no doubt that in formal terms Islam is incomparably more advanced than the Orthodox faith" and that "anyone would prefer Islam, with its single dogma, one God, and one Prophet to . . . the complicated and confused [Orthodox] theology."[19] Contemporary interpreters of the classics maintain such statements demonstrate the impartiality and even the sympathy of these authors to the noble enemy.

Yet the classics also show a loyalty to what the Russian troops were doing in the Caucasus and, in a sense, romanticize the unavoidable brutalities of war. In fact, many of those who wrote about the Caucasus had participated in the fighting themselves or felt closely associated with the military action there. They were fulfilling their duty and some even derived an odd satisfaction from the fighting. Lermontov, for instance, wrote to a friend in 1840: "I have developed a taste for war, and I am sure that for one who becomes accustomed to the strong sensations of that game, few are the pleasures that would not seem bland."[20]

Gordin has written "Pushkin's and Lermontov's views on the Caucasian drama were based on the conviction that the Caucasus would inevitably be incorporated into the Russian world."[21] The conviction that the Russian army was bringing civilization to the Caucasus was deeply rooted in the minds of the intellectuals of Russian society. With no means of mass communication available, society at that time was hardly concerned over the price being paid to incorporate the Caucasus. If opinion polls had existed, most "thinking" people would probably have spoken resolutely for the annexation of the Caucasus; this was the period of Russian imperial expansion.

The current conflict in the Caucasus is unfolding in a totally different historical context. In the 1990s, Russia, no longer an empire or authoritarian (totalitarian) state, looked hard for a new basis for national solidarity. In a sense, Russia's survival as a country was at stake. From the opinion poll results cited earlier, many Russians in the mid-1990s were ready to give up a part of the Caucasus in exchange for general stability and an early cessation of the war.[22] Public opinion is fluid, however, and is affected by military results. When an army is successful, the public is inclined to support a fight to the finish, which is exactly what happened in 1999–2000. The media, too, play a major role.

War and the Russian Mass Media

The image of a noble enemy was propagated by Russian journalists and television hosts, particularly during the first Chechen campaign and especially on NTV, a television station that remained independent until the spring of 2001. War reporters like Yelena Masyuk, who brought the reality of Chechnya into living rooms across the nation, were later accused of a lack of patriotism and even of collusion with the enemy. Actually, the main motivation of journalist was probably a desire to advance professionally and to influence government policy. Many Russian journalists were deeply impressed by how the Cable News Network (CNN) and its war correspondents, particularly Christiane Amanpour, influenced U.S. policy during the Bosnian crisis of 1992–1994. The Chechens' heroic image was further promoted by several incidents in which journalists and politicians had volunteered to take the place of civilian hostages held by rebels, thus effectively offering themselves as human shields to the terrorists as they were retreating from Budennovsk and Kizlyar.

The image of "proud highlanders" was also actively exploited by the Chechen propaganda chief, Movladi Udugov, whose aggressive information campaign was much more successful than the clumsy and inefficient official government reporting, and was juxtaposed to that of "bloodthirsty Chechen bandits" that was being created and propagated by Russia's progovernment, or nationalist, mass media. The most striking and even grotesque example of that image was presented by Alexander Nevzorov, a journalist and Duma member, in his television production *Purgatory*, released in the late 1990s with the obvious purpose of fomenting more enmity toward the Chechens while justifying atrocities by federal forces. In frequent media reports Chechen brutality was demonstrated by Chechens' treatment of women, who were referred to as "Russian slaves" in the Russian press.[23]

Nonetheless, these newspapers and television stations that tried, deliberately or otherwise, to romanticize Chechen separatism, also had to report the darker side of a "free Chechnya": public executions, kidnappings, and tortures. Several Russian television crews, including those from NTV, were also held captive against payment of a huge ransom.

Remarkably, to date the war in Chechnya has failed to produce an objective image of the average Chechen rebel, a person drawn into the war by circumstances after the war had destroyed his life and the lives of his relatives and friends. Independence fighters of this type have easily made up the largest part of the rebel forces. Russian society has developed a stereotyped image of a Chechen: a professional guerilla whose "peaceful" daytime life is only a pause before more nighttime fighting. This situation, however, can also be considered from a different angle: that of someone who cannot find a useful daytime occupation and is forced, therefore, to take up arms at night. Various reasons exist for taking up arms, ranging from the desire to avenge the dead, to fear of a local field commander, to the simple desire to make money.

In any postconflict reintegration effort, it will be crucial to eliminate the black-and-white pictures drawn by official propaganda bureaus and to look at the Chechen resistance as it truly is. For the Chechens themselves, a no less difficult question will arise: Should former rebels see their past as a senseless tragedy, as a heroic saga, or as something else? The answer to that question will largely determine future relations between Chechens and the rest of Russia's population.

It is still too early to make final conclusions about how the Chechen tragedy has influenced Russian society. It is still too early to predict for how long that influence will be felt. Still, some preliminary conclusions can be drawn.

Conclusions

The war in Chechnya has resulted in thousands of deaths and a tremendous loss of material resources. It has destabilized the situation in Russia's southern regions, and it has contributed substantially to the development of ethnic and religious phobias, which might have dire consequences for a multiethnic and multidenominational country like the Russian Federation.

The Chechen conflict undoubtedly played into the hands of the hardline forces, which demanded tighter rules and a crackdown on civil rights including (or perhaps primarily) the freedom of the media, which had been quick to point out Moscow's failures in the North Caucasus region. In the fall of 1999 and winter of 2000, the political strength of the Russian government was largely measured by the apparent success of the Chechen campaign.

Vladimir Putin's promise, or threat, to destroy the terrorists became his most popular statement as prime minister and later as president, as well as a symbol of strong government resolve. After the 2000 elections, however, the Chechen conflict ceased to be the determining factor in assessing the performance of the second Russian president. After it had become clear that, contrary to numerous promises, the Chechen problem could not be solved over a period of several months, the Kremlin stopped using it as its trump card and devoted itself fully to constructing a hierarchy of power. Public opinion also switched to more mundane issues.

Fed by the Chechen conflict, the Caucasian and Islamic phobias grew increasingly stronger. Between 2000–2002, Russia, including Moscow, saw a wave of minipogroms at street markets, where Caucasian vendors were prime targets, although other nationalities, mostly Asians and Africans, also suffered. In 2001, this enmity culminated in the creation of an exclusive Moscow bar that officially refused to serve Caucasian patrons.[24] More than a decade after the dismantlement of the Soviet Union, Russians continue to view the Caucasus and Central Asia increasingly as foreign and even alien lands.

This situation had repercussions for the several million migrants in Russia, most of them illegal, from the former Soviet republics. Tolerance is giving way to harsher treatment. Registration with the police, always obligatory, began to be enforced. Bribe sums grew. In 2002, a citizenship law was adopted that ended the practice of privileged naturalization for ex-Soviet citizens. A further strengthening of border controls with both Central Asian and the states of the Caucasus is now perceived as a must if Russians are to have easier access to European Union countries. Still, Turkmenistan's decision in 2003 to drop local ethnic Russians' right to dual citizenship led to a strident public outcry in Russia against "oriental despots."

Russian society continues to accustom itself to the war in Chechnya. Its members have gradually developed a shield protecting them from the pain of seeing the deaths of Russian soldiers and the plight of civilian and internally displaced populations. People now perceive the events in Chechnya as part of their daily lives. Their attention to Chechnya is heightened only if they are directly affected by the conflict: for instance, when another round of conscription begins. Not infrequently, however, popular annoyance is directed not so much at Chechen separatists as at the Russian military and politicians who are unable to put an end to the Chechen struggle for separatism.

It took the Russian authorities a long time to realize that they were unable to deal with separatism in a resolute and professional manner. The Chechen crisis has proved to be a chronic disease for which no effective remedy is in sight. In turn, Russian society has also proved ill-prepared to judge the developments in Chechnya precisely. Even during the first Chechen campaign, when the ruling elite was concerned about losing power as a result of popular antiwar sentiments, these sentiments were softened by half measures that could not bring the conflict to an end. During the second Chechen campaign, public opinion was passive and produced no practical influence on the development of the crisis.

After several years of the second campaign, the Russian population has gotten used to terrorism. Russians have had to accept that no place in their country is safe from terrorists. They have also seen that nothing can stop suicide bombers from carrying out their missions. Thus, many ordinary Russians now share the experience of the Israelis and Americans. They *know* they are at war, but they do not *feel* it. Psychologically, they prefer to leave it to the government and the army to wage war and fight terrorism. Strangely, Russia is at peace during the world's war on terror.

4

The Islamic Factor

No study of the conflict in Chechnya is complete without an analysis of the Islamic factor. For many Russians, a bearded man holding a Kalashnikov automatic rifle and wearing a green headband has become the symbol of Chechen separatism and the stereotypical image of a Chechen. Today in Russia the word *terrorism* is rarely used without the adjective *Islamic*.

What is the exact meaning of the Islamic factor? Does it stand for the Islamic tradition's influence on developments in a particular Muslim society, country, or region? Does it relate to Islam's well-known refusal to differentiate between the secular and the spiritual, which makes Islam a "total religion"? The Islamic factor is probably best explained as Islam seeking to address secular social problems through the consistent promulgation of an ideal of social justice not attainable outside the context of an Islamic state. Conversely, the true Islamic state derives its strength from the unity of religious and secular power, something that Muslim liberals actively object to. Finally, Islam has a code of laws, the Shariah, that imposes strict rules on the lives of individuals and communities.

Like any religion, Islam claims to be the source of absolute truth. As an extremely secularized religion, however, Islam's claims of absolute truth extend beyond concrete, practical matters. Religious motivation stimulates and guides political ambitions. These entities claim that their actions are sanctioned by a higher authority, and therefore they have the right to use any and all methods, including kidnapping and hostage

71

taking, necessary to achieve their ends, even if they exceed the moral limits of Western societies.

The call to Islam is especially resounding because most Muslim countries have been either formally dependent or informally dominated by Christian powers. Today, the technological gap between the Muslim world and the West is widening. Hence we see an energetic push to prove Islam's "right to the absolute truth," and the individual's desire to believe that it is Islam and Muslims who will ultimately prevail. However incredible this may seem against a background of the Muslim world's growing backwardness, numerous Muslim ideologues have welcomed the twenty-first century as the beginning of "an Islamic era."

The conflict in Chechnya relates to the call to Islam and may be considered under the rubric "Chechnya's Islamic factor." It involves the way the conflict fits into political and ideological trends in the Muslim world; how much the conflict influences internal processes in the Muslim world; and the extent to which the conflict is itself an extrapolation of contemporary Muslim trends in the Russian Caucasus region. A companion group of issues relates to how the general condition of the Muslim world influences the situation in Chechnya and how the situation in Chechnya bears on developments in Muslim regions and countries in the Caucasus, Central Asia, and Russia. This problem is essentially political, and not theoretical, and it concerns the practical interaction of political forces acting under Islamic slogans, primarily that of a global jihad.

In terms of duration, severity, and the extent of casualties, the conflict in Chechnya stands out from other crises in the Muslim world. An important element is that the separatists have declared jihad on Russia and proclaimed Chechnya, under the name Ichkeria, an Islamic republic, complete with Shariah law. By doing so they created the precedent of an Islamic state forming within the former Soviet Union, a precedent that can be a model elsewhere in the former Soviet southern regions. Moreover, Chechnya has become, within certain limits, an exporter of radical Islam to Muslim regions of Russia and the Commonwealth of Independent States. It is in Chechnya that the Islamic threat—the trump card that security elites in Moscow have played since the mid-1990s—first turned into a clear and present danger.

Islam in Chechnya: Taking a Closer Look

There are several approaches to analyzing the Islamic factor in the Chechen conflict. According to one, while Islam is not the root cause of the conflict, it is a main factor in its continuation and its main ideological tenet. Thus, the conflict is seen in terms of a "clash of civilizations." Initially, this approach was common among both radical leftist journalists and the conservative military in Russia. In due course, the ruling establishment in Moscow also fell in with this approach. The vigorous Islamic threat became a justification for fighting the war until ultimately victorious and for maintaining the toughest stance possible in order to prevent religious extremism from spilling over into other regions. The concept of an Islamic threat was extrapolated to all Islam, which certainly upset Russia's Islamic community.

Another approach holds that Islam is but a cover for very secular pragmatic objectives in economic and political spheres and that the religious renaissance is merely a convenient tool for attaining separatist ends. Despite the differences between these two approaches, both equate Islam with militant fundamentalism and imply Islam's hostility to Russia.[1]

A third approach is based on the view that as a religion, Islam should not be involved in political squabbles and can be useful only as a peacekeeping force in conflict situations. This idealistic stand is characteristic of many Muslim clerics, as well as of secular politicians with a Muslim background. To an extent, this approach extends to popular acceptance, reflecting how Moscow politicians want Islam to be seen—as politically neutral—and proffers a distorted and obscure view of the true role of religion in Muslim society.

The proponents of a fourth approach insist that the Islamic factor can and must play a positive role in the creation of a new Russia and that it can be a line of defense against globalization and Western (primarily American) expansionism. This anti-Western bias is coupled with affirmations of a neo-Eurasian idea and the special role of Russia, which could use the Islamic factor in realizing its binary nature of belonging to both Europe and Asia.[2] (This argument is often associated with the affirmation of Russia's inherent "imperial nature.") The Islamic factor is thus seen as an appropriate tool for strengthening Russia's position. The chief advocate of this approach is Heidar Jamal, the founder of the Islamic Renaissance Party and the head of the Islamic Committee of Russia. Jamal believes that "it is in the interest of Russia to rely on the true Islamic factor in the Caucasus."[3]

Among these four main approaches are a wide spectrum of shades and nuances, which can often be confusing. We stress that the use of Islam as a political instrument has been largely a reaction to or a consequence of the war and not its cause. As Chechnya's first elected president, Johar Dudayev, said: "Russia . . . has forced us to take the Islamic path."[4] It was after Dudayev's death that the conflict, which began as a secular separatist bid, assumed clear religious overtones.

Chechnya's Islamic Project

Although Islam had proved to be an efficient tool in mobilizing Chechens toward war, it later failed to serve the same function for their internal political consolidation. The Islamic national project has failed in Chechnya because most Chechens are simply too individualistic to embrace the idea of an Islamic state complete with Shariah law.

Moreover, Chechen society, at least its urban areas and the diaspora, gradually warmed to democratic values. In the early 1990s, an Islamic republic in Chechnya looked like a nonstarter. Dudayev thought little of the idea. Initially, Aslan Maskhadov also took an anticlerical stand, though later he had to bow to pressure from Islamic radicals.

There have been attempts to implement the Islamic project both at micro- and macrolevels. Islamic rules were enacted in Shatoy and Urus-Martan in Chechnya; in the Kadar Valley, Tsumadinsky, and in some other rayons of Dagestan. At the opposite end of the spectrum, there was an attempt to unify Chechnya and Dagestan into a single imamate.[5] This pattern is common to the entire post-Soviet southern region and, indeed, to the rest of the Muslim world. There have been continual attempts to create Muslim enclaves and a proliferation of states calling themselves Islamic; there are also transnational organizations whose declared aim is to create an Islamic megastate based on radical ideologies and the universal introduction of Shariah.

Olivier Roy, a noted French academic who spent a lot of time studying Afghanistan before switching his attention to Muslims in the former

Soviet Union, believes that Islamic radicals, who sought to transform state structures from secular to religious structures within a nation state, have suffered a defeat. He also insists that any attempts to implement pan-Islamic ideas are doomed to failure and are, indeed, failing.[6] In principle, this is correct. However, it would be premature to think that the Islamic movement has been politically defeated. Even if it is involved in a secular political process, Islamic radicalism will not abandon its aims, and the neofundamentalists will not throw in the towel. A more likely scenario is that Islamists will step up their activities in conflict-prone regions where local populations adhere to traditional ways and are receptive to calls for reform by the public in Islamic wrappings. On the one hand, the experience of Middle Eastern countries demonstrates that it is impossible to create a so-called genuine Islamic state with the absolute dominance of Shariah, the elimination of banking principles from the economy, and the construction of an insurmountable barrier to external influence. So far, no country has succeeded in returning to the golden age of Islam. Indeed, the Islamic Republic of Iran itself is proof that total Islamization and the implementation of the Islamic project at the national level are impossible. Even the Taliban regime, which served as the most uncompromising example of adherence to the Islamic tradition both domestically and in relations with the outside world, failed to mobilize Muslims to fight the U.S.-led military action.

In Iran, the trend is toward a gradual liberalization of the regime and a grassroots yearning for democratization. Further, radical revolutionary rhetoric is being forgotten. Afghanistan's Taliban regime increasingly looks like a historical aberration, brought about by decades of civil war. Under normal peacetime conditions, when Islam is no longer an instrument of military and political mobilization and the banner of jihad becomes irrelevant, extremist principles will almost inevitably dissipate, thus eroding interest in creating an Islamic state. Islamic radicals, as a minority, would be overwhelmed by nonradical average citizens.

In fact, this is exactly what happened in Chechnya after the 1996 Khasavyurt peace accords. Once military operations under jihad slogans had ended, the desire of local radicals to play the Islamic card was consistently rejected by a secular majority in Chechen society. Still, small groups of Islamic militants vowed to fight for an Islamic state. These groups migrated from one "local project" to another (that is, from Bosnia to Chechnya to Afghanistan), fighting for a cause that is now essentially lost.

The terrorist attacks in New York and Washington, D.C., challenged the entire world and particularly the West. The tragedy of September 11, 2001, demonstrated how difficult, if not impossible, it is to predict where Islamists will strike next. Yet the attacks confirmed that the terrorists realize their own failure and inability to reach strategic objectives.

Despite the particularities of the Chechen conflict and that Chechnya is a problem specific to Russia, it is not exceptional in the "Islamic political game." The protagonists of that game understand that their strategic objective—the creation of an Islamic state system—is unattainable. The *struggle* for an Islamic state is the essence of the contemporary Islamic movement, regardless of the impossibility of attaining an Islamic state. It is through this unending struggle that Islamists and their followers, both current and future, find a way to self-realization.

The Roots of Islamic Radicalism

Chechen separatism can be managed with sufficient political will, courage, and diplomatic talent. It can also be suppressed by military force, and for a long time. It will likely be impossible, however, to eradicate Islamic radicalism. Islamic radicalism is a self-regenerating phenomenon. The twenty-first century may well be remembered as a century of regular political activity by Islamists at many levels, local and global.

The factors responsible for the growth of Islamism involve internal social and economic factors: First is the frustration of most Muslim populations over their dire economic conditions and their disappointment in the ruling elites, who are often aloof, corrupt, and inept at dealing with those conditions. For the populace, the general crisis of their lives becomes associated with religious apostasy and moral degradation among the ruling classes, elites who often ignore Islam's ascetic values. The resulting social protest assumes a religious form, and calls for social justice and the establishment of fair government increase.

The second cause of increasingly active Islamism is the Muslim resistance to external pressures, traditionally exercised under the flag of jihad. The Chechen case is a perfect example. From the Caucasian war of the nineteenth century to the anti-Bolshevik resistance in the 1920s and 1930s to the current conflict, Chechens likewise couch their resistance in terms of jihad.

Yet in the twentieth century, jihad as the ideology of a national liberation movement did not necessarily postulate the creation of a state based on religious tenets. Rather, this ideology was typical of such nineteenth-century movements as those led by Abd al-Kader in Algeria, Mahdi in the Sudan, and, of course, Imam Shamil in the Northern Caucasus. Along with Afghanistan under the Taliban regime, Chechnya is one of the few places where a similar evolution took place—and failed.

The export of radicalism is the third cause of the rise of Islamic militancy. Various radical Islamic organizations have tried to project their influence in the former Soviet territory. While these organizations initially confined themselves largely to educational and religious activities, as political tensions rose, more Muslims became involved in politics. The Islamic organizations launched radical propaganda and financially supported their brethren in the faith. Later they gave assistance (however limited) in the recruitment and training of rebels.

In pursuit of their cause, Islamic radicals do not shy away from cooperating with criminal elements, especially those involved in drug trafficking. In particular, such unholy ties have formed in the Caucasus and Central Asia, the more so because the plants from which drugs are produced are grown chiefly in territories controlled by Islamists. (In the late 1990s, the Taliban movement in Afghanistan controlled 97 percent of the Thebaic poppy, the main raw material for heroin production.[7]) After the defeat of the Taliban, drug trafficking passing through Central Asia has grown worse. Russian expert and journalist Igor Rotar reported that in the North Caucasus, "the criminal circles march to power under the green flag."[8] According to witnesses, in Chechnya "each field commander necessarily has plantations and facilities to produce drugs in the area he controls."[9]

The most important question about radical Islam's activity and growing influence is whether its causes are primarily internal or external. In Russia, there is a wide difference of opinion. According to the official view, the radicalization of Islam is first and foremost the result of external influence, without which the fundamentally anti-Russian idea of creating an Islamic state in the North Caucasus would never have appeared. External influence is also blamed for the religious form of Chechen separatism. In line with this logic, "It is time that everyone realized clearly that it is not only Basayev and Khattab that Russia is fighting in Chechnya. The much more serious enemy is Islamic radicalism. Chechnya is only part of radical Islam's grandiose plans to reshape the political map of the world so that green becomes the dominant color."[10] The influential business weekly *Kommersant-Vlast* published a map of the Greater Middle East (including Central Asia) that featured the borders of the proposed "Wahhabite Empire." The note to the map read: "The seemingly isolated events are, in fact, all related. From all these points are threads leading to the Middle East and the Arab monarchies of the Persian Gulf."[11]

Russian liberals see Islamic radicalism as a challenge to European civilization and as a threat to the stability and territorial integrity of the Russian Federation. Nationalists, communists, and even some "statists" believe that Islamic radicalism is a component of a global anti-Russian conspiracy, led by the United States, that uses Islamists for its political ends. "Unlike in 1991–1996 when [Western-led] anti-Russian military actions were largely carried out under the flag of secular nationalism, today Islamists and Wahhabists have begun to play an increasingly important role," writes Communist *Pravda*. According to *Pravda*, "In the West and in Wahhabist circles, it is in Chechnya that lie the principal hopes of dragging Russia into a long and crippling war."[12] These speculations are consonant with belief in an anti-Russia, Islamic-Catholic conspiracy, which is often propagated by the left-wing conservatives and Orthodox ideologists, who share a similar xenophobic sentiment.

This logic received a powerful, fresh impetus in connection with the American counterterrorist operation in Afghanistan. In fall 2001, the entire Russian left-wing nationalist press shouted that the United States was trying to set Russia on a collision course with the Muslim world.

This view easily accommodates the idea that the Chechen crisis is primarily a result of external intrigue by a variety of forces: the United States, Ukraine, Iran, the Persian Gulf states, Afghanistan, Turkey, and other countries. This view concurs with the opinion, often found in left-wing nationalist circles, that NATO and Islamists have concerted plans to destroy Russia, and that, consequently, they must be resisted. "It was in Dagestan [the Basayev incursion of 1999] that Russia stopped its geopolitical retreat under pressure from NATO and its satellites in the Arab world," wrote *Dagestanskaya Pravda*.[13] Thus, the common conspiratorial approach to Islamic radicalism unites pro-Western liberals, left-wing radicals, and Russian statists, especially those who adhere to the quasi-imperial nationalist outlook. One of the most colorful representatives of this school of thought is Sergey Kurginian, "a conspiratorial genius" of the Russian analytical community.[14]

Even if one agrees with these views, one must admit that the basic conditions for radical Islam's political and ideological expansion were created by internal forces, not least the Kremlin. One cannot fail to notice the reemergence of the typical Soviet approach where the adverse consequences of domestic policy errors, corruption, and the abuse of public funds are presented as "evil intrigues by the enemy."

On occasion, the phenomenon of Islamic radicalism has been exploited by non-Islamic states. The USSR welcomed Iran's 1979 Islamic revolution, which ended Tehran's pro-American orientation. In his 1981 report to the Soviet Communist Party Congress, Leonid Brezhnev proclaimed that Islam could occasionally play a progressive role. The Soviets assisted various Islamic radicals in the Middle East in order to undermine Israel, America's regional ally. On the other hand, the United States and other Western countries supported the anti-Soviet Islamic resistance in Afghanistan in the 1980s. There were hopes that the 50 million Soviet Muslims, awakened by the Iranian revolution and angered by the Afghanistan invasion, would present a major challenge to Moscow that would fatally weaken the Soviet monolith. The lesson to be drawn from this experience is clear: at the end of the day, all attempts at cooperation with Islamic radicals by Soviet and Western special services, strategies notwithstanding, Islamists are always guided by their own agenda and logic.

To recap: the Islamization of the conflict in Chechnya was a reaction to conditions rather than a cause, and any external factor was always of secondary importance. The very involvement of external forces was a consequence of domestic developments. That involvement, however, played into the hands of Russian political leaders and, especially, of the military establishment, offering them an opportunity to blame their own errors on external forces. It is clear that tensions in Chechnya resonate in the rest of the Muslim world. It is equally clear that Chechnya's influence on the Muslim world is limited and not comparable with the conflicts in the Middle East, Afghanistan, or Iraq.

That said, the isolated nature of the Chechen conflict does not mean that it is somehow a minor problem. The war in Chechnya has not only stimulated an Islamic renaissance in neighboring regions, it has determined the high level of politicization and the confrontational nature of the Islamic renaissance. It has turned the Islamic factor into a factor of instability in the south of Russia and the entire Caucasus.

Islamic Radicalism in the North Caucasus

The transformation of Chechen ethnic nationalism into a religious movement catalyzed the rise of nationalist and religious sentiments among other Muslim peoples in the North Caucasus. As the conflict continued and became progressively more violent—and as Russian forces suffered more losses—certain groups, especially young people, were overwhelmed with the euphoria of national and religious self-assertion. Solidarity with the Chechens became their rallying cry. Open support for Chechen separatism was also a way to overcome indigenous inferiority complexes, a compensation for diminished social status and second-rate treatment outside the region. Supporting the Chechen struggle against Moscow was retribution for the inability to find a comfortable niche in post-Soviet society.

A common way for people to associate themselves with the Chechen resistance was to participate in various Islamic classes and training camps. In these camps religious studies were combined with military training. The activities were financed from abroad as well from Chechen sources.

The business of recruiting and training rebels from among young people in the North Caucasus is one of the most complicated aspects of the Chechen conflict, one clouded by numerous stories and bold lies. The explanation is found in the odd situation where Russian special services and Chechen rebels have shared a desire to exaggerate the level of support that Chechen separatism has enjoyed among other peoples of the North Caucasus. For Chechens, emphasizing the support of people from outside Chechnya has confirmed their own importance in the region and has presented the conflict between Chechnya and Moscow as the forerunner of a regional conflict in which Chechens will play the leading role. As for Russian officials and especially the military, they have used the alleged involvement of other Muslim peoples in the conflict to boost their own status as defenders of Russia's territorial integrity. In addition, the spillover from Chechnya of externally supported Islamic radicalism has been exploited by the local ruling elites, who have missed no chance to sell themselves to Moscow as the prime bulwark against Wahhabism.

It is difficult to assess objectively the influence that radical Islam has had in the North Caucasus. Any assessment must rely on indirect evidence and often intuition rather than hard facts and statistical data (which are frequently doctored).[15]

Chechen radicals used to have their strongest ties with "fellow sympathizers"—one who sympathizes with communist doctrines but is not a member of the Communist party—in Dagestan. In Dagestan, however, radical Islam's emergence as an ideology and movement (eclectic and fragmented, without any one institutional form) was in no way connected to events in Chechnya, and radical Islamic leaders had never put forward separatist banners. In Dagestan, radical Islam had social roots. Originally, the local Islamic space was free of the confrontational ideas of jihad. Islamic politicians and ideologists in Dagestan, including such influential figures as Ahmed-kadi Akhtayev, one of the founders of the Islamic Liberation Party, and Bagauddin Muhammad, an Islamic fundamentalist cleric who commanded the greatest authority in the North Caucasus, had never called for the secession of Muslim enclaves from Russia. Their objectives were religious, educational, and social.

Until the mid-1990s, Daghestani Islamic radicals entertained an ambivalent attitude toward Chechen separatism. Although they recognized the Chechens' right to self-determination in terms of Chechnya's independence or continued membership in the Russian Federation, and cooperated with the Chechen resistance, Daghestani Islamists were not enthusiastic about the spread of irredentist ideas across the entire North Caucasus. At a meeting of the heads of Daghestani jamaats (Islamic student communities) in the mid-1990s, the participants agreed that an armed conflict with Moscow was possible, but only if Moscow took the same action against Dagestan as it had against Chechnya. Islamic radicals realized only too well that in Dagestan, separatist sentiments would inevitably destroy a fragile ethnic balance, thus sparking a civil war. As well, the radicals realized that they were in the minority in the republic.

Daghestani Muslims identify themselves on four levels: ethnic, Daghestani, Muslim, and as full-fledged members of the Russian Federation. Their self-perception as a people associated with "Russia as a whole" is the basis of their social stability. It is telling that both the followers of radical Islam and their opponents in the traditionalist and institutionalized clergy see Russia as their native country and strongly object to being regarded as aliens. As State Duma Deputy Nadirshah Khachilayev, a known proponent of radical Islam who headed the Muslim Union of Russia in the mid-1990s, said: "Muslims should not feel like unwanted children in their home country."[16] Sayid-Muhammad Abubakarov, an opponent of the Wahhabists and chair of the Spiritual Muslim Council of Dagestan, bitterly remarked: "The understanding that followers of the Islamic faith are full-fledged Russian citizens and masters of the state, rather than outcasts, will still take quite some time to take root in some government agencies and, especially, in the mass media."[17]

The question of whether Chechen separatists relied on the support of Daghestani fellow sympathizers and hoped to create a unified Chechen-Daghestani state outside Russia is not as simple as some analysts insisted in the late 1990s. Indeed, the creation of such a state was much debated in Chechnya. In April 1998, a congress of the peoples of Chechnya and Dagestan was convened in Grozny. The congress leadership, and primarily Basayev, repeatedly insisted that the unification of Chechnya and Dagestan was necessary and inevitable. Speaking at the congress, Movladi Udugov, Ichkeria's foreign minister, said: "The victory of Islam in the Caucasus will be inevitable if the peoples of Chechnya and Dagestan break free from the influence of Moscow and Moscow's puppets in Makhachkala [Dagestan's capital]." Gusseynov, the chair of the executive committee of the Union of Avari Jamaats, agreed with Udugov: "Dagestan has been blessed with a historical chance of becoming free and independent, and to translate this chance into reality, we must unify with Ichkeria under the flag of Islam."[18]

How ethnic elites and ethnic communities inside Dagestan perceived this idea is a different story. Their reaction to Chechen calls for unification was cautiously negative. The elites were fully aware that creating a single imamate would effectively mean the redistribution of their political and economic power in Dagestan in favor of the more ambitious Chechens. Chechen leaders dreamed of gaining access to the Caspian Sea, which would give Chechnya an opportunity control the oil pipeline in Daghestani territory as well as rich fisheries. It would also give Chechnya much easier access to the outside world (Chechnya's 80-kilometer border with Georgia passes over extremely difficult terrain, and transportation links are few and unreliable), a development that separatists saw as a way to strengthen Chechen sovereignty. The Daghestanis were not at all happy about this, nor were they happy about Chechen-Daghestani unification on the basis of Islamic principles: a development that would inevitably trigger a harshly negative reaction from Moscow. In fact, the Chechen initiative of creating a single state was dragging Dagestan into a bitter confrontation with Moscow. No matter how that confrontation ended, the republic would be seriously destabilized.

There had never been a unified approach in Dagestan to the Wahhabis. Some members of the local elite preserved their contacts with Wahhabbis—for various reasons, including family ties convenience. Also, in Dagestan a religious and political counter-elite had emerged that relied on Chechens to boost its influence. Daghestani Islamists and Chechens continued to cooperate, and Basayev and Khattab considered Daghestani Islamists as a bridge between Chechnya and Dagestan. They also hoped that cooperation with Daghestani religious leaders would strengthen their authority with their own followers in Chechnya and across the North Caucasus.

In their turn, Islamic radicals persecuted by Daghestani authorities also needed support in the form of propaganda, political assistance, and even military assistance. In 1996, the famous *Hejira* took place.[19] Bagauddin Muhammad and hundreds of his followers relocated to Chechnya, where they were effectively granted political asylum. From this safe haven they could continue to influence affairs in Dagestan. Despite having different internal roots—separatist aspirations in Chechnya and social frustrations in Dagestan—the two Islamist movements supported and benefited each other. Still, the alliance between Chechen and Daghestani Islamists reduced the latter's support base at home, a trend that became especially visible after Basayev-led incursion into Dagestan in 1999, when most of the local population opposed the Chechen action. As well, the invading army included a large number of Daghestani muhajirun who had been forced to emigrate to Chechnya and who were seeking revenge for past offenses.

The Religious Basis of Islamic Radicalism

Most Russian experts and the mass media fear the dangers of exporting Islamic radicalism from Chechnya to other Muslim republics of the North Caucasus, of the eventual destabilization of the region, and of the growth of interethnic and interreligious tensions. From this perspective, it is important to understand to what extent radical Islamic ideas are compatible with the traditional mentalities of Muslim peoples of the North Caucasus, what social and ethnic grounds exist for the proliferation of radical Islam, and what forces oppose that proliferation.

The religious basis of Islamic radicalism is *Salafiya*, an ideology of returning to early Islamic values, which dates to the time of the Prophet Mohammad and the righteous caliphs. Salafiya's theological and legal basis is the negation of the differences among the four main Mazhabi (the theological and legal schools of Islamic thought) of Islam. In the eighth and ninth centuries, four mazhabs were formed in Islam: the *Khanbalite*, *Maslikite*, *Shafiyite*, and *Khanafite* mazhabs. Shafiyism and Khanafism are the most widely spread religious trends in the North Caucasus. Both of these, especially Khanafism, are also the most liberal trends of those schools of thought adhered to by Russia's Muslim community. The Salafites proceed from the conviction that the Islamic faith is unique and is based on the principles outlined in the Qur'an and Shariah. Uncompromisingly, they oppose any external borrowing of non-Islamic, especially ethnic, traditions that bring syncretic elements to Islam. Salafiya is therefore strongly opposed to the local Islamic tradition of the North Caucasus, which is based on a synthesis of classic Islam and local ethnic and cultural traditions. The Salafites insist that Muslims live strictly in line with Islamic principles and harshly criticize anyone having liberal attitudes to public and private behavior.

In the eastern part of the North Caucasus (Chechnya, Dagestan, and Ingushetia), Salafiya's main opposition is *Muridism*, which is a variety of Islamic *Sufism*. In the western part of the region, the local ethnic (though not necessarily religious) cultural tradition plays a special role in resisting Salafiya.

In the sphere of social and political relations, the Salafites advocate an Islamic state based on Shariah laws, which would require a radical overhaul of the existing system of government. Such an overhaul would be difficult without a civil war, an option rejected by most Muslims in the North Caucasus.

Local Muslims are biased against Salafites, who are known as Wahhabists in the North Caucasus. Most Muslims dislike the religious rigidity of Salafiya, its rejection of a so-called people's Islam, and its call for radical actions against local authorities. Many people worry that the scenario in Chechnya will occur, with a struggle for an Islamic state turning into separatism.

Yet such factors as frustration over the failure of recent reforms, a worsening economy, unemployment, and the disintegration and distortion of traditional ideological and moral imperatives have forced local populations to seek religious solutions. This is especially true of the young, who, despite massive official propaganda, see radical Islam in a heroic light, as a struggle for justice.

Moreover, there are lingering political tensions, especially but not only in Karachayevo-Cherkessia and Kabardino-Balkaria related to a continuing power struggle. Islamic radicals have repeatedly tried to interfere in the political intrigue in these republics, although not publicly. Public opinion inside these republics, however, holds that secular politicians, including those who publicly condemn radicalism, would not hesitate to use Islam, when expedient, as a means to attain their ends. This is especially true of Ruslan Aushev, the president of Ingushetia from 1992 to 2001, who has often spoken of reintroducing Islamic law to daily life, including legalizing polygamy (the attitude toward women is a litmus test in the region of a politician's Islamism). In Dagestan, the same can be said of the powerful mayor of Makhachkala, Said Amirov, and of the former secretary of the Republican Security Council and Hero of Russia, Magomet Talboyev. Sometimes non-Islamic politicians are also suspected of using Islam for political ends. For example, in 1998, after the situation in Karachayevo-Cherkessia intensified, such accusations were leveled at president-to-be Vladimir Semenov (the general of the army and former commander-in-chief of the Russian Ground Forces), who is an ethnic Karachai known for his extremely cautious attitude to "politicized Islam."[20]

How Many Salafites Are There in the North Caucasus?

Experts, politicians, and special service officers cannot specify the number of Wahhabi Islamists operating in the North Caucasus or what percentage they are of the region's Muslim population. Estimates vary from 5 percent to 20 percent. In absolute terms, the numbers sometimes run to hundreds of thousands. It is even more difficult to estimate the number of armed Islamists. It is likely that several thousands are dispersed across several areas. Different sources put the number of potential and active Salafite "soldiers" at between 2,000–10,000.

Available statistics are not accurate, and it is difficult to establish criteria for identifying Salafites, who refer to themselves simply as Muslims. Still, data for the period 1998–2000 helps to roughly estimate the number of Islamic radicals. Igor Dobayev, an expert with the North Caucasus Academy of Civil Service, wrote that in Dagestan "there were up to 5,000 Wahhabis who call themselves Islamists."[21] Yuri Snegirev, of the leading Russian daily *Izvestia*, wrote that there were 3,000 Wahhabi rebels in the republic.[22] It is remarkable that in some areas the number of Wahhabis is known to the last man. Ilya Maksakov, an experienced and usually well-informed analyst with Moscow's *Nezavisimaya gazeta*, believes that in 1998 the Wahhabis totaled 2,795.[23]

In the North Caucasus republics of Kabardino-Balkaria, Karachayevo-Cherkessia, and Adygeya—to say nothing of the predominantly Christian North Ossetia—the number of Wahhabis is small and measures in triple-digit figures. According to the interior minister of Kabardino-Balkaria, Gen. Hachim Shogenov, for instance, during "routine checks of people showing an inclination toward extremist and nationalist ideas," the police created a database of three hundred names.[24] The authors of *The Herald of the Russian Academy of Sciences* also found three hundred Wahhabis in Karachayevo-Cherkessia.[25] The Wahhabi presence is more noticeable in Ingushetia owing to a massive influx of Chechens—as many as a thousand Wahhabis—although it is difficult to know how many are Ingush and how many Chechens.

Still, the influence of radical Islam in the North Caucasus is hardly confined to the presence of several hundred trainees from "Wahhabi camps." In various locations across the region, there is a trend to follow Islamic norms of behavior and observe Islamic canons, including Shariah prohibitions, in daily life. Local mass media often carry reports about young people who are referred to as role models and who in every possible way emphasize, and sometimes overemphasize, their adherence to Islam in contrast to the religious indifference and immorality prevailing in society. One newspaper in the North Caucasus published an article about a high school in Nalchik, the European-style capital of Kabardino-Balkaria, where a group of Muslim seniors set themselves against their schoolmates by stressing Islam's superiority over other religions and their own prevalence over other people because of their adherence to Islam. The article carried the headline: "The New Muslims."[26] This happened in a peaceful republic where most people have a negative attitude to Salafism.

Across the North Caucasus young people ages fourteen to seventeen are increasingly attracted to Islam. (Ironically, this attraction coexists with an interest in Western culture.) Further, their Islam is not the traditional "Islam of their forefathers," but a politicized Islam, one dominated by the ideas of Shariah, the Islamic state, jihad, and even Islamic revolution.

The "New Muslim" phenomenon is not confined to young people. In the North Caucasus, Islamic radicals enjoy significant support in local Muslim communities. For instance, in 1998 in Dagestan the number of Muslims with a negative attitude to Wahhabism decreased from 74 to 63 percent, while the percentage of its radical proponents grew from 3 percent to 5 percent.[27] Although attitudes toward Islamic radicals worsened immediately after Chechen rebel groups invaded Dagestan, only a year later a greater understanding had evolved between the radicals and the rest of society, in part because the government's harsh suppression of Wahhabism made the public more sympathetic to it.

Proponents of radical Islam continue to enjoy considerable and sustainable influence in all the North Caucasian republics except for North Ossetia.[28] Until recently, Islamic radicalism was least visible in Adygeya. It has, however, gained strength in Karachayevo-Cherkessia and Kabardino-Balkaria. General Shogenov has identified eight areas of Kabardino-Balkaria where the Islamists were "especially active," including the capital city, Nalchik.[29] In Kabardino-Balkaria, the growth of Islamic radicalism is assisted by the sporadic intensification of ethnic tensions between the Kabardins and the Balkars. Some experts believe that the more radical Balkars may eventually respond to radical Islamic rallying cries. The Balkars are known to have sent letters of support to the radical Islamic and pro-Chechen Caucasian Conference.[30]

In Ingushetia, Islamic radicalism is also spreading, presenting what Ruslan Aushev called "a serious threat to stability in society."[31] In Ingushetia, Islamic radicalism feeds on three sources: the Chechen crisis, the socioeconomic situation, and the still-unresolved border conflict between Ingushetia and North Ossetia. The significance of the third factor cannot be overestimated or ignored. According to political analyst Eduard Skakunov, "Fundamentally, the conflict between Ingushetia and North Ossetia is a conflict of values, in which each side is measuring up the other in accordance with its own social and cultural values, which are different from, and, most important, incompatible with those of the opponent."[32] Moreover, Chechen field commanders have recently spoken of their "readiness to support the Republic of Ingushetia in reclaiming territories that are historically hers."[33]

While the Chechen war helped spread Islamic radicalism across the region, the failure to create an Islamic state in Chechnya set limits to that radicalism. Chechens rejected the idea of an Islamist state , and attempts to impose Islamic rule by force have further discredited the Islamists. In this sense, Chechnya is like Tajikistan, where the 1992–1997 civil war between the Islamists and their opponents helped to prevent potential Islamic revolutions in other Central Asian countries, so powerful was the Tajik conflict's effect on the region. One must remember that conflict in Tajikistan was resolved only after the Islamists were recognized as legitimate participants in the political process. Tajikistan remains a secular state, within which Islamists have a recognized role.

Thus, although the number of Islamists in the North Caucasus is difficult to estimate accurately, Islamization is spreading noticeably. It affects the youth, including those in urban centers, who are beset by high unemployment rates. The continuing Chechen conflict, which since the late 1990s has assumed Islamic overtones, helps in recruiting new followers to the Islamist cause. Nevertheless, the failure to create an Islamic state in Chechnya leaves new recruits few options but an endless, and essentially hopeless, struggle. Gauging the effects of long-term instability caused by those promoting Islamic states will be important in the life of the entire Russian Federation.

Chechnya and Russia's Muslim Organizations

The conflict in Chechnya touched off a process of Islamic radicalization in the North Caucasus as well as across the Russian Federation, and it contributed to a schism in Russia's Muslim community. According to the beliefs of the institutional clergy, inside the Muslim community "trends have emerged whose further development may result in a confrontation among Muslims and between Islamic believers and the followers of other religions. They may also jeopardize the stability and peace of some regions."[34]

After the breakup of the Soviet Union, Chechnya, as well as the rest of the North Caucasus, was no longer isolated from the greater Muslim world. Moreover, regional developments cannot be separated from developments in other Muslim countries or regions. The Muslim world can be compared to an ocean where a tidal wave originating off one coast eventually hits the other.[35] A more accurate analogy might be to compare the Islamic world to a complicated system of communicating vessels, each one a Muslim society, state, or whole region. Anything important that happens in one vessel resounds to the other vessels: the rest of the Muslim world.

In this connection, it is appropriate to discuss the impact of the Chechen conflict on the Russian Federation's Muslim community, and Russian Muslims' reaction to the conflict. Originally, it was not a religious conflict, and Chechen separatists were not focused on engaging the sympathies of their fellow Muslims in the rest of the federation.

The Tatar and Bashkir populations of Russia have failed to build sustainable ties with their fellow Muslims in the North Caucasus and have no material interests there. The attempts by Russia's Muslim clerics and politicians to create integrated organizations have not met with meaningful success. Created in the mid-1990s, the Muslim Union of Russia and the Nur movement have failed to develop well-coordinated activities, a situation complicated by the personal ambitions of Muslim leaders. While much work has been done to create an institutional framework for the so-called all-Russia Muslim community and the gap "between the peoples of the Caucasus and Tatars" has been narrowed, Islamic believers in Russia continue to be divided into two communities: one in the North Caucasus and the other spread across the rest of Russia. North Caucasian Muslims account for about one-fifth of Russia's 25 million Muslims.

The ethnic, cultural, economic, and political isolation of these two Muslim enclaves has trumped their religious commonality. In the Chechen conflict, the role of Muslim solidarity is weakened by political and religious differences. One can speak of three levels of Muslim solidarity. In predominantly Muslim regions, local leaders tend to have dual outlooks: they condemn separatism and related Islamic radicalism, yet they are unhappy about Moscow's actions against Chechnya even as they demonstrate loyalty to the central government and seek to appear impartial. At the second level, where Muslim movements and organizations cooperate with authorities, protests are heard more distinctly. The leaders of these movements and organizations openly side with Chechen Muslims and see in Moscow's negative attitude to Chechens a manifestation of Islamophobia. In the mid-1990s, this type of Islamic solidarity was demonstrated by the Muslim Union of Russia, the Islamic Culture Center, and many Islamic clerics in Russia. The same can be said of the Refah movement, which was created in 1999 to gather Muslim support for Vladimir Putin but which has strongly criticized Russian authorities for their refusal to negotiate with Maskhadov and his entourage. These Muslim leaders, including Ravil Gaynutdin, also urge more compromise from the Chechen side.

Solidarity with Chechen separatism based on religious belief can be observed among Muslim opposition groups rather than mainstream Islamic organizations. The leader of the Tatar national movement, Fauziya Bayramova, known for her radical views, is convinced that the Islamic factor will eventually be seized by the Muslim peoples of Russia as they struggle for national independence. She also believes that the use of Islam in that struggle is a natural reaction to the "Russian Orthodox fundamentalism" that seeks to become Russia's official and only religion.[36] Religious solidarity with Chechnya has been manifested in mosques across Russia, especially in those that have young imams who have studied abroad: a factor not unnoticed by either the institutional clergy or the relevant government agencies. The least well-behaved Muslim preachers have been cautioned against such attitudes. In cases where radical Islamic ideas coupled with pro-Chechnya solidarity refuse to be dissuaded by words of caution, authorities have resorted to stronger methods. In 2000, the Yaldyz Islamic school in Naberezhniye Chelny was closed down after thirteen *shakirds* (students) left for Chechnya to fight for the separatists.

It is no wonder that Chechen politicians have been disappointed by the level of support they have received from Russia's official Muslim community. Maskhadov had counted on Muslim sympathies, especially from Tatarstan and its president, Mintimer Shaymiyev. Shaymiyev, however, traditionally concerned with a more informal Islam in Tatarstan, has never supported Chechen nationalist efforts. His actions were aimed at mediation and negotiation: his representatives have met with Chechen politicians, including Maskhadov, and he has criticized Moscow for preferring excessive force to negotiation. In 1999, the State Council of Tatarstan went so far as to adopt a resolution, "On Suspending Conscription in the Territory of the Republic of Tatarstan," in order to prevent Tatarstan-born Muslims from confronting their fellow Muslims in

Chechnya in battle. That, however, was the limit of Islamic solidarity shown by Tatarstan. In 1999, Shaymiyev and other prominent Muslim politicians, including Bashkortostan President Murtaza Rakhimov and Ingush leader Ruslan Aushev, supported Fatherland–All Russia, an electoral coalition created by Yuri Luzhkov and Yevgeny Primakov to challenge the pro-Putin Unity movement. This coalition had for some time aspired to become one of Russia's leading political forces; in these circumstances, any solidarity with separatists would certainly have been inappropriate.

Later the Muslim elite unanimously threw its support behind new president Putin's policy in Chechnya, and the question of Muslim solidarity with the Chechens withered away. The Kremlin, for its part, publicly acknowledged that Russia, with its 20 million Muslims, "is, in a certain sense, part of the Muslim world."[37] The Russian leadership also reached out to the *Muftiyat* to bridge the gap to the wider Muslim world. Moscow had not forgotten the ostracism it experienced after the invasion of Afghanistan. Anti-Soviet Muslim solidarity was one of the factors that contributed to the Soviet Union's failure in Afghanistan. Having learned those lessons, the Russian government has focused on reducing the support the Chechen rebels receive from outside the country.

International Islamic Solidarity

Even without Russian interference, external Islamic support is questionable. Generally, Chechnya's influence on the Muslim world and the Muslim world's influence on Chechnya have been occluded by misinterpretation. The most important misinterpretation is the exaggerated impression of an international Islamic presence in the North Caucasus. While official Russian propaganda tries to present the conflict in Chechnya as the result of an international "Islamic conspiracy," this perception is unsubstantiated.

To realistically assess the extent of external influence on Chechnya, one has to ignore the propaganda about that influence and to objectively assess the information of mass media and other sources, especially regarding financial support and the number of Muslim mujahideen fighting in the North Caucasus from abroad.

The Chechen conflict seemingly fits within the general trend toward a radical Islam used by various Islamic organizations and movements as an instrument of political struggle. At the same time, the conflict is an intra-Islamic conflict. Because it also takes place in the so-called Christian-Islamic borderland, it occupies a certain geopolitical niche that determines its link to developments both in the Muslim world and in the post-Soviet political arena. A hypothetical final resolution of the conflict in Chechnya will certainly not be a turning point in the development of neither the Muslim world nor, indeed, of the post-Soviet regime. An intensification of the conflict, however, is possible and will adversely affect both Russia's national security and its relations with Muslim countries. (See chapter 5.)

International and national Islamic organizations provide the most support to the Chechen resistance. Do such organizations act independently, or do they have a mandate from their governments? Konstantin Polyakov, an expert who has long studied the presence and activities of various Islamic organizations in Russia, admits that although the most influential and richest Islamic organizations—including the World Islamic League, the International Islamic Rescue Organization al-Igasa, and the World High Council for Mosques—have headquarters in Saudi Arabia and benefit from Riyadh's financial support, "They do not always follows the recommendations of the Saudi government."[38] These organizations have considerable autonomy, especially because they are directed by influential local politicians. Yet this is exactly what enables the Saudi regime to use its influence to limit their autonomy, and it has done so to avoid confrontation with Moscow.

Besides these organizations, other centers and foundations are trying to develop activities in Russia, including the Caucasus region. The most prominent are, among many others, the International Charity Association Taiba, the Ibrahim al-Ibrahim Foundation, the International Association of Islamic Appeal, the Sudan-based World Islamic Appeal League. These provide assistance by training Muslim clerics, by financing new religious schools and universities, and by sponsoring various scientific and religious seminars. In the North Caucasus, rich Muslim organizations provide humanitarian assistance to internally displaced persons. Some of these organizations, for example, the British-based Islamic Relief organization, use every opportunity to stress their activities are nonpolitical and are supranational.[39] Charitable Islamic organizations have been known to cooperate with Russian government agencies. For instance, in March 1999, the International Islamic Rescue Organization worked with the Daghestani Ministry of Emergency Services to distribute food and clothing in Kizlyar, Kumtorkalinsky, Kizilyurtovsky, and other areas of Dagestan that had been hardest hit during the Basayev incursion and the ensuing fighting.

An expansion of Russian Muslims' contacts with the outside world is as inevitable as is the growing attraction of Russians to Western values. When the Iron Curtain was lifted, the USSR was no longer protected from Western and Islamic influences. The proliferation of religious ideas from abroad that are different from indigenous Russian Islam should be viewed in the context of an unavoidable cultural dialogue in a society that claims to be open. Indeed, in the pre-Soviet period, when Islam in Russia was not as isolated from Islam abroad as it was during the Soviet period, Russia's Muslim community experienced trends similar to those underway in the Near East, the Muslim parts of India, and elsewhere. In fact, even the variety of ethnic cultures and affiliations with different schools of religious thought is not an insuperable barrier to an exchange of ideas among religions.

Chechen Separatists and Outside Financial Assistance

Foreign funds have been flowing to Chechnya through various channels: bogus firms or intermediaries (both in Russia and abroad); foreign emissaries bringing cash directly to field commanders; Chechen communities in the Middle East that collect money; and Chechen politicians on fundraising missions. What is not known is how much money is being transferred. No Islamic organization supporting Chechen resistance has ever revealed specific amounts.

Polyakov has made some calculations based on Russian press reports. According to Polyakov, the Kuwait-based Islamic Center transferred about $13.5 million to Chechnya through Aslan Maskhadov's representative, Islam Khalimov. By December 1999, $8 million had been collected in Qatar. The Jordanian branch of the Muslim Brotherhood had given the Chechens $20 million by the end of 1999, when a Qatar-based charity organization collected thirty kilograms of gold jewelry worth $1.2 million.[40] In the spring of 2001, Basayev's and Khattab's associates had reportedly received $5–$20 million (note the large variance) to step up military and terrorist activities in and around Chechnya. Compared with this kind of money, the $15,000 allegedly collected for Chechens in Bahrain's capital, Manama, looks ridiculously small.[41] Amid reports of tens, if not hundreds, of millions of dollars pouring in from the Gulf States, the story about an Arab named Omar who delivered $850,000 in cash to Maskhadov, but who was killed by field commanders who divided the money among them is believable.[42]

How do the numbers on Chechen financial assistance quoted in media reports compare with the reported financial assistance given to the Taliban regime? There is credible information that in 1996 Osama bin Laden gave the Taliban $3 million to storm and take Kabul. The scale and success of the Taliban action, which eventually enabled it to seize control of an entire country, are incomparably larger than those of Chechen separatists, although some military personnel and journalists continue to insist that much more was and continues to be spent in helping Chechen rebels.

Still, the reported level of funding to Chechnya is simply too high. There are strong reasons to believe that the reported amount of assistance has been overstated and that what reaches Chechnya is often stolen. (Compare Moscow's funding of the reconstruction of Chechnya). For instance, it remains unclear what happened to the money—a hefty $12.5 million—from a special humanitarian assistance fund set up by Saudi King Fahd.[43] Information about how the money makes its way into Chechnya is not always reliable either. It would be logical to ask: If Russian special services know about these channels, why do they not clamp down on them? Too many people on all sides continue to cash in on the Chechen war.

Rebel Training Camps and Foreign Volunteers

Reports about the foreign financing of rebel training camps and of the foreigners volunteering to fight in Chechnya are similarly dubious. In the 1990s, according to Russian special services, 1,600–2,500 rebels were trained at Khattab's camps. Shortly before the Chechen incursion into Dagestan, there were more than twenty such camps, each one specialized: experts in psychological warfare were trained at Camp Dagvat, mountain fighters at Camp Abudjafar, and so on.[44] In Serzhen-Yurt (near Urus-Martan, the center of Chechen Islamism), Khattab set up a so-called war college, which trained Chechen recruits ages fifteen to seventeen, as well as recruits from Tajikistan and Uzbekistan.[45]

There are many stories circulating on how people are trained at such camps. One concerns Zamir Ozrokov, age twenty-four, from Kabardino-Balkaria, who had been told that "in Chechnya they teach the purest Islam of all." In May 1999, he "took a bus to Grozny, then a taxi to Serzhen-Yurt" [this is a nice correlation with stories about secret paths leading to the rebellious Chechnya comment]. He was taken to a certain Ibrahim, a Karachai who gave him a place in the barracks with bunk beds. During the first few days there were seven or eight people in the camp, but soon the number of trainees increased to about a hundred. The training included Qur'an studies, Kalashnikov stripping and assembly, [and] target and mine practice. . . . Among the trainees were Daghestanis, Nogais, Karachais, [and] a man from Kabardino-Balkaria. Three weeks later, Ozrokov said it was time for him to return home, and they returned his passport to him and let him go. At home he was appointed the imam of a mosque in the upper part of the village of Baksanenok."[46] Similar stories can be, often enough, read in other publications or heard from those who come to the North Caucasus. Based on conversations with some of the former trainees, one can conclude that many of them treated their training there as staying at some kind of a summer Boy Scout camp.

One develops the impression that combat training at such camps is light and that the camps do not train professional mujahideen but a type of local militia that can carry out attacks in the areas controlled by federal forces. In fact, the graduates of these training centers are reservists, to be used if the conflict accelerates. They would use their hastily learned skills in setting mines where they may be the least in danger, regardless of whether the mine hits the enemy. There have been reports that each participant in a mine-laying operation receives $100. Compare this to reports that a Chechen rebel receives between $100–$1,000 per month and that a field commander up to $3,000 a month. Naturally, Basayev, Gelayev, Madzhidov, and other rebel "generals" would receive far larger amounts.

The Russian media also reports the price of "conversion" to Wahhabism. Mullahs who agree to side with Wahhabis are paid a lump sum of $1,000–$1,500 and thereafter a monthly fee of $50–$100. Within a Wahhabi community, compensation for bringing people into the fold is based on the principles of a pyramid scam. Thus, a community member who recruits a new person receives $100–$150, and that recruiter then receives a percentage for each newcomer recruited by the person he recruited.[47] One recruiter and several people who had been offered money to convert to Wahhabism reported that these numbers seemed right, except that the percentage fees for neophytes are never paid individually, but randomly, for groups of converts. It is true, however, that in predominantly Wahhabi communities, mullahs can expect to receive sizable remuneration.[48]

Training camps welcome not only Chechens but also people from other North Caucasian ethnic groups, mostly Daghestanis. It is hard to assess the number of trainees or, more important, the practicality of their training. According to the Ministry of Internal Affairs of Kabardino-Balkaria, only some twenty to thirty residents of the republic have fought in Chechnya.[49] People from Adygeya and Karachai-Cherkessia are also known to have fought on the side of the Chechens, but their number would hardly exceed several dozen.

Information on foreign volunteers is particularly vague. According to Russian government sources, which could not be independently confirmed, Khabib Ali Fathi from Jordan was the first foreign combatant in Chechnya. He spent time as Dudayev's religious adviser (although sources insist that Dudayev often ignored Fathi's advice). Fathi was also the religious leader of a small combat group of North Caucasians and Arabs. Beginning in 1995, Khattab, who had come to Chechnya from Afghanistan, took command of the group. The number of rebels in that group grew considerably. Of three hundred fighters, about fifty were Arabs. (In 1997, Khattab was promoted to lieutenant colonel and was awarded two Chechen commendations.)

During the 1999 incursion into Dagestan, "Emir Khattab's Peace-Making Army" suffered heavy losses. Yet only a few foreigners were killed or taken prisoner during the antiterrorist operation, which is an indication that the number of foreign volunteers may be grossly exaggerated.

At the 1996 international conference of Islamic radicals in Mogadishu, Somalia, attended by representatives of radical groups from Somalia, Sudan, Ethiopia, and Yemen, there was a decision made to send five hundred to seven hundred fighters to Chechnya in the fall of that year.[50] The authoritative London-based Arab newspaper *Ash-Shark Al-Awsat* reported that thirty-seven Arabs were killed in Dagestan during Russia's antiterrorist operation.

There has been no official statement of the total number of mercenaries fighting for the separatists. Chechens, however, do not usually welcome Muslims who are not natives. Even Khattab, who was killed in 2002, was popular. He was accused of arrogance and reluctance to recognize local traditions: "For all the people of Ichkeria, Khattab remains a wandering alien who is barely tolerated. His very appearance is an irritant: a man with hair that falls below his shoulders—what could possibly be uglier for a Chechen?"[51]

Chechen rebels are particularly annoyed when their military successes are ascribed to the Arabs, Afghanis, and others. In the summer of 1998, President Maskhadov, as well as several influential field commanders, called on the local youth to leave rebel groups commanded by foreigners, saying that "Arabs, Tajiks, and other scum have no business here."[52] (In Afghanistan, there was a large number of foreigners among the Afghan Taliban—both true mercenaries and fanatics—and their contribution to both military and punitive operations was much more significant than that made by the natives. During the antiterrorist operation in Afghanistan, foreigners put up the stiffest resistance to Northern Alliance troops. Yet in Chechnya the locals, including Taliban supporters, dislike foreigners.) According to Chechen rebels, foreigners account for 1–2 percent of the total rebel strength and, therefore, they cannot decisively influence the course of the war. Local politicians privately agree with that estimate.

Interestingly, the Russian ultranationalist weekly *Zavtra*, which never misses an opportunity to highlight a "global conspiracy against Russia," at one point reported that no more than two hundred foreign mercenaries are fighting in Chechnya.[53] By contrast, speaking at the Parliamentary Assembly of the Council of Europe in January 2000, Russian Foreign Minister Igor Ivanov said that there were about two thousand "mercenaries." He did not specify, however, from which countries the mercenaries came. He may have meant Daghestanis or people from other republics in the North Caucasus.[54] Note that the use of the word "mercenaries" is misleading. Many paid soldiers are fighting for ideals rather than money, which makes them especially dangerous.

At the end of 1999, when relations between Russia and Georgia had reached a new low, some of the Russian media reported that a thousand "Taliban fighters" had crossed the border between Chechnya and Georgia. Later, however, Russian military authorities reduced that figure to three hundred, making the claim only a little less preposterous. "Three hundred Taliban fighters riding three hundred donkeys, plus 24 Stringer SA missiles mounted on Arabian thoroughbreds—this is something

Georgia has not seen so far," the Georgian newspaper *Svobodnnaya Gruziya* remarked ironically.[55] Yet both the Russians and Chechen separatists tend to exaggerate the strength of the Ichkerian fighting force. Thus, according to Chechen sources, more than one thousand people took part in the July 1998 maneuvers of the so-called Peace Making Brigade of Chechnya and Dagestan led by Basayev and Khattab.

The participation of foreigners in the Chechen conflict has made the conflict an international affair and has proved that Islamists from other Muslim countries are involved. Yet neither the true magnitude of their involvement nor the amounts of financial assistance is sufficient grounds for considering Chechnya a target of international Islamic influence. The same applies to speculation on sustainable and intimate cooperation among Islamists in the North Caucasus and Central Asia.

Indeed, Chechen separatists and Islamic radicals in Central Asia— first and foremost the Islamic Movement of Uzbekistan (IMU) and Khizb at-Tahrir al-Islamiy (the Islamic Liberation Party)—have repeatedly and publicly avowed solidarity with the Chechen cause. Khattab and IMU leader Juma Namangani have often voiced the idea of a global jihad against the infidels, which include Russia, the West, and the Central Asian regimes. Further, Central Asian Islamists have treated Chechens with a kind of reverence for their occasional successes in fighting Russian troops. The demonstration effect of the conflict in Chechnya for Islamists in the Ferghana Valley is confirmed by the fact that in 1999, when the IMU planned to invade the Uzbek enclaves of Sokh and Shakhirmardan in Kyrgyzstan, the intention was to declare "an Islamic state based on the Chechen model."[56]

In the early 1990s young Chechens used to come to Central Asia to study Islam. Field commander Salman Raduyev studied in a religious school in the Uzbek city of Namanghan. To this day, the leaders of local Islamists cherish the memory of Raduyev, who they see as the kind of leader they need to defeat their enemies. Indeed, Central Asian Islamists have lacked professional soldiers with combat experience. The separatist government of Chechnya, however, was always reluctant to deploy Chechen "specialists" to the region, and after the Taliban regime was defeated, the issue withered away.

Under the Taliban regime, Islamic rebels from Chechnya and Central Asia were trained in the same camps in Afghanistan. Likewise, several Uzbeks were trained at Chechen training centers under Khattab's command, as were fighters from Islom Diniy Kharakati (the Islamic Movement of Eastern Turkestan), which advocated the secession of China's Xinjiang province. Moreover, it is likely that Central Asian radicals who had trained in Chechen camps participated in hostilities in the North Caucasus. The usually well-informed *Kommersant-Vlast* weekly noted cautiously "some of Namangani's people may be fighting in Islamic brigades in Daghestan."[57]

It would be far-fetched, however, to insist (as *Dagestanskaya Pravda* does) there is a connection between "the offensive of rebels from the radical Islamic Movement of Uzbekistan, which is ideologically close to the Taliban and Wahhabis," and the "more active resistance of the remaining bandit groups in Dagestan."[58] Indeed, the existence of a single authority controlling all, or at least the most important, actions of Islamic radicals is highly doubtful. That is a role too large for even the so-called Supreme Steering Council, formed in 2000 in Kandahar, Afghanistan, and composed of Osama bin Laden, Mullah Omar, and representatives of nearly all the radical movements of Central Asia, Chechnya, Egypt, Yemen, Iran, China, Lebanon, Sudan, and elsewhere. It is unlikely that this committee ever played a coordinating role. Nor is there evidence or reason to believe that a central international terrorist committee exists.

Islamic Radicals in the South Caucasus

Not until 1999–2000 did the penetration of radical Islam into the South Caucasus cause Russia concern. Two states were targeted in particular: Georgia, whose Pankisi Gorge was used by Chechen separatists for rest and regrouping, and Azerbaijan, the only Muslim state in the region.

In Azerbaijan, where the Islamic renaissance peaked in the late 1980s and which the followers of the Iranian revolution failed to turn into a base of operation, the problem of Islamic radicalism does not seem too serious at present. Even in the conflict with Christian Armenia over Nagorny Karabakh, religious confrontation has never been strongly pronounced. Initially the conflict in Chechnya left Azerbaijan virtually unaffected. Later, however, economic hardship and the presence of about a million refugees from Armenia and Karabakh in the country led to calls to resolve the conflict on an Islamic basis. The previously banned Shiite

Islamic Party of Azerbaijan stepped up its activities. Azerbaijani security services insisted that the party was in the process of preparing an Islamic revolution, but its plans were subsequently upset.

At the same time Islamic Sunni radicals also came to the fore. They have close bonds with fellow Muslims in the Northern Caucasus: Chechens and people from Dagestan, primarily Lezghins. Radicals promoting an independent Lezghinistan are becoming increasingly likely to use extremist Islamic slogans to persuade the five hundred thousand Lezghin population, divided nearly evenly between Russia and Azerbaijan.

Tofik Babayev, the deputy minister of national security of Azerbaijan, has said seven thousand Wahhabis were in the republic, concentrated near the Abubekra Mosque in Baku and the Gei and Shahdilyar Mosques. Three hundred Azerbaijanis were trained at Wahhabi centers in Dagestan.[59] In the summer of 2001, Azerbaijani news agencies reported bin Laden's emissaries had frequently visited Azerbaijan to explore opportunities to buy components for chemical weapon production. Even earlier, in 1998, rumors circulated that U.S. special forces had thwarted attempts by Islamic terrorists to blow up the U.S. embassy in Baku.[60]

For Azerbaijan, the Chechen conflict brings more problems than benefits. The instability generated by the conflict allows local oil exports to bypass Russia more easily, thus reducing Baku's reliance on Moscow and fostering economic contacts among Azerbaijan, Georgia, and Turkey. Yet the current secular government, which misses no opportunity to demonstrate how pro-Western it is, truly fears the spread of Islamic radicalism, which could upset the current political arrangement. Finally, Azerbaijani authorities are concerned about the possible infiltration from the North Caucasus of Chechen and other criminal elements, which also tend to use Islamic symbols. Thus, although the current government in Azerbaijan would like to see the struggle for Chechen separatism suppressed, it rarely says so in public.

The ever-intensifying activities of radical Islamists in the Muslim countries that were part of the former Soviet Union raise the issue of joint resistance. Obviously, Russia has an important role to play here. Yet circumstances related to the conflict in Chechnya prevent Russia from becoming a bulwark against radical Islam. First, for many years Russia has failed to elicit a decisive turning point in the struggle against Islamic radicalism on her own soil. Second, Russia's stubborn fight against

Chechen separatism is sometimes perceived as evidence of recidivist imperial aspirations that might engulf the rest of the CIS. Third, local elites, especially in Uzbekistan, are opposed to Russia's massive involvement in repelling Wahhabism in Central Asia. Such involvement, they believe, might result in Russia's having excessive military and political influence in the region.

Some Conclusions

By the mid-1990s, the Chechen issue of separatism had acquired an Islamic dimension. As a result, the demand for Chechnya's independence has become coupled with the cause of creating an Islamic state. Chechnya, however, is nowhere near having an Islamic revolution. After more than a decade of conflict, Chechen society is deeply divided and utterly disoriented. Radical Islam has also spread to other North Caucasus republics, where it has a considerable following, particularly among the young. What is referred to in the region as Wahhabism is in fact Islamic radicalism. Despite its name, it has indigenous roots. Islamist activists and the Russian special services alike exaggerate the foreign support of Wahhabis.

It is wrong, of course, to think toppling the Taliban regime in Afghanistan means that Islamic radicalism has been utterly defeated. On the contrary, Islamic radicalism still has a broad social and ideological base, and its politicians and ideologists are skillful in appealing to the Islamic tradition that highlights those elements that justify their struggle. The solidarity and even admiration shown by many Muslims to the acts of fellow Muslims who are terrorists is strong evidence of the support for Islamic radicalism.

When discussing post–September 11 Islamic radicalism, note that:

- Islamic radicals are becoming increasingly active at a time when several Muslim countries, including those in Central Asia and enclaves in the North Caucasus, face dire economic conditions.
- The activities of Islamic radicalism overlap the process of Islamic renaissance in the former Soviet Union, with religion becoming increasingly politicized.
- The Muslim religion is asserting itself in Europe, where Muslim states were created in the 1990s for the first time since the

Ottoman Empire, and where the number of fundamentalist-minded migrants has recently soared. These migrants are progressively less inclined to adapt to European traditions; on the contrary, they seek to preserve their religious and cultural identities.

All these factors may have an unpredictable influence on the situation in both the North Caucasus and Central Asia.

In turn, the events in these regions are part of the political process in the Islamic world in general and are therefore also capable of producing a reaction in other regions. Despite tragic events, the Northern Caucasus remains on the periphery of the Muslim world. Still, it has a distinct role in the wider context of the geopolitical changes unfolding in Southeast Asia, the Caspian region, Central Asia, and Western Eurasia.

5

War and the Military

The Chechen campaigns have constituted a turning point in Russia's military history.[1] For half a century before "Chechnya," the armed forces were exclusively focused on a world war scenario. This stance was not immediately altered after the collapse of the Soviet Union. It took two Chechen campaigns before the strategic focus budged. Even as the old Western front became quieter and the Eastern front also quiescent, Russia's exposed southern flank became the prime source of concern. The first Chechen campaign signaled the beginning of a change in Russia's geostrategic environment, and the second campaign made that change official.

The change was not totally unexpected. Even though the decade-long Soviet engagement in Afghanistan was seen at the time as little more than a temporary diversion from Russia's main strategic theater, it pointed to a new trend. Ever since the 1979 storming of the presidential palace in Kabul, Muslim mujahideen became the only enemy that Soviet, and then eventually Russian Federation soldiers, encountered on the battlefield. Afghanistan was succeeded in short order by involvement in Tajikistan, and then in the North Caucasus. The military's obvious problem, of course, was that it had been designed, equipped, and trained for altogether different wars.

The federation's armed forces were hardly in a unique position. The end of the Cold War required all its antagonists to revamp their military systems. Gorbachev decreed military reform in 1988; Yeltsin in 1992. Gorbachev's reform failed amidst the debris of the crumbling Soviet

Union. Yeltsin's reform never took off because of an unwritten compact between "czar Boris" and his generals. The top brass stayed loyal to their commander-in-chief. The president, in a quid pro quo, allowed them to run their fiefdoms as they saw fit. As a result, even as the federation's armed forces were progressively reduced, the structure—albeit downsized and downgraded—remained that of the Soviet military.

The failure of military reform is often explained by a shortage of financial resources for national defense. Here, the main reason is not so much a shortage of money as the lack of a clear idea of what kind of military force Russia needed at the beginning of the twenty-first century. Initially, Russia adopted de facto the last version of the Soviet military doctrine, which focused on stabilizing the East-West conflict. The "Foundations of the Military Doctrine of the Russian Federation," a nebulous November 1993 catalogue of risks and threats, did nothing to change that traditional orientation. The West—that is, the United States and its NATO allies—(though unnamed), continued to be the most likely adversary of the Russian armed forces.

In the minds of the Russian military leadership, the first wave of NATO enlargement in the second half of the 1990s, plus the 1999 Kosovo crisis, led to a revival of the traditional Western threat. This restoration of Cold War strategic thinking would have been complete were it not for Chechnya. The brutal war in the Caucasus and the rapidly deteriorating situation in Central Asia exposed the gap between the potential and the real dangers. The paradox of the last decade of the twentieth century was that, against the background of an anti-American, anti-NATO military doctrine and a program of military exercises and weapon purchases to counter that perceived threat, the Russian military organization was increasingly forced to turn its attention southward.

Apart from this strategic about-face, the Chechen conflict remains profoundly significant for the Russian military organization in several ways. As with any military campaign, the first phase of the conflict revealed the true state of the entire Russian military organization (the armed forces, internal and border troops, and security forces): its combat-readiness, the quality of its officers and enlisted staff, the competence of its military, and its political leadership. The first campaign demonstrated the general unpreparedness of the military to meet the challenge to national security. As a result, it was specifically Chechnya and the prospect of engagement in Central Asia that stimulated profound military reform in Russia, which was pursued incrementally by the Putin administration.

Clearly, military reform cannot be reduced to reform only the armed forces, especially its structural optimization, but must take account of the government's resources. Chechnya clearly showed that in Russia, in contrast to the Soviet Union, a unified military organization did not exist. The Ministry of Defense, the Interior Ministry, the contingent of border guards, and the security services, once held together by the iron discipline of the Communist Party, became in the 1990s a gaggle of lobbyists competing to influence the president, parliament, and the government.

Internal conflicts are not new in Russia's history, but the political context has changed. Waged under conditions of democratization, the Chechen war posed anew the various political, legal, and ethical problems that occur in civilian-military relationships.[2] The war revealed and even intensified the difficulty of managing the military organization. The Chechen war led to the appearance of populist generals, some of whom (Lev Rokhlin, Vladimir Shamanov, and others) sought a political career. At the same time, compared with the Soviet period, the capability and readiness of government leaders to exert day-to-day control over the military organization weakened.

The second Chechen campaign saw two other new phenomena: the rise to power of a group of officers working in security services, and the establishment of army generals as representatives of centralized power in the regions. Ultimately, Chechnya became a source for a new round of struggle between democratic and authoritarian tendencies within the Russian political system. The war clearly challenged the emerging civil society, and by challenging it, also stimulated its development.

At first the Russian army fought the war with weapons designed for large-scale war. It was not so much the weaknesses of this weaponry that were revealed as its inappropriateness for a new generation of low-tech conflicts in which the "Kalashnikov culture" prevailed. While recognizing this, the cash-starved Russian defense industry could not provide the military forces with the command, control, communication, and intelligence systems so badly needed on the battlefield. This in turn contributed to heavy casualties and costly failures. Yet the Chechen war resulted in only superficial changes in the Russian military-industrial complex and did not arrest its profound degradation.

Above all, war is a severe test of military personnel. In Chechnya, the mission of the armed forces changed radically. Historically the Russian military took on the world's strongest military powers, whether to protect the homeland from invasion or to extend power deep into Europe and Asia. In post-Soviet Russia, the military was needed for smaller-scale engagements, often in civil wars or ethnic conflicts, on both Russia's borders and in its own territory—actions that require a different military ideology and a different training system for officers and men. The war in Chechnya also presented the Russian military for the first time with an "information war" for which it was totally unprepared. An antiquated propaganda apparatus could not adequately respond in such a war.

Having lost the first campaign in Chechnya, the military recovered by the start of the second campaign. It became tough and decisive in waging an information war against the enemy on the field of battle as well as against "the enemy within." This "counterattack" threatened not only the free access to information, but freedom of speech itself.

In this chapter we describe those processes of military reorganization that were provoked, inhibited, or deformed by the Chechen war. What did the war mean to those ordered to wage it? How did it change the army and its soldiers? And what does all this mean to the country at large? We begin by considering war itself as the only true test of a country's armed forces.

Diagnosis: The State of Russian Military Organization

The 1994–1996 campaign began without serious preparation, was waged ineptly, and ended with a disgraceful outcome for the federal government. Typically, the military blames the politicians who acted in their own interest, betrayed their own army, and acquiesced in the Khasavyurt debacle. Society at large blamed the generals, who had forgotten or never learned how to fight—witness the disastrous New Year's Eve storming of Grozny and (more ominously) the massive draft dodging that resulted. Both groups of accusers, those in and out of uniform, are right. The first Chechen campaign proved the Russian military organization to be grossly deficient at all levels, from the commander-in-chief to the drafted private.

The Russian military that went into the first Chechen campaign, exactly three years after the fall of the Soviet Union, was the disorganized and heavily degraded rump of the Soviet army. The strength of the armed forces had declined from 4.3 million in 1988 to 3.4 million in 1991 and 1.7 million in 1994. The true reduction was considerably less because the 1992 law on defense excluded the Ministry of the Interior (border and Railway troops) and the armed branches of the security services from the main corpus of the armed forces. Thus, though the total military strength remained large, it was no longer unified and its capabilities were being reduced even faster than its number of bayonets.

The military reform announced in 1992 by President Boris Yeltsin and Defense Minister Pavel Grachev amounted to reorganization and redeployments on a gigantic scale but of a fairly mechanical nature. Masses of people were relocated across the vast territory of northern and central Eurasia. The reunification of Germany and the withdrawal Soviet troops from its eastern part (1990–1994); the ratification of the Conventional Forces in Europe (CFE) treaty in Europe (1991); the dissolution of the Warsaw Pact and the withdrawal of troops from Eastern Europe (1991–1994); and, finally, the disintegration of the Soviet Union itself led to the pullout of thirty-seven divisions from Germany, Poland, Czechoslovakia, Hungary, the Baltic States, Azerbaijan, and Mongolia. Another fifty-seven divisions remained in Belarus, Ukraine, and the Central Asian states under the flags of these newly independent countries. Moscow asserted control over the forces in Georgia, Armenia, Moldova, and Tajikistan, as well as the greater part of the Black Sea Fleet.

Regrettably, this truly titanic reorganization effort lacked a strategy. As they reshuffled divisions and headquarters, the federation's military leaders strove to preserve the army's former structure in the vain hope that eventually everything would return to normal. The army quickly became an empty shell. The number of "cadre"-level (understaffed) divisions, brigades, and regiments grew dramatically, from 20 percent to 50 percent. In the confusion of feverish reorganizing and redeployments, some units simply disappeared from the General Staff's radar screen, although they continued to exist, physically. Others continued to be listed on rosters but had long become the equivalent of Gogol's "dead souls." By the mid-1990s, the Russian armed forces had few combat-ready units.

There were major changes in the conscription system: university students and several other categories of potential conscripts, making up

85 percent of the entire pool (compared with about 55 percent in the 1980s), received the right to defer military service. The 1993 constitution provided the right to alternative service. Many officers, including many who were younger and better qualified, rushed to take advantage of this right. As a result, the quality of enlisted men and officers rapidly deteriorated. Commissioned officers were allowed to retire or resign, thus abolishing the previous near servitude of twenty-five to thirty years in the ranks without an option to leave.

As the Russian military proceeded with these measures, the strategic vision of both the high command and the political leadership blurred. A real war was far from their minds. They believed that the end of the Cold War with the West and the normalization of Sino-Russian relations gave them a period of peace and tranquility. Still, the post-Soviet world teemed with ethnic and civil conflicts (called hot spots by the Russian media). The reluctant participation of the military in these conflicts since the 1980s was regarded as police action.

In defending the country from outside aggression, the armed forces felt that domestic matters should be handled by the Interior Ministry and the security services. Russian army professionals, from company officers to a members of the General Staff, were disgusted by the tendency of politicians to send them into various local conflicts as a "fire brigade," to extinguish the conflagration as quickly as possible. Worse, if the mission met with criticism, the political experts blamed the military for the "dirty" business and abandoned them.

The Kremlin launched the campaign in Chechnya in late 1994 in a somewhat emotional response to the disgraceful failure of the Federal Counterintelligence Service's (the FSK) covert mission.[3] When the Russian Security Council discussed using military force in Chechnya, Defense Minister Grachev—who had publicly boasted days earlier that his own airborne troops would defeat the rebels within two hours—tried to delay the operation until the following spring. The impatient civilian hawks, however, took Grachev at his word. Why wait months if the mission could be accomplished in a couple of hours? The hawks won the day. The goal was to restore Russian constitutional order in Chechnya and disarm the illegal units by deploying regular forces in Chechnya.

The problem was the gap between the ends and the means, or between the goal and the federation's military capability. Soon it became clear that neither the political leadership nor the military commanders had an accurate picture of the real state of the federation's armed forces—and for a long time afterward General Grachev was reminded of his irresponsible boast. Grachev was not the only one lost in reveries of former power and glory who refused to believe what he saw with his own eyes. Decision makers had been blinded by lingering myths of Soviet military might.

Not until the disaster of the first Chechen campaign did President Yeltsin awake to the "monstrous unpreparedness" of the armed forces he had commanded for the past three years.[4] Yeltsin never fully recovered from that belated discovery. According to Yevgeny Primakov, in 1995 Yeltsin had even talked of retiring "because of Chechnya."[5] Regardless of his admission of guilt, Yeltsin remained cool and aloof toward the armed forces until the end of his presidency.

In retrospect, the lack of preparation is curious. Soviet forces, after all, had been fighting in Afghanistan for a decade. Withdrawal from Afghanistan coincided with deployments to destinations along the Soviet Union's southern periphery: Tbilisi, Baku, Sumgait, Osh, Nagorny Karabakh, Abkhazia, Northern and Southern Ossetia, Ingushetia, and Tajikistan. The missions ranged from breaking up demonstrations, separating warring factions, and fighting cross-border incursions, to helping one side of a conflict to prevail. Although the deployments provided a wealth of experience in managing imperial decline and disintegration, that experience was never analyzed for the benefit of military officers and political leaders. Thus, the same mistakes were repeated. As Russian officers bitterly remarked, Moscow was stepping on the same old rake, only to be hit in the forehead again.

Another problem was the availability of forces. Although on paper it had more than 1.5 million personnel in its ranks, the Russian military command in 1994–1995 had to scurry to compose units and even tank crews in the heat of battle: cadre units were not able to fight. To quell a rebellion in the North Caucasus, the General Staff had to search for personnel from the Baltic to the Pacific. The motley force thus assembled, were not combat-ready. Infantrymen, marines, paratroopers, border guards, and Interior Ministry soldiers were gathered on the same battlefield for the first time since the 1941 Battle of Moscow. What had been a tragedy in 1941 was a farce half a century later.

Inevitably, then, the prime casualty of the first Chechen campaign was the myth of the indestructible Soviet army. The once-legendary force now belonged to history. The 1.5 million in uniform did not amount to a cohesive military organization. Events had now impartially created a new army, but its formation clashed with special interests, which effectively barred reform. In the wake of the first Chechen campaign, however, it was no longer possible to be complacent over the state of the military. An example of the extent of the desperation is reflected in the title of a 1997 report by the nongovernmental Council on Foreign and Defense Policy: "The Current State of the Russian Army as an Impending National Catastrophe."[6]

Pressure for reform did bring some results. Of course, Yeltsin's 1996 election campaign decree on completing the transition to an all-volunteer force by 2000 was never taken seriously. A more important step was the sacking of the two men most closely associated with failures in Chechnya, Defense Minister Grachev and Oleg Lobov, the secretary of the Security Council. The new Security Council secretary, General Alexander Lebed, was tasked with finding a way out of Chechnya and giving a boost to stalled reforms.

As described in chapter 1, Lebed negotiated a troop withdrawal from Chechnya, leaving the republic in the hands of the separatists, and succeeded in having his protégé, Igor Rodionov, appointed defense minister. Both the larger Chechen settlement and Russian military reform eluded Lebed, however. His ambitions to succeed the ailing president ensured Lebed's swift downfall. Even after Lebed's dismissal, the recovering Yeltsin and the Kremlin administration remained suspicious and hostile toward Rodionov. The defense minister's proposals for reform projects fell on deaf ears. In the end, Yeltsin sacked Rodionov in May 1997.

By this time, many believed that the war in Chechnya had already become a thing of the past. The newly appointed defense minister, Igor Sergeyev, and General Staff Chief Anatoly Kvashnin were given the job of optimizing the structure of the armed forces. Lacking an alternative, that assignment passed for reform. Sergeyev and Kvashnin were an interesting combination. The former commander of the Strategic Rocket Force, Sergeyev was the first so-called missileman ever to hold the job, and Kvashnin was a Chechen war veteran. While the soft-spoken Sergeyev was interested in ensuring that nuclear deterrence and strategic parity worked and would give Russia international prestige, the gruff Kvashnin, the former commander of the North Caucasus military district, emphasized conventional forces for local conflicts. These two different perspectives were bound to clash. For a while, however, the two worked together to create at least a few combat-ready formations.

Between 1990 and 1999, the number of divisions in the armed forces decreased from 212 to 24. Those remaining were little more than cadre units. By early 1999, the General Staff formed three divisions and four brigades at constant readiness (manned at 80 percent, with matériel at 100 percent). In the future, it was assumed there would be 8–11 full-fledged formations. Another 21 divisions and 10 brigades were to constitute as bases for future mobilization. They would be manned at 10–15 percent and be fully stocked with weapons and equipment.[7] Yet the new formations were built by simply concentrating resources within the military organization. Thus the enhanced capability of the few was paid for by an even lower capability of all the other units.

Fundamental disagreements between Sergeyev and Kvashnin on the force development policy led to a gridlock within the military. Sergeyev's plan to create strategic deterrence forces was shelved, and the General Staff failed to receive the full operational control of the military organization that Kvashnin had sought. Given the situation, the August 1998 financial collapse was the coup de grace. The government ran out of funds across the board.

Meanwhile, in 1998, preparations for a new military campaign in Chechnya were well under way. The Defense and Interior Ministries had concluded that a new clash with the Chechens was inevitable, since stability in Chechnya proved elusive and the radical Islamists were gaining influence. Both ministries also sought retribution for the recent failure of their forces in Chechnya. The army leadership headed by Kvashnin tried to learn from the mistakes of the first campaign. They knew there would be a next time, and soon. While proceeding with its optimization effort, the General Staff gave priority to the North Caucasus military district, emphasizing antiguerilla warfare and counterterrorism.

Thus, by spring 1999, the Russian military had formed and trained a more or less combat-ready force, which inspired confidence in the potential for the success of the new operation. The kidnapping in March 1999 and subsequent killing of General Gennadi Shpigun, the Interior Ministry representative in Chechnya, was blatant provocation. The Kremlin, however, required persuading that the only solution in Chechnya was military. An unlikely obstacle was Interior Minister Sergei Stepashin, who was committed to negotiations with Aslan Maskhadov and was ready to make serious concessions to the Islamists, particularly in Dagestan. From the point of view of the military command, this merely encouraged Wahhabis.[8]

The rigidity of the top echelon of the Russian government in the last months of Yeltsin's tenure, as well as the president's lack of concentration and his vacillation, made persuading the Kremlin more difficult. The Kremlin's pursuit of a political solution in Chechnya probably ended in the wake of NATO's seventy-two-day air war against Yugoslavia in the spring of 1999.[9] Official approval of military boldness was evident in the June 1999 march to Pristina, when a small party of Russian paratroopers drove from Bosnia to Kosovo to secure a major airport ahead of NATO forces. This daring operation, bringing Russian peacekeepers to the threshold of confrontation with U.S. soldiers, was masterminded by Kvashnin and sanctioned by Yeltsin, while the rest of the government, including Defense Minister Sergeyev, was kept in the dark. It signaled a new direction in the General Staff and the Kremlin's willingness to condone and follow it.

Just two months later, when Basayev and Khattab's troops invaded Dagestan, the Kremlin gave the long-awaited go-ahead to the military. Moreover, Stepashin, who had become prime minister (and heir apparent to Yeltsin) in May 1999 was immediately removed from his post. Director of the Federal Security Service Putin, who had assumed the toughest stand since the beginning of the Chechen conflict, became the new head of government. With Yeltsin's approval, Putin gave the Russian military its most decisive task since 1994: to wipe out the Chechen armed units and take control of the entire territory of Chechnya. Kvashnin received his coveted carte blanche.

From the beginning of the second Chechen campaign, the Russian army was considerably different than it had been in the first campaign. It acted with purpose and brutality. The syndrome of defeat was overcome in quick order. The verity of the well-known adage was again confirmed: the Russian army is never as strong as it describes itself, but it is never as weak as it seems from the outside.

Non–Ministry of Defense Forces?

The war in Chechnya tested all the other forces in the Russian military organization. These "other forces" included Interior Ministry troops, border guards, and railway troops, as well as the military branches of the security services: the FSK, the Federal Agency of Government Communication and Information (or FAPSI, which was merged into the FSB in 2003), and various other federal security services. In the 2001–2002, these other forces numbered about half a million, compared with the 1.2 million of armed forces.

The interior and border troops survived several budgeting ups and downs during the 1990s. From 1993 to 1997, Yeltsin pampered them while giving the armed forces a cold shoulder. This reflected the president's grudge against the army for its "too cautious" stance during the October 1993 political standoff in Moscow, and also the armed forces' early reluctance to become involved in domestic conflicts. This hesitation naturally made the president turn to the interior troops, and the border guards benefited from the successful lobbying activity of their first director, Andrei Nikolayev.

The first Chechen campaign and the civil war in Tajikistan, however, showed the inadequacy of these other forces. The interior troops, despite better financing and new heavy weaponry, lacked the training to quell armed separatism. The border guards were unable to secure the Tajik-Afghan border without the support of the army's 201st Motorized Division in Tajikistan because they were precariously sandwiched between the Tajik opposition in Afghanistan and the ruling clans in Tajikistan.

The security services were not particularly efficient and at times were even helpless against Chechen separatism and later against terrorism. It was precisely the FSK's inept covert attempt to overthrow Dudayev, reminiscent of the CIA's unsuccessful Bay of Pigs operation in April 1961, that led to war. The daring, far-reaching raid by Basayev's rebels in Stavropol (Budennovsk) in the summer of 1995 made then-FSK director Sergei Stepashin (who had been negotiating with Maskhadov) resign. The operation to free hostages in Pervomaysk in January 1996—which was personally led by Mikhail Barsukov, the new head of the service (now called the FSB)—ended in utter disgrace. Despite heavy Chechen casualties, the Russians were unable to stop their escape into Chechnya. The federals let the terrorists escape into Chechnya, and Barsukov was fired in the summer of 1996.

The formal transfer of the Chechen operation to the FSB at the beginning of 2001 did not produce an immediate positive result. The liquidation of several rebels and the arrest of others was not a prologue to the end of the war or a political solution. Moreover, terrorist acts against Russian troops and Chechen administration employees loyal to Moscow became even more frequent. Regardless of the formation of a "unified staff to lead the counterterrorist operation," the main Russian figures in Chechnya remained Ministry of Defense generals. In October 2002, a Chechen group of fifty took hundreds of people hostage at a Moscow theater, which sent the message that there was no place in Russia secure from Chechen attacks. However, in mid-2003, just before the elections in Chechnya, the FSB passed the baton to the Interior Ministry as a sign of further normalization. This did not impress the terrorists, who shortly afterward blew up a military hospital in Mozdok, just outside Chechnya's border.

Thus, the Chechen war has revealed a continuing and deepening crisis in the Russian military organization. This crisis remains unresolved. Initially its main cause lay in the disappearance of a traditional enemy and the inability of the political leadership to clearly define where threats to the national security of Russia lay in the twenty-first century and how and for what kinds of wars and conflicts Russia must prepare.

Chechnya: A Model of Future Wars or a Special Case?

The unprecedented conflict between two of the highest-ranking officials in the military hierarchy—Minister Igor Sergeyev and the chief of the General Staff Anatoly Kvashnin—while purely personal on the surface, reflected the key problems of Russian military reform.

Official military historians point out that in 1991 there was a "deep schism" in the national defense strategy, after which "all the strategic values formed after October 1917 lost meaning, and the official system of defense objectives was fully reevaluated."[10] The reference here, of course, is to the rejection of such communist-era tenets as the struggle against world imperialism, the defense of the socialist Fatherland, the promotion of proletarian internationalism, the extension of internationalist aid to participants in the anti-imperialist struggle, and so on.

While valid goals, one must remember that as early as the 1930s the working-class character of Soviet military doctrine had been effectively replaced by a more traditional geopolitical approach. At the turn of the 1990s, with the formal rejection of long-defunct Marxist-Leninist thought,

Russian strategic thinking openly adopted traditional geopolitics as its guiding light. The revived interest in such notions as the balance of power, spheres of influence, and buffer states led one to conclude that having left the twentieth century, Russian strategic thought was now entering the nineteenth century.

No one denied that the end of the Cold War sharply minimized the chance of a war between Russia and the West. For a brief period between 1989 to 1992, an idea prevailed of creating a unified security zone, a zone of stable peace stretching from Vancouver to Vladivostok, encompassing North America, Europe, and Russia.[11] In the early 1990s, Russia was mostly concerned with managing ethnic conflicts in post-Soviet territories. From 1992 to 1993, Russian forces took up several peacekeeping operations simultaneously: Moldova, the South Caucasus, and Central Asia. The Chechen conflict was then considered by Moscow part of a larger pattern, a case of aggressive nationalism that threatened the integrity of CIS states. The 1993 "Fundamentals of the Military Doctrine of the Russian Federation," approved by Yeltsin less than a month after he had used force in Moscow to suppress a parliament-led revolt, contained a provision about the use of the armed forces in conflicts inside Russia. In a little more than a year, this provision gave the Kremlin legal ground for sending the army into Chechnya.

The new military doctrine, however, did not delineate the character or sources of military threats to Russia. Conflicts involving Soviet succession had either exhausted the parties involved (as in Karabakh) or were being neutralized by Russian peacekeeping. Meanwhile, relations with the United States and other NATO countries had not reached the partner level and were beginning to stagnate. The Russian military was turning a suspicious eye to U.S. and Turkish "encroachments" in the Caspian basin.

The first Chechen campaign coincided with a new dip in Russian-Western relations. Commenting on NATO's plans to expand eastward, Yeltsin warned at the December 1994 summit of the Organization for Security and Cooperation in Europe (OSCE) about an era of "Cold Peace" succeeding the Cold War. The phrase stuck, but Yeltsin went further. Protesting U.S. air strikes on Bosnian Serb positions in 1995, the Russian president warned Washington against sliding into World War III.

The emergence of a new-era contingency (in the Caucasus) and the revival of the old strategic worldview led to internal debate. More liberal government figures, pointing to the Chechen experience, insisted that internal threats should take priority. Witness to this approach was the National Security Concept, drafted under the direction of Security Council Secretary Ivan Rybkin and formally approved in December 1997. The professional military, on the other hand, gravitated to giving priority to world power conflicts. In an unusually frank statement in December 1996, Defense Minister Rodionov listed an array of Russia's potential adversaries that included NATO countries, Iran, Pakistan, China, and Japan—the full Soviet-era list (which included nearly all Russia's neighbors.)

By the time the second Chechen campaign had begun, NATO had expanded against Moscow's vehement protests, to include three Central European nations. Even worse from Russia's point of view, it had launched an air war against Yugoslavia, Europe's most serious armed conflict since the end of World War II. Russian-Western relations became strained as never before since the end of the Cold War. On the ground in the Balkans, a Russian-NATO military clash was narrowly avoided.[12]

Taking its cue from these developments, in the summer of 1999 the Russian military conducted its largest exercises in a decade. War games included strategic aviation mock launches of nuclear-tipped cruise missiles aimed at NATO targets. In addition, the general staffs of Russia and Belarus, in a command postexercise, were deciding on the use of tactical nuclear weapons to defend the Kaliningrad enclave against a Western invasion. In late fall 1999, when Yeltsin went to Beijing on what turned out to be his last foreign visit as head of state, he publicly warned President Clinton never to forget, "not for a minute, not for a second," that Russia was a nuclear power. It appeared as though, ten years to the day after the fall of the Berlin Wall, that everything had come full circle.

The official Russian blueprint approved in 2000 included a new military policy and a new national security concept. It identified U.S. global hegemony and "NATO centrism"—that is, the alliance's dominant security role in Europe linked to the use of force to resolve crises—as threats to Russian interests. These policy mandates were reflected in the pattern of military exercises and in the purchase of new weapons. Yet as the Kremlin and the General Staff seemed to be reactivating the Western front, a new front was being formed to the south of Russia's borders. What had been regarded as a diversion from the main (Western) strategic axis was turning into a clear and present danger.

In the 1980s, Afghan mujahideen were still seen as agents of the United States and its partners in the informal anti-Soviet coalition along with Pakistan, Saudi Arabia, and China. At the beginning of the 1990s, with Afghanistan "written off," Russian mainstream politicians and the military turned a wary eye on Ankara's pan-Turkic expansionism into Central Asia and the Caucasus. At the same time, most liberals, led by Foreign Minister Andrei Kozyrev, saw the prime danger as being Tehran's revolutionary fundamentalism. Governments could be deterred, of course. Thus, Turkey was warned, as early as 1992, of a third world war if it interfered in the Karabakh conflict. The federation befriended Iran through arms sales. Moscow, however, found it more difficult to handle separatist rebels (as in Chechnya) and Islamic militants (as in Afghanistan and Central Asia), who liberally used terrorism to achieve their aims. The southern front would be different from the western one.

In the dramatic summer of 1999, when the Kosovo crisis seemed to confirm the worst fears of the Russian military over NATO's concept of "humanitarian intervention," Basayev and Khattab completed preparations for an incursion from Chechnya into Dagestan, and the militants of the Islamic Movement of Uzbekistan (IMU) infiltrated Kyrgyzstan from Afghanistan for an attack in the Ferghana Valley. Both groups struck nearly simultaneously in August. The southern front was opened, the enemy was almost immediately identified as international terrorism.

That concept had been in gestation for some time. General Staff saw the Bosnian crisis (1992–1995) largely as a traditional tripartite geopolitical contest for regional supremacy: U.S.–Turkey (for Bosnian Muslims), Germany–Western Europe (the Croats) and Russia (the Serbs). That the first two eventually united against the third was regarded as thoroughly predictable. The Kosovo conflict led Russian observers to a different conclusion, even before the 1999 crisis. They saw two dangers: NATO's interventionism outside its sphere, and the rise of Muslim (in this case, Kosovar) radicalism, with its international connections.

The Russian national security and military policy documents approved in 2000 included, along with criticism of U.S. and NATO policies, a reference to a new threat from "extremist, nationalist, separatist, and terrorist movements, organizations, and structures."[13] While not dropping altogether the ideal of a struggle for spheres of influence in the former Soviet regime, the policy papers acknowledged that economic crisis and social dislocations in the newly independent states had stimulated belligerent nationalism, religious extremism, and such nontraditional dangers as cross-border crime and international terrorism.[14] The strategic worldview was indeed changing.

The General Staff's World War III maps become outdated, both figuratively and literally.[15] Putin loyalist Sergei Ivanov, who in the spring of 2001 succeeded Igor Sergeyev as defense minister, identified two military security priorities in his inauguration address: the North Caucasus and Central Asia.[16]

Still, it took September 11, 2001, to make Russia's political leadership finally dissolve the notion of NATO as Russia's principal potential enemy. Lacking clear guidance from the Kremlin, the General Staff had been developing a "one-and-half war" strategy: an "aggression of the Balkan type" (that is, a Kosovo-type NATO move against Russia or its CIS allies, such as Belarus), coinciding with an Islamist offensive in the Caucasus or Central Asia. This scenario was used in a CIS air defense exercise staged in early September 2001.[17] Even as the forces on the ground practiced a two-front war, the Russian air force was engaged in a strategic exercise that had the United States as the enemy. It was this exercise that Putin immediately aborted on the news of the September 11 attacks, relieving U.S. forces of the need to remain on alert status and winning President Bush's gratitude.

Thus, despite deeply ingrained strategic stereotypes, the military security axis gradually shifted from its traditional Western aim to the south. The Chechen campaigns and growing instability in Central Asia achieved a strategic reorientation that no amount of liberal rhetoric could. The East-West standoff was consigned to the history books. The "Time of the South" had begun.

Military Aims

Throughout the 1990s, Russian military thinking was largely lost in the late nineteenth century. Simply holding the common center together, however, was hardly a reasonable objective. In the late 1980s, Russia decided to abandon, as a result of fatigue, and not defeat, the heavy burden of empire. Most striking and contrary to the expectations of Western intelligence services, the army preferred to remain an apathetic observer rather than a last-minute savior of the empire.[18] If the army could not intervene to avert the Soviet Union's collapse, what would be its mission in the local conflicts in the Caucasus and Central Asia?

From 1994 to 1996, the Russian leadership, which for the three preceding years had not only condoned Chechen separatism but also even openly armed it, finally decided to use military force to "restore constitutional order" in Chechnya. The vagueness of the mission, however, no less than Moscow's equivocal behavior both before and during the first campaign, greatly contributed to Russia's military and political defeat in the summer of 1996.

By contrast, in the second Chechen campaign, Russia officially defended itself from attacks by "international terrorist gangs" and "armies of killers."[19] The military was assigned the clear-cut task of "liquidating the center of international terrorism in the Northern Caucasus region."[20] The mission was backed by political will and material resources, an approach that was more realistic. It helped, of course, that the Russian army had gone into battle to defend its own territory (Dagestan) before taking on the separatists inside Chechnya.

Vladimir Putin compared the actions he had ordered in Chechnya to the security service operation in the Baltic's and the Western Ukraine that had been conducted by Stalin's secret police (the NKVD, or the People's Commissariat for International Affairs), aimed at eradicating anti-Soviet resistance lasting from 1944 to the mid-1950s. This "technocratic" comparison by Putin is telling, in that he does not distinguish between separatists and terrorists; they are both enemies to be eliminated, and separatists are not considered participants in a dialogue. Nonetheless, separatists sometimes achieved their goals: four decades after the surrender of the Lithuanian "forest brothers" and the Ukrainian followers of Stepan Bandera, Lithuania and Ukraine achieved independence from Moscow.

Putin's counterterrorist operation was designed to preserve Russia's territorial integrity, protect the population, and show the political will of the government. The issue of territorial integrity transcended the actual physical size of Chechnya, which was merely 15,000 square kilometers. Putin and his associates feared the Islamic factor. Prime Minister Putin's vision was: "If we don't stop the extremists now, then some time later we'll be faced with another Yugoslavia in the entire territory of Russia, the *Yugoslavization* of Russia . . . First Dagestan would be overrun. Then the entire Caucasus would separate; that's clear. Dagestan, Ingushetia, and then up the Volga River to Bashkortostan [and] Tatarstan. This means advancing right into the middle of the country."[21]

This passage is also revealing. For Putin the commander-in-chief, Chechnya is a symptom of a far larger and more serious problem. Russia's southern border coincides with much of the arc of instability, stretching from North Africa and the Balkans to the Greater Middle East and all the way to Southeast Asia, and including the newly independent states of Central Asia, Russia's neighbors and associates in the post–Soviet commonwealth. Should these former Russian borderlands give way, Russia's Muslim republics will be dangerously exposed. Thus, like Chechnya, Central Asia is Russia's first line of defense.

With regard to Central Asia, just as with the Caucasus, Moscow's prime concern was the utter permeability of its long borders. To isolate Chechnya physically, as some Russian politicians, including Moscow mayor Yuri Luzhkov, had suggested, was simply not feasible. Money and other key resources were not available, and fencing off the problem was seen as dangerously defeatist. Moreover, the mountainous sectors of Ingushetia and Dagestan were indefensible, with limited resources. Moreover, the eighty-kilometer border with Georgia, a foreign country, presented a diplomatic challenge. Similarly, dividing the rebel republic into two zones—the pacified north and the contained south—as other Russian politicians, including the Union of Right Forces leader Boris Nemtsov, had suggested, was rejected as a half-measure. Putin and Kvashnin decided to go for the final solution.

By comparison, action in Central Asia was to prevent an even more serious cross-border challenge: Russia's longest (more than 7,000-kilometers) and thoroughly permeable border with Kazakhstan. Kazakhstan is vast, sparsely populated, and of vital importance to Russia. Geographically, it is a buffer between Central Asia and Russia; strategically, it is an ally within the Collective Security Treaty; politically, it is a binary state composed of Turkic-speaking Kazakhs (about half the population) and Slavs (mostly of Russian and Ukrainian stock, one-third of the population); and economically, it is an oil-rich country whose industry is closely tied to that of southern Siberia. Should ethnic tensions in Kazakhstan rise, Muslim extremists gain a foothold, or Slav separatists attempt to secede, Russia would be massively affected. Simply put, Kazakhstan's stability is key to Russia's own.

To keep Kazakhstan out of the fray, therefore the Russian strategy was to strengthen the frontline states of Tajikistan, Kyrgyzstan, and Uzbekistan. The first two, although Moscow's military allies, are more important to regional security. It was Uzbekistan, defiant vis-à-vis postimperial Russia and itself a would-be regional hegemon, that was the prime target of the Islamists. Russia sought to secure the Afghan border, improve defense and security cooperation with its allies, and thus reduce the threat to Uzbekistan, which rejected Moscow's meddling.

New Wars, New Enemies

The Chechen army, and then the Chechen guerillas, turned out to be an unusual and inconvenient enemy for the Russian federal forces. The education of Soviet and Russian military officers was primarily derived from World War II experiences. Until the late 1990s, the military training curriculum largely ignored local wars and conflicts. Not only the Caucasian war of the nineteenth century and the NKVD special operations in the 1920s, but such conflicts as Vietnam, the Middle East, and Afghanistan, were considered largely irrelevant.

Only after the first Chechen campaign did this view begin to change. The Defense Ministry finally announced to the academies: "There will be no global war. You must prepare the army for local conflicts."[22] The military doctrine of the year 2000 contained a passage about the need to fight against irregular armed units. New things, however, were seen as a complement to, rather than a substitute for, the old missions. Army general Makhmut Gareyev, a noted and influential military theorist, wrote that "the Russian armed forces need to acquire *primary readiness* for local wars and conflicts, and *mobilization readiness* for a large-scale regional war [emphasis added]."[23] The latter, of course, meant conflict with the United States.[24]

Thus, the Russian armed forces should be capable of nuclear, space, and strategic theater operations, while also being able to engage in peacekeeping and counterinsurgency tasks. In other words, repelling an "aggression of the Balkan type" was no less relevant than "fighting international terrorism."[25]

The new enemy was no match for the NATO armies that had been faced during the Cold War, but it was different. The regular army of separatist Ichkeria had 15,000 men at the beginning of 1995 and between 10,000–11,000 in 1999, supported in either case by around 30,000 militia.[26] Their inferiority in number was compensated by small-group tactics that would constrain and wear down the larger federal forces. The

Russian superiority, however, was often a statistical, not a military, fact. Just before Chechen troops took Grozny in August 1996, Defense Minister Igor Rodionov estimated the number of "rebels and armed criminals" to be between 3,000 and 3,500. The Russian garrison of the city numbered 7,500: the vast majority of those troops, however, were not combat forces.[27] For a long time during the second campaign, despite heavy Chechen losses (according to Russian data, 14,000 separatists had been "eliminated" by January 2001[28]), the rebels continued to pose an imposing military challenge.[29]

The situation that Central Asian states faced was different, but broadly similar. At the beginning of 2001, the Islamic Movement of Uzbekistan (IMU) was believed to have between 300 and 600, or 2,000 and 7,000 fighters.[30] Much smaller than the regular armies they opposed, the Islamists were better organized and equipped than the government forces, and some had experience in the Russian army. The IMU's Juma Namangani, for instance, served as a paratrooper during the Soviet occupation of Afghanistan.

A major difference is that whereas in Chechnya separatists operate from a home base, Central Asian Islamists have no homeland. Instead, they use bases in neighboring countries to strike and fall back to prepare for the next attack, hoping that one will lead to a takeover of the target country. Taking out those bases was vital for the Russian strategy in the region, and in 2000 Moscow contemplated air and missile strikes at Afghanistan as well as the deployment of reinforcements to Tajikistan. Russia's resources, however, were inadequate for the mission. It was the U.S. Operation Enduring Freedom, that secured Central Asia by destroying the Taliban.

Over time, the Russian view of the Chechen rebels hardened. In the first campaign, Dudayev and Maskhadov were still treated as fellow officers who had gone astray. That was not so in the second campaign. "There's nothing human about them," scoffed General Valery Baranov, commander of a unified force in Chechnya, referring to the rebels.[31] Government officials in Central Asia made similar comments. "Our peaceful people have to wage a war against foreign riff-raff," complained Kyrgyzstan's ambassador to Russia.[32]

After 1999, the rebels were officially labeled terrorists and criminals fighting exclusively for money. This cut off the path to negotiations and refined the goal as complete liquidation of the enemy, no matter how long it took. Ironically, such a hard line, no-interference-from-wobbly-politicians-or-the-public approach eventually caused military officers to realize there was no such thing as a purely military solution to the Chechen problem.

What troubled the Russian military most was the support for the rebels by many people in Chechnya, Ingushetia, and Dagestan. Law-abiding during the day, Chechens became saboteurs after night fell. Throughout the republic, Russian troops were being watched, and their movements immediately reported to the rebels. Even Grozny, despite a heavy troop presence, routinely escaped Russian control at sundown.[33] Brutal retaliatory actions by federal forces served only to recruit more supporters for the rebel cause. The families of rebels were commonly thought to be hiding in the refugee camps of Ingushetia, which also provided food to the mountain fighters.[34] In response, the Russian military often treated Ingushetians as Chechens allies, which did little to endear them to the local population.

A year after the Wahhabi enclaves in Dagestan were overrun, the Russian military was still reporting continuing tensions.[35] Two and a half years later, in 2002, presidential aide Sergei Yastrzhemsky cited support of the rebels by some of the local population as one of Moscow's main problems. Winning hearts and minds had become important. Unsure how to proceed, the military and security services sought to divert attention elsewhere.

Chechnya's border with Georgia presented problems. Rugged terrain and the near-absence of roads made it difficult to control. The Russian military had a vicious and deeply ingrained hatred of Georgian President Eduard Shevardnadze (formerly Gorbachev's foreign minister and responsible for signing treaties that resulted in the swift withdrawal of Soviet forces from Central and Eastern Europe). On the defensive, Shevardnadze sought to check the imperial ambitions of Moscow reactionaries by developing closer ties with the United States and Western Europe. To make things more complicated, the Georgian territory adjacent to Chechnya was outside Tbilisi's control. The Pankisi Gorge was in the hands of Chechen field commander Ruslan Gelayev—or so Russian military intelligence claimed.[36] The Georgians, for their part, had always suspected that Gelayev was a Russian agent provocateur.

Whereas during the first campaign Georgia allowed Russian border guards to close its border with Chechnya from the south, during the second campaign Shevardnadze balked at a repeat. Although the reasons cited had to do with protecting Georgia's sovereignty, in reality Tbilisi was frustrated with Moscow's double standard in dealing with Chechnya and Georgia's own rebel province, Abkhazia. In response, Moscow began treating Georgia as the rear base of Chechen terrorists, and their communication channel to the outside world, a move that seriously complicated Russian-Georgian relations and made the United States and the European Union wonder about Russia's ultimate goal regarding Georgia (see chapter 5).

Generally, it is important to consider the perceived international context when distinguishing the second Chechen campaign from the first. While the Russian military considered the first war an isolated event, or at worst, part of a regional tendency of ethnic fragmentation, the second campaign was immediately perceived in the context of Islamist extremism. This gave the Russian military a new mission, one larger than a single campaign. Chechnya was but one front in the new confrontation; Central Asia and the all-too-familiar Afghanistan was the other. From now on, the Russian military had a new adversary, the Islamic terrorist-separatist-fundamentalist: an implacable, treacherous, and merciless enemy. This was clearly a caricature: Chechnya was not primarily a military threat, but a political challenge; the Taliban had no wish to take over Central Asia or invade Russia. There was also no coordination between Chechen rebels and Uzbek Islamists. International terrorism coordinated by Muslims was a figment of the imagination. Yet, it was convenient to believe in an enemy that was "larger than life." Fighting this new enemy provided a sense of urgency to the changes required in the Russian approach to waging war.

Operational Art and Tactics

Beginning in 1990, Russian (and worldwide) military thinking was influenced by U.S.-led operations in the Persian Gulf (twice against Iraq), the Balkans (against Yugoslavia), and in Afghanistan (against the Taliban and al-Qaeda). The Russian military paid particular attention to such tactics as engaging the enemy without entering into direct contact, using precision-guided munitions, and employing mobile forces.[37] Yet, except for in Afghanistan, as the Russians noted, the Western coalition was fighting a conventional enemy: the armed forces of the modern state.

In contrast, since Afghanistan in the 1980s and Tajikistan in the 1990s, the Russians were facing various rebel groups using guerilla tactics, sabotage, and terrorism. The Russians found Chechen tactics more advanced than those used by the Afghan mujahideen in the preceding decade. The Chechens hit and run, staged surprise attacks (so-called bee-swarm attacks) on military convoys, laid ambushes on roads, used snipers, and laid mines. By some accounts, up to 60 percent of all Russian casualties in Chechnya and Afghanistan were the victims of mine wars.[38]

The Russian army found it difficult to apply its obvious advantages with such foes who operated out of the general population. Pavel Grachev complained in the fall of 1995 that the political leadership's directives to "attack where the enemy congregates, taking care to avoid shooting peaceful civilians" violated "the laws of war."[39] In 1999, many of these constraints were removed, and the military was given a freer hand. Nonetheless, the use of almost World War II methods had a limited effect. The use of aircraft and artillery, of course, allowed the military to destroy rebels from a distance, but actions in populated areas and in the mountains presented a serious problem. The Russian military concluded, for example, that storming villages was pointless if the number of rebels holding out there was less than 1.5 percent of the population.[40] Such precision in defining criterion, of course, was fascinating. How could such calculations be made on the battlefield? One thing was clear, however. The use of heavy weaponry and the resulting destruction of homes rarely led to the destruction of rebel forces; instead, it guaranteed local hostility to the Russian military.

Russian military theorists have claimed that, using the experience of the Chechen campaigns, the military developed a new theory of special (counterterrorist) joint-force operations, bringing together forces from the Defense and Interior Ministries, the FSB, the Federal Agency of Government Communication and Information, and the Ministry of Emergency Services.[41] The path from theory to practice, however, was difficult and thorny.

The tactics of the Russian forces underwent considerable change compared with those devised for war with the West. Military operations in Chechnya were episodic and reactive: that is, the operations were responding to Chechen flare-ups. The field of battle was so wide and configured so erratically that traditional military concepts of the "front" and the "rear" proved irrelevant, and the traditional concepts of "attack" and "defense" were absent. Forces often had to attack and defend in separate, isolated sectors. The chief methods for liquidating the enemy were through artillery and air attacks, enemy containment, and blockades. Russian troops were also forced to change to small-group (squad) tactics. Sometimes groups of only three soldiers were formed, an unthinkable move for Soviet tacticians. Forces became task-specific.[42]

In the view of the Russian command, the major lessons of the Chechen campaigns can be summarized as follows.[43]

- Emphasize preventative measures.
- Set decisive goals when using force.
- Isolate the area of military operations from the outside world, depriving the enemy of reinforcements and supplies.
- Engage in joint operations with the ministries of Defense, the Interior, the FSB, and border guard forces.
- Value the sustainability of operations over the massive use of weaponry.
- Use heavy weapons selectively, except in mountainous or forested areas.
- Minimize collateral damage to the population and civilian infrastructure.
- Set priorities for the use of precision-guided weapons.

Considering the practices of the first and second Chechen campaigns, this list amounts to wishful thinking.[44] In particular, neither high-precision weaponry nor precision-guided munitions are available for federation soldiers fighting in Chechnya. Thus collateral damage to the Chechen population is much more extensive than need be.

The success of U.S. military operations in Afghanistan and Iraq both surprised and shocked the Russian military. In September and October 2001, many Russian experts predicted a difficult and drawn-out war with massive U.S. casualties. The rapid rout of the Taliban with minimal loss of American lives led Russian military observers to talk of the "commercial" (rather than military) nature of the U.S. operation. The only solace for the Russians was that the Americans were unable to capture either Osama bin Laden or Taliban leader Mullah Omar. This colossal misjudgment was repeated in February and March of 2003 when most Russian military commentators predicted "a new Vietnam" for the United States in Iraq. True to form, the subsequent, rapid fall of Baghdad was ascribed to the Pentagon bribing Iraqi generals. American success and especially when compared to Russian failure, led more hard-thinking military specialists, however, to call for fundamental structural changes in the Russian military.

Drawing on the Chechnya experience, they argued for modifying the force structure. While not calling for the abandonment of regiments and divisions (the sacred cow of a large-scale war against NATO or China was still in place), they demanded increased flexibility. As a result, the principle of a module-type organization was accepted, with the battalion as its basic element (something akin to how the U.S. army is organized). This plan agreed with the general optimization trend. A serious reorganization of the Russian military structure, however, proved to be more difficult.

The first Chechen campaign effectively buried Pavel Grachev's idea of creating mobile forces comprising airborne troops, *Spetsnaz* commando-type formations, and marine forces. Instead of emphasizing coherent rapid-deployment forces capable of lightning strikes, Russian commanders had to deal with joint operations by different types of forces. Moreover, and somewhat ironically, the second Chechen campaign led to the revival of Land Forces, which had less of a priority in the 1990s in the eyes of the political and military leadership. In 2001, after a three-year hiatus, the high command of these forces was restored. A few combat-ready motorized infantry units were brought to full strength, and the importance of combat support was rediscovered, sometimes the hard way.

The Role of Nuclear Weapons

Under the condition of Moscow's practical concentration on local wars, the problem of nuclear weapons in Russian military policy resurfaced. As early as 1993, in "Fundamentals of the Military Doctrine," the Russian leadership was emphasizing nuclear deterrence to balance the weakness of the conventional armed forces. Russia candidly abandoned the propagandistic Soviet-era obligation not to use nuclear weapons first. The 2000 national security concept and military policy documents highlighted the enhanced role of nuclear weapons. Going further, some Russian experts argued that to deter the new threats from the south,[45] medium-range missiles of the type banned by the 1997 Intermediate-Range Nuclear Forces Treaty (INF) should be resurrected. It is difficult to see, however, how INF weapons might deter Islamists or separatists. Rather, they could be used to deter those states considered to be their sponsors.

In 1992, Marshal Yevgeni Shaposhnikov, then commander-in-chief of the Joint Armed Forces of the CIS, threatened Turkey with a third world war to deter Ankara from intervening militarily in the Karabakh conflict. No other state considered a supporter of Chechen separatism or militant Islamism—namely Pakistan, Taliban-ruled Afghanistan, Saudi Arabia, and the United Arab Emirates—was ever directly threatened by Moscow, but Russia's nuclear strategy, although still shackled from the Cold War, was loosening. To some, the U.S. 2002 Nuclear Posture Review was showing the way.

Yet having seen the futility of deterring stateless actors, official Russian military thought still has not crossed the threshold from nuclear deterrence to preventive strikes. It must also deal with attempts by separatists and terrorists to deter the Russians. In 1996 Shamil Basayev's agents placed radioactive materials in Moscow's Izmailovsky Park. Ever since, Russian special services have had to consider the possibility that nuclear devices might fall into the hands of Muslim extremists, which, in turn has led Moscow strategists to consider issues of nuclear proliferation and missile defense more seriously.

Although the Russian military generally did not perceive either Saddam Hussein's Iraq or present-day Iran as a direct danger, Pakistan's 1998 aggressive entry into the nuclear weapons club alerted them to new dangers. Ever since 2000, President Putin has been proposing cooperation with Europe, NATO, and the United States on missile defense.

Force Deployment Patterns

Based on the Chechen experience, the Russian military has concluded armed forces should not be deployed in the center of a country, as advocated by the proponents of mobile forces, but close to areas of potential conflict. Thus, the Russian military has been slowly but steadily turning south and southeast, and away from its traditional Western focus. The process, however, has been anything but well directed or well organized.

Before mid-1992, Moscow planned a clean withdrawal from the ethnic conflict-ridden Northern Caucasus and Central Asia. In May 1992 in Tashkent, under an agreement dividing up among the CIS countries the resources of the Soviet army, Russia agreed to Uzbekistan becoming totally sovereign in the defense field. In Kazakhstan, the Russian military presence was largely tied to the Baikonur space launch center. The formation of a joint Russian-Turkmen command was the first step toward the full security independence of Turkmenistan, achieved in 1999. Russian border guards in Kyrgyzstan had been phased out by 1998. The Russian regular forces would have also left Tajikistan, but for the civil war there that lasted through 1997. Even then, their future remained unclear until the late 1990s. A similar pattern was seen in the Caucasus. In June 1992, federal forces left Chechnya, abandoning equipment and weaponry.[46] In 1993, Russian regular forces and border guards left Azerbaijan, prodded by the national democrats then in power in Baku. The full removal of the Russian army from Georgia was put on the official agenda.

Ethnic conflicts in the post-Soviet territories slowed down this trend and created a need to deploy peacekeeping forces in order to isolate areas of tension and protect Russian interests, but it was Chechnya that substantially reversed the trend. The North Caucasus military district became the only regional command with a fighting mission.

In 1995, there was a decision to form the 65,000-strong Fifty-eighth Army, with headquarters in North Ossetia's Vladikavkaz. In 1998, an operational group of Defense Ministry forces was formed in Kaspiysk, Daghestan. While most soldiers still did tours of duty in Chechnya, returning to their home regiments at the end of a few months' stay, it was decided in early 2000 to deploy two large units permanently in Chechnya itself—the 15,000-strong Forty-second Motorized Infantry Division, headquartered in Khankala, and the 7,000-strong Forty-sixth Interior Forces Brigade—as well as a border guard detachment with 1,400 authorized personnel, headquartered at Itum-Kale.[47]

On the southeastern axis facing Central Asia, the districts of the Volga and the Urals were merged in 2001. Farther south, Moscow won Dushanbe's agreement to establish, with the division-strong Russian peacekeeping force in Tajikistan, a regular military base with headquarters in Khudzhand in the Ferghana Valley. In 2003, a token Russian air force presence reappeared in Kyrgyzstan, with the potential for subsequent expansion. But there were also false starts. The decision in 2000 to deploy a rapid reaction corps of 50,000 headquartered in Omsk in southern Siberia and dedicated to action in Central Asia, fell flat because of lack of funding. In March 2001, a modest plan to station five battalions (3,000 personnel) of Russian paratroopers in Tajikistan had to be called off for a similar reason.[48]

These moves to redeploy forces to the southern sector had consequences for international agreements. Russia's new requirements did not fit the flank limitations required under the 1990 Conventional Forces in Europe (CFE) treaty. The Russian leadership had to plead with and cajole other parties to the treaty to agree to an increase in the Russian quota during the treaty review. Moscow discovered, with some surprise, that to get what it wanted in the post–Cold War world, it had to deal not so much with the United States (which did not see Russia's needs as its problem), as with Turkey (which saw a problem), and even with Georgia, which was unwillingly hosting Russian forces.

During the second Chechen campaign, Tbilisi was so hostile over the in-country Russian military presence that Moscow had to reduce its garrison, withdrawing troops to neighboring Armenia, which welcomed the Russian presence. Other units went to the North Caucasus. This was the end of a long era. For the first time since 1800, Tbilisi ceased to be the headquarters of a Russian military presence in the Caucasus region. The new headquarters was being built some five hundred kilometers farther north, in Rostov-on-the-Don, where the North Caucasus military district was headquartered.

During the 1990s, the Northern Caucasus command turned from a sleepy backwater posting into a frontline force, effectively the only truly combat-ready element in the Russian military establishment. Besides Chechnya, it watches over the separatist enclaves of Abkhazia and South Ossetia that are outside Tbilisi's control and are policed by Russian peacekeepers. It has a mission to protect and defend Russia's border, especially since Azerbaijan in 1993 and Georgia in 1999 saw Russian border guards leave. In this period of Russian military history, a new frontier means one closer to home.

Under new conditions, the North Caucasus military district has also become a training ground for the post-Soviet military elite. As in Afghanistan two decades earlier, officers go there for combat experience and to earn major promotions. In 1997, the then-commanding general of the district, Anatoly Kvashnin, was appointed chief of the General Staff. His successor, Viktor Kazantsev, was selected by Putin in 2001 as the presidential representative in the south of Russia and de facto governor-general, if not viceroy, of the unruly region.

While the heart of the Caucasus story is in its shifting borders, in Central Asia the idea of a borders, fronts, and rear locations is almost entirely absent. The Russian military presence is extremely thin throughout the region. Uzbekistan categorically refused to turn to Russia for troops, even in the high-risk environment of terrorist raids during 1999–2000. Only Russian weapons were welcome. By that time, Turkmenistan had completed a three-stage dismantlement of the Russian presence, and Kyrgyzstan (where there had been no regular Russian units) waved goodbye to Russian border guards. Kazakhstan still has around 15,000 Russian military personnel, nearly all of whom serve at the Baikonur space launch center or at several test ranges in the Kazakh steppes, including Sary-Shagan and Emba—which hardly constitutes a combat force. Thus, Russia's only deployable military force in the vast region was the 201st Motorized Rifle Division (with approximately 8,000 personnel, mostly Russian nationals) and Russian-led border guards (approximately 14,500 personnel, 95 percent of which were Tajik nationals).[49]

This curious, quasi-colonial arrangement highlights a major demographic limitation Russia is now facing. The decrease in the birthrate at the end of the 1970s and its sharp decline in the 1980s, coupled with both the exemption of significant categories of Russian citizens from military service, and the health and crime problems, have produced a conventional military force far inferior to anything Russia had seen since the 1918–1920 civil war. In the 1990s, the semiannual intake into all the armed services (including the interior forces and border guards) was limited to between 180,000–190,000, which forced the army command to take anyone available and to compete against other (often better-connected) services for a scarce resource of diminishing quality. This was another first in Russian military history.

At the beginning of the first Chechen campaign (December 5, 1994) the operational group of federal forces in Chechnya numbered 24,000.[50] By the time of the storming of Grozny (December 31), that number had increased to 38,000 (with 230 tanks, approximately 450 armored fighting vehicles, and almost 400 pieces of ordnance and mortars) and eventually it reached 80,000. During the second campaign, the Russian leadership gave up the tactic of escalation and resorted to mass invasion. As a result, the ranks of federal forces at the start of the operation approached 100,000, half of which were Defense Ministry personnel. Nevertheless, this number represented the limit. Russia is not capable of participating in two local conflicts like that in Chechnya simultaneously. During the second campaign, the principle of the volunteer participation of conscript soldiers in combat, which had been proclaimed though not always adhered to in the first war, was abolished.

Thus, in the 1990s, the war in Chechnya and the conflicts in Central Asia led to the partial redeployment of Russian forces toward the southern (Caucasus) and southwestern (Central Asia) sectors. Although the main forces remained, particularly after Kosovo, oriented toward a Western enemy, the Russian command had to create new groups of conventional forces in those two sectors.

The Problem of Borders

A distinctive feature of these new conflicts in the south, even when compared to the war in Afghanistan, is the absence of reliably protected frontiers. In the first years after the collapse of the Soviet Union, the Russian Federation's borders with former Soviet republics were absolutely impermeable. Under those conditions, the Russian leadership tried to realize a concept of two borders. The first border contains the Republic of Russia. The second border, that of the former Soviet Union, would become the outer frontier, Russia's strategic buffer zone, behind which CIS countries would be reliably protected from attack or other malignant influence. Using Soviet-era infrastructure, the main border forces and resources would be concentrated along this cordon sanitaire. The border troops of all CIS states were to become fully integrated under de facto Russian command. In this scheme, the borders between the CIS countries themselves would remain absolutely passable.

This concept was immediately rejected by several CIS countries (Ukraine, Moldavia, Azerbaijan, and Uzbekistan), which saw it as a threat to their independence and a step toward the reintegration of the former Soviet territories under Russia's tutelage. The refusal of several governments to accept the Russian plan forced Moscow to rely on its border troops, which were then stationed in the territories of Georgia, Armenia,

Turkmenistan, Tajikistan, and Kyrgyzstan. Still, a continuous frontier was not possible owing to the gaping holes made by the CIS countries that refused to cooperate. The first Chechen campaign demonstrated that both internal and external borders had become too permeable for Russia's security. On the one hand, Chechen separatists received aid and support from the Middle East; on the other, Russian towns situated as far as 120 miles from Chechnya became targets for armed raids by Chechens. In Tajikistan, Russian border guards routinely came under fire from both the front and the rear.

By the beginning of the second Chechen campaign, Russian border forces remained only in Armenia and Tajikistan. Moscow had to take steps to fortify those borders, which had been intended to be internal. This was anything but easy. Rugged terrain and strip farming are the main problems for border demarcation and control in the Caucasus. In the Central Asian sector, there is a mammoth problem of controlling the enormous border that separates Russia from Kazakhstan.

Lacking the personnel and other resources to control the Kazakhstan border reliably, Russia was forced to accept that the only substantial barrier between Moscow and Taliban-controlled Kabul was a few thousand border guards and motorized riflemen stationed in Tajikistan. Providing some political stability in Tajikistan itself, this garrison was nevertheless incapable of shielding Russia from the increasing flow of narcotics from Afghanistan.[51]

Since 1996, heroin has replaced raw opium as the primary illegally trafficked narcotic. Although Russian and Tajik military personnel talk about a "heroin jihad" against the infidels,[52] they have little to fight it with. The methods for conveying the narcotics not only to CIS countries but to countries within the federation are becoming ever more subtle.[53] A major contributing factor is the corruption within CIS government bureaucracies, including both their security services and armed forces.

Relations within the Military Community

The collapse of the Soviet Union meant the collapse of a unified military organization. The 1992 Law on Defense defined the armed forces as purely Defense Ministry structures. The Interior Ministry troops, the Federal Border Service troops, the Federal Agency of Government

Communication and Information troops, the FSB, the Federal Security Service, the Ministry of Emergency Services, and the railway troops all began to act independently and as counterbalancing members of an extended military community. The Chechen war illuminated the other side of this fragmentation: the problem of how to command forces during joint operations.

Joint operations turned out to be one of the weakest elements of Russian strategy. For the first time, in March 1994, a joint grouping of Northern Caucasus command and Interior Ministry forces was established on the territory of Northern Ossetia and Ingushetia. Still, the coordination of operations during the Chechen war, which began nine months later, ultimately was not provided, a main reason for the failure of the entire campaign.

In accordance with the laws of the Russian Constitution, the president is the commander-in-chief of the armed forces. He controls other forces as chief executive. The so-called power block of the government (the Defense Ministry, the Interior Ministry, the Ministry of Emergency Services, the security agencies, and the Foreign Ministry) are placed under the direct control of the head of state. The president can coordinate the actions of various power block departments through the National Security Council, which he heads. The Security Council prepares decisions and ensures their execution.

In reality, this scheme was fraught with problems during the 1990s. President Yeltsin had little interest in military issues and paid more attention to creating a system of "checks and balances" within the executive branch, including the military community. The Kremlin encouraged rivalry among the Defense Ministry, the Interior Ministry, and the Federal Border Service in the corridors of power, but strangely enough, the Kremlin then expected these rivals to cooperate smoothly on the Caucasus battlefield.

The role of the Security Council as coordinator and executor of approved decisions more often than not remained on paper. After first making sure that the senior members of the national leadership were collectively responsible for the start of the Chechen war, the Security Council rarely dealt with Chechnya, and worse, failed to coordinate the day-to-day activities of the ministries and departments. By contrast, for two years (1996–1998) after the Khasavyurt agreements, the council became a kind of "ministry for Chechen affairs," managing relations with

Maskhadov. The Security Council secretary at the time, Ivan Rybkin, yielded the practical side of his duties to his nominal deputy, the tycoon Boris Berezovsky. Under Putin, the new Security Council figured prominently for fifteen months before again losing key personnel and much of its influence.

In crisis situations, the peculiar new Russian system of checks and balances demonstrated utter dysfunctionality. The decision to begin operations in Chechnya (November–December 1994) was taken without a serious discussion of the options available and the consequences involved, as though people had forgotten the Soviet politburo's "Afghan experience." The hostage crisis in Budennovsk (June 1995) caught the highest government bodies unaware. President Yeltsin was away, Prime Minister Victor Chernomyrdin personally negotiated with terrorists, and the various power block principals gathered, only to step on one another's toes. Checks and balances had turned into chaos.

Making the Interior Ministry responsible for Chechnya in 1994–1995 was an unfortunate choice. In combat, Interior Ministry troops submitted with great reluctance to the armed forces command. At the beginning of the second campaign, this changed; the Ministry of Defense was made top dog. The mission of Interior troops had been defined as conducting clean-up operations in populated areas and keeping order after the end of hostilities.

The 2000 military policy attempted to designate a specific mission for each component of the military community. Thus, the armed forces were to "rout illegal armed units and create conditions for a full-scale resolution of the conflict." Interior Ministry troops were to restore law and order and provide public safety and stability. The intelligence services were to fight terrorism.[54] (The latter assignment had been established in the 1998 law on fighting terrorism.)

In practice, achieving such a distribution of labor turned out to be difficult. Not until six months after the announcement of the end of military actions (in January 2001) did the FSB officially receive responsibility for counterterrorist operations. Even then, however, the Ministry of Defense remained the most visible federal agency in Chechnya, and all other agencies stayed effectively autonomous and independent of one another.

The poor coordination of the power structures is a product of the collapse of the previous authoritarian control model and the weakness and underdevelopment of democratic institutions, and there is a temptation to recentralize according to the traditional model. Thus the General Staff seeks to gain control over the Defense Ministry, Interior troops, and railway troops, while many in the security establishment support a "restored KGB" model, uniting the FSB, the Federal Border Service, the Federal Agency of Government Communication and Information (FAPSI), the Federal Protection Service, and the Foreign Intelligence Service. The General Staff has yet to achieve its goal; the FSB, however, took control of the border guards in March 2003 and the dissolved FAPSI.

Arms and Equipment

Burning tanks on Grozny's streets on New Year's Day 1995 is one of the most vivid images of the first Chechen campaign. Tanks—the potent symbol of recent Soviet military power—became easy targets for Chechen rebels. Altogether federal forces lost more than two hundred tanks and armored infantry vehicles in the first campaign. The problem was not only in the construction of the battle machines (they were eventually upgraded) or their employment. Instead, the weapons and tanks designed to destroy large regular enemy forces on European plains were useless in guerilla warfare. Something similar had occurred in the early 1980s in Afghanistan, but Afghanistan was considered an exception, and the "norm" remained a large-scale war in Central Europe and Asia.

The hallmark of the second campaign (at least in the beginning) was artillery and missile attacks on Chechen rebel positions. The rebels were forced to retreat, but many populated areas received extensive damage. On the eve of 1999–2000, Grozny was so demolished that not until the middle of 2001 could it function even nominally as the administrative center of Chechnya. The capital was transferred to the largely untouched Gudermes, where federal forces had entered by arrangement with local city elders.

Likewise, the Russian army in Chechnya during the second campaign was ineffective. Although ostensibly equipped with large firepower, it lacked high-precision weaponry, modern communication equipment, modern command and intelligence resources, and the weaponry needed for nighttime operations. The contemporary weaponry of the Russian Land Forces averaged 22 percent, but only 7 percent was in military intelligence and 2 percent in army aviation.[55] The condition of the tank inventory and the air fleet had remained substantially unchanged since war in Afghanistan. In February 2002, after a series of five crashes of military transport helicopters, federal forces requested the immediate replacement of army aviation. The needed matériel (the Ka–50, Ka–52, Ka–60, and a field command module), however, was issued in paltry numbers. The first few "black sharks" (Ka–50 helicopters) were delivered to Chechnya only in January 2001. Apart from finances, another impediment was the reluctance of military industrialists to combat test equipment that was already selling well on international markets under "unusual" conditions of guerilla warfare. There were other considerations. Gennady Nikonov, the engineer of the modern submachine gun Abakan (a follow-up to the Kalashnikov), complained that his creation must be sent to Chechnya in strictly limited quantities to avoid its falling into the hands of the enemy.[56]

As a result, in the second campaign, as in the first, the military was forced to cannibalize parts to repair weapon systems.[57] Some improvements were made. In 1994, the army entered Chechnya lacking basic protection (flak jackets), wearing overcoats that impeded movement and uncomfortable footwear. In 1999, soldiers had somewhat better protection, uniforms, and footwear. Nevertheless, the lack of modern weaponry and equipment remains one of the most important reasons for so many casualties among soldiers and Chechens as well as the wide-scale destruction that took place in Chechnya. Commanders, however, are looking worriedly beyond Chechnya, at the fast-growing technological gap between the Russian military and that of the United States.[58] "For the first time in the history of our country," notes Gen. Makhmut Gareyev, the president of the Academy of Military Science, "the Russian army is lagging considerably behind a potential enemy in several parameters: communication, intelligence, electronic warfare, high-precision munitions, and so on."[59] This statement implies who the high command still considers to be a "potential enemy."

Weapons are not the only weak point in the Russia-U.S. military comparison. The gap in the quality of personnel is even more evident. Complex and expensive equipment breaks easily. Officers and soldiers expose themselves to unacceptable risk. In aviation, for example, the number of flight hours logged by pilots is an average of 20–30, compared with 120–150 in the aviation forces of NATO countries. Although helicopter crews in Chechnya and Tajikistan spend considerably more time in the air, the combination of idling and then long hours cannot be productive for any military organization.

Most Russian arsenals are not only designed for continental war but are outdated. New weaponry has not been produced, not so much because of a lack of resources as from inefficient spending. Finally, more than half of what is produced by the Russian defense industry is exported.

The second Chechen campaign allowed the military to proclaim its needs more loudly. According to calculations made in 2000 by the then head of weapons of the Russian army, Anatoly Sitnov, $16 billion was needed for the "normal manufacturing" of weapons and military equipment,[60] or twice the yearly military spending budget. Nevertheless, a specific plan was made to rearm the Forty-second Division, which was marked for continuous deployment in Chechnya. Proposed spending to purchase communication equipment, armor, motorized matériel, and individual flak protection was 2.5 billion rubles, or nearly $100 million. That amounted to more than 1 percent of total defense spending. Procurement rose somewhat in 2000–2003, but it was nowhere near Sitnov's figures.

The war did force shifts in the Russian military budget. Funds for personnel maintenance and day-to-day needs were reduced by nearly 10 percent.[61] As a result, funds for procurement and research and development increased somewhat. Military manufacturing, having received a shot in the arm, rose from 8 percent to 25 percent in various regions. Nevertheless, no realistic military industrial policy was designed. Not having clearly determined the extent of the threat, the enemy, the nature of the war, or the specifics of the theaters of operation, the Russia's military and political leadership to this day cannot decide which weapons are needed or in what quantities.

Military Morale

Wars shape the attitudes of officers and soldiers, who form a special military culture and spawn informal associations, from clubs to clans. In this sense the southern wars have great significance for what could be referred to as the human element of the Russian military organization.

In the Caucasian war, Grand Duke Konstantin appointed General Alexei Yermolov proconsul of the Caucasus. In fact, Yermolov had an ambition to wage war on his own terms, even to the point of meddling in the affairs of neighboring governments. He was not an exception. Other governor-generals, such as Baryatinsky, Tsitsianov, and Vorontsov, acted independently of St. Petersburg and made their own decisions. Regardless of modern improvements in communication, the independent action of military leaders has grown in the transition from continental confrontation to local wars.

Portraits of generals Yermolov and Baryatinsky now hang on the walls of the Russian military headquarters in the Northern Caucasus. The army holds competitions named for General Skobelev, the conqueror of Turkestan. In the 1980s, about six hundred thousand Soviet soldiers passed through Afghanistan, including a large part of the officer corps of the Land Forces. Since the 1990s, members of the officer corps fulfilled a Chechen "internship." According to some calculations, only 8 percent of those officers gain the skills and judgment expected of them. Unlike their nineteenth-century predecessors, they are not used to the Caucasus, because many are sent on only short-duty assignments. Senior officers appear only briefly at well-guarded headquarter offices and then claim combat experience as well as the perks involved. They are hardly romantic knights of the imperial mold with "the conscience of a soldier—perhaps a kind of stoicism in service."[62]

For the first time in the history of Russia, the Chechen war raised the issue of remuneration for the military in combat conditions. Time-and-a-half officer pay plus a per diem are inadequate compensation. At the start of the second campaign, the government attempted to equalize the pay scales of those serving in Chechnya with the salaries paid to Russian peacekeepers in the Balkans. Thus, many officers asked to be sent to Chechnya. Still, although the armed forces needed soldiers owing to large staff reductions, the number of servicemen who enlisted did not meet the need. Contract soldiers openly went to Chechnya to earn money.

Delays in the payment of "combat" renumeration began in 2000. Russian authorities were not able to fully meet their promises. Lawsuits resulted as well as protests, such as the picketing of the Northern Caucasus military headquarters. The situation was reminiscent of the mercenary armies of eighteenth-century Europe: the recruitment of mercenary soldiers from pools of adventurers and poor men, the refusal to discharge them after the campaign, and ensuing soldier mutinies. In spring 2001, President Putin felt constrained to visit Chechnya personally to sort out the problem of paying officers.[63] The acuteness of the problem abated only after large-scale military operations had ended.

In Chechnya, as in the Russian army as a whole, there exists an enormous (50 percent) shortage of company- and platoon-level officers. Nonetheless, group tactics require soldiers to have great independence and responsibility. Commanders admit, however, that the professional level and moral caliber of military academy graduates do not meet the requirements of the armed forces.[64] The Chechen war exposed a fundamental flaw in the Russian military; it lacks a strong corps of professional noncommissioned officers. In combat conditions, particularly like those in Chechnya, where the role of sergeants is growing, this deficit is disastrous. After the end of the first Chechen campaign, newly appointed defense minister Igor Rodionov tried to create a professional sergeant corps but he received little support.

Improving army leadership proved too difficult for the military department. The southern wars stimulated the practice of hiring under contract. However, the experience of mercenaries was not a positive one. In Tajikistan, the 201st Division, which is often considered one of the most combat-ready, battle-worthy, and disciplined units in the Russian army, is nearly fully manned by contract soldiers. It is nevertheless unclear whether the division is ready to fight and to take casualties. In Chechnya, where this risk is high, contract soldiers do not play a decisive role. Their presence in the forces leads to consequences that lose the hearts and minds of civilians: the contract soldiers, many of them in Interior Ministry forces and armed police units, often excel at inflicting unnecessary cruelties on the local population.

The Chechen war has become the stimulus for the mass evasion of the draft. The semiyearly draft is 180,000 men; the average number of draft dodgers is between 20,000–25,000, and reached 36,000 in 1998. Even the Northern Caucasus, where the local population has every reason to be on the defensive, young men avoid army service.[65] The quality of the draft contingent continues to fall. An eyewitness who is far from being anti-army said a few months before the second Chechen campaign that "having almost half of the new recruits suffer serious somatic or mental illness has become commonplace."[66]

The first Chechen campaign exposed a vacuum that had formed after the abolition of the Soviet system of appointing political officers and the end of Communist Party cells in the barracks. With the power of commanding officers unrestrained and virtually autocratic, a feeling of tension prevailed among the troops that was compounded by the conviction that the authorities and society had abandoned the fighting army. Even awarding the Hero of Russia honor to 120 men did not help.[67] The country did not care about the war, or the army, for that matter.

The second campaign, in contrast, jump-started official patriotic propaganda. In Yeltsin's memoirs the grandiloquent "figure of the Russian soldier defending the country and establishing order on his territory . . . becomes a strong, unifying national symbol."[68] Sentimentality, however, cannot replace systematic attention to the needs and problems of soldiers. Yeltsin's successor took several perfunctory steps to raise the morale of forces, beginning by flying to Chechnya on December 31, 1999, a few hours after having assumed the duties of president. A year later, the red standard with the star and the double-headed eagle was approved as a symbol of the Land Forces. (Tanks and armored vehicles in Chechnya often carried the red flag without the Russian tricolor.) The president approved a new statute regarding the composition of the military guards. Although it was unclear what troops would constitute the new guards, they would probably include those who had distinguished themselves in southern wars. Finally, Putin required affluent businessmen to make "voluntary" donations to assist servicemen and their families. Veterans also received aid (mostly in-kind) from the Russian Orthodox Church.[69]

Yet there was no success in improving the morale of the armed forces. More than half the casualties in the second Chechen campaign (and up to 80 percent in some units) are the result of hazing, violations of safety regulations, and other noncombat situations.[70] The federation as a whole generally supports the war effort, but since the taking of Grozny, it has again lost interest in the war and the army.

War Crimes

In an interview with Radio Liberty, Ruslan Khasbulatov (the former head of the Russian parliament) relying on eyewitness accounts, put the number of casualties in the second Chechen campaign at one hundred thousand, which is more than in the first campaign. According to Russian generals, no more than one or two thousand civilians died as a result of counterterrorist operations. The discrepancy is great, but unlike army casualties, civilian dead and wounded are not subject to an official count.[71]

The Chechen war is the first to pose serious legal problems for Russia involving national and international law. First, the government does not have an adequate legal basis for military action. Both campaigns of the conflict were conducted without a declaration of a state of emergency in Chechnya. Instead, the war was begun under the slogan "protecting constitutional order." The Yeltsin administration sought to avoid placing the war issue before a hostile Duma, however, which would probably not have approved a state of emergency and in any event would have insisted on having a say in the conduct of the war. The war was later labeled a "counterterrorist operation." The Putin administration exploited the popularity of engaging in an antiterrorist fight. In either case, the Kremlin concluded that its hands would be much freer without a state of emergency. Thus many legal "formalities" were sidestepped.

A gap exists between Putin's legal reform effort and the reality in Chechnya. Although the president preaches the primacy of law, as commander–in–chief he is apparently unable to ensure discipline among his troops in the (officially nonexistent) war zone. Hundreds of Chechens disappear without a trace, some to be released for a ransom.

Finally, there is conflict with Russia's international obligations. Russia joined the Council of Europe at the beginning of 1996, but since the fall of 1999 the Parliamentary Assembly for the Council of Europe (PACE) has consistently criticized the methods of the military operation in Chechnya. It has even raised the possibility of applying sanctions against Russia. The Organization for Security and Cooperation in Europe (OSCE) has levied similar criticism.

Consequently, the Kremlin has felt a need to show that it is law-abiding. In early 2000, after the scandal of the arrest, transfer to the Chechens, and rearrest of Radio Liberty correspondent Andrei Babitsky, a court hearing eventually exonerated the journalist. President Putin appointed Vladimir Kalamanov as his special representative on human rights in Chechnya. (In 2002, Kalamanov was succeeded by Ella Pamfilova.) It was also in 2000 that regimental commander Colonel Yuri

Budanov was arrested, accused of having killed a Chechen girl, and put on trial.

The trial of Budanov was the first court case against a senior officer accused of a crime in the Chechen war. The trial polarized Russian society. Defense Minister Ivanov stated "Budanov is a victim of circumstance and the inadequacy of our existing legislation" and further said he "felt compassion for him."[72] Senior generals, including then-commander of the Northern Caucasus district Gennady Troshev, commented harshly on the possibility of Budanov's conviction. Ulyanovsk governor and Chechen war veteran General Vladimir Shamanov took a similar stand. Vladimir Zhirinovsky's party (the Liberal Democratic Party of Russia) and the extreme right-wing Russian National Unity party conducted a noisy nationalistic campaign. The Kremlin found itself caught between its own military, the exigencies of the rule of law, and international public opinion. Under such conditions, the authorities tried to put the brakes on the case. Budanov was given several psychiatric exams, pronounced temporarily insane at the time of the crime, and re-examined. He was ultimately found guilty in July 2003, stripped of his rank, and sentenced to ten years in prison. Insightful observers connected Budanov's conviction with a need to bolster Kadyrov's position before Chechnya's presidential elections. The Budanov case provides insight into the problems of the transition period in the Russian legal sphere.

The so-called cleanup operations in Chechen cities and towns were often accompanied by rape and theft. Although most of these claims were made against servicemen from the Interior Ministry forces and OMON special police, by April 2001, at the end of the intense phase of the second campaign, there were sixty-four cases were pending against members of the armed forces.[73] Altogether, from August 1999 to December 2000, 748 criminal cases were opened.[74] Only a small number of those, however, concerned crimes against civilians: fourteen in July 2000 and six months later, thirty-five.[75] Before the Budanov trial, only seven senior servicemen had been convicted.[76] According to General Troshev, no legal measures had been in force to prevent looting by government personnel.[77]

Army corruption under conditions of insufficient control is a considerable problem for commanders and their political masters. The view that the war has a commercial nature on both sides is well documented. Accounts that oil acquired using primitive drilling methods continued to enter Dagestan and other regions of the Northern Caucasus illegally were commonplace. Such activity was now protected by the military.[78] An especially dangerous phenomenon was the sale of arms, matériel, and ammunition to the enemy. There were even instances of selling Russian soldiers to the Chechens as slaves.[79]

Trafficking in humans, and even in corpses, became an everyday occurrence. A particularly acute issue is the number of people missing after clean-up operations; this number was 930 by the summer of 2001, according to official data.[80] The authorities were inundated with complaints about the OMON special police and especially contract soldiers, who were accused of theft, torture, and even mass killings.[81]

"The Chechens see that Russian officers look much like their own field commanders," summarized journalist Shamsudin Mamayev. "They love money just as much and respect not the law, but the fist. But the rebel chieftains come from one's own people, and the officers are outsiders."[82] Real crimes, and even rumors of crimes, drew Chechens into the ranks of the rebels.

Despite the government's considerable "administrative resources," the outcome of federation trials cannot always be predetermined. The Russian criminal justice system is constrained to do as much as the media had in the first campaign: to investigate crimes and violations of law. The process of installing a "third power"—a strong judiciary—in Russia will depend largely on how objectively the courts fulfill their obligations in the forthcoming Chechen cases.

The religious factor is a particular problem. As noted, beginning in Afghanistan, first the Soviet Union and then the Russian Federation has waged war with one and the same enemy, the Islamic mujahideen. When official atheism was abolished and parallel Russian Orthodox and Islamic revivals emerged, the beginnings of religious conflict in the army appeared. Approximately one in ten Russian soldiers is a Muslim, but among officers and especially the generals, the number of Muslims is considerably less. Moreover, the Russian Orthodox Church is active in the armed forces. Turning the Russian army into a force of "Orthodox Christian soldiers," however, may cause serious problems, including problems for servicemen themselves. Recognizing this, the Kremlin has made concessions to the Muslims. Under Yeltsin, it tolerated polygamy, which had been openly instituted by Ingushetia's first president, Ruslan

Aushev. Under Putin, it considered allowing Muslim women to wear head scarves in their official passport photos.

Information Wars

The first Chechen campaign took place under remarkably open conditions—directly in front of the cameras of Russian and international media. As a result, the authorities, lacking a clearly defined policy for managing information, suffered a crushing defeat in dissemination and control. This defeat, in turn, created a severe credibility gap, fostering a mistrust of both the government and the army among members of the ruling elite and a lack of faith in their capabilities. Comparisons were made to Russia's astonishing and shameful defeat in the 1904–1905 Russo-Japanese war.[83] New difficulties overlaid old ones not yet overcome. The internationalism of the Soviet period died, but Russian self-awareness was occasionally degenerating into nationalism.

With Putin's appointment as prime minister, the authorities examined the causes of the government's failure in information management and it learned some bitter lessons. Determined to prevent a "Vietnam syndrome," they began to use information blackouts, making the battlefield off limits to most journalists, and using "friendly" media to tell the official story. As a result, the second campaign, in terms of information flow, was the exact opposite of the first. Journalists were given particularly selective access to information. Attempts to circumvent the official line were abruptly muzzled. The military leadership began to work actively with journalists, gaining their cooperation in creating a positive image of the army.

The thesis of the "enemy within, seizing control of the press and television and blurring the moral points of reference,"[84] had already appeared in the first campaign. At the time, many in the Kremlin saw antiwar journalists as traitors. Only Yeltsin's firm stand prevented a suppression of freedom of speech.

The situation began to change at the beginning of the Kosovo crisis. Russian public opinion unambiguously sided with the Serbs. Anti-Western, anti-American sentiments reached an unprecedented peak. Under these conditions, the raid by Russian paratroopers from Bosnia to Kosovo was successfully presented as a "PR stunt," showing the military action as a triumphant move. There was no propaganda czar, however; instead, the government gave its propagandists and their private counterparts carte blanche in manipulating the nation's image of itself as a superpower and in drawing the "correct" picture of the counterterrorist operation. They needed to coordinate only key details with the political leadership.[85]

The strategies for information management used during the second Chechen campaign were based on the following main principles:

- Limiting access to first-hand information.
- Having the military itself prepare information with subsequent release for general use.
- Excluding the showing of any of the horrors of war, including suffering soldiers and command blunders.
- Emphasizing the savagery of the Chechens.
- Creating a new image of the Russian army "defeating a sworn enemy in a just war."[86]

Reporting on the conflict from the Chechen perspective by the Russian media became problematic because of the sharp rise in anti-Chechen sentiment. A new law on fighting terrorism made objective reporting dangerous for those who risked it. Not many journalists dared to criticize the military, as had *Novaya Gazeta* correspondent Anya Politkovskaya. The newspaper, highly outspoken and critical of the war, came close to being shut down. Although the foreign media were clearly free of such limitations, with the exception of Radio Liberty, they had little impact on the Russian public.

The only television channel that refused to follow the authorities' new rules was Vladimir Gusinsky's NTV. The harsh criticism of the war in Chechnya on NTV pushed the Kremlin to replace the channel's owner, and thereby change its journalistic policy. The Russian government elite's hatred of NTV arose during the first Chechen campaign; the channel had been labeled a "Russian apologist for Ichkerianism."[87] A widespread theory circulated that NTV was an enemy of the rebirth of Russia as a great power. While Yeltsin remained in power, Vladimir Gusinsky's media empire was safe. When Putin came to power, however, calls to "transfer [NVT] into good hands"[88] coincided with the authorities' intention of destroying the independent political influence of the "oligarchs."

The official military press (chiefly *Krasnaya Zvezda*, the Ministry of Defense mouthpiece) and veterans' organizations took a belligerent stand on "cases of crude insults to the army" in NTV's programs. It was not merely a matter for debate. "An information war has been imposed on us," said government representatives, "and everything is it should be when at war. Preemptive strikes are needed."[89] In April 2001, the government, acting through Gazprom (the government-controlled natural gas company) took control of NTV and also press publications belonging to Gusinsky. The public barely reacted to this threat to the right of freedom of speech.

After the ownership of NTV was changed, public criticism of the methods used in the Chechen war was much more muted. Even the coverage of Chechnya by channel TV6, which belonged to another opposition oligarch, Boris Berezovsky, was sketchy. (TV6 went off the air in early 2002.)

The continuing war has produced a feeling of hopelessness in both Russian and Chechen society. Neither political nor combined military and police measures have inspired much hope of stabilizing the situation in Chechnya in the near future. Under such conditions, most Russians are ready to accept a continuation of the war as long as it does not affect them personally. Despite the current public tolerance of the war, the authorities and the military are clearly nervous. Politicians see the lack of prospects for the full eradication of separatism but are powerless to do anything about it. Meanwhile, the military is afraid of betrayal by politicians who would blame them anew for failure.[90]

In neutralizing the perceived ideological enemy, the authorities worked to create a positive image of the army, making up for some fifteen years of the purported "blackening" of Russian history. The following passage illustrates this broader context. It was said by Colonel General Valery Manilov when he was the first deputy chief of the General Staff (1996–2001) and the leading ideologue of the Russian military establishment (now retired and a member of the upper chamber of parliament).

> Our ancestors . . . and everyone in the world knows this very well . . . acted as true humanists. If they acted on their own territory, then they defended their land and their countrymen and their people from the enemy. If they had to act on the territory of other states, then they came there as warrior-liberators . . . The fuller and more vivid humanism of our officers and soldiers is evident in the

counterterrorist operation in Chechnya . . . Separate cases of not adhering to norms and principles of humanitarian law and the law of armed conflicts, which are committed by individual soldiers, have become the object of intense and important investigation by law enforcement bodies.[91]

These theories have a long resonance. In December 1999, in the heat of the second Chechen campaign, the Russian government decided to renew the military training of students in the eleventh grade. At the beginning of 2001, a government program for the patriotic education of Russians citizens was approved for 2002–2005,[92] presuming the collaboration of the Defense Ministry and the formation of a program of Russian military history education to instill spiritual values. Financing for the project, however, turned out to be meager (between $5 and $6 million).[93] One of the project's aims was to prepare a new comprehensive textbook of contemporary history and, accordingly, to draft an official version of Russian history. In early 2002, the head of the Russian Orthodox Church, Patriarch Alexis II, raised the issue of the desirability of teaching the fundamentals of Russian Orthodoxy in public schools.

An Attempt to Construct the "Right" Version of History

Military propagandists act both independent of and with civilian colleagues. They received a directive to combat "various kinds of political speculation, which in the long run might be used by political extremists to inflame violent events." Moreover, "a representation of the real history of the Caucasus" was considered "one of the most important conditions of the successful conclusion of the counterterrorist operation, a confirmation of peace in the region." The main theories of the "real history" of Russian-Caucasian relations were set forth on the pages of *Krasnaya Zvezda* at the beginning of 2001 by leading military personnel at the Defense Ministry.[94] They are summarized as follows:

- Wars have not been the only interaction in the history of Russia and the Caucasus. Russians (Cossacks) peacefully settled the region north of the Terek River in the sixteenth century. Russia indirectly liberated the Chechens from the threat of the Golden Horde.

- Caucasian peoples themselves invited Russia to the Caucasus, seeking its help against marauders: Turks, Persians, and Crimean Tatars. Even when local rulers supported the Turks or the Persians, the common people counted on Russia.
- The rivalries between Russia and Turkey and Russia and Iran have deep historical roots. In the Northern Caucasus, Turks were anti-Russian agitators seeking to "increase the spread of Islam . . . and to establish an anti-Russian tenor."
- Western countries (primarily Britain and France) unequivocally supported Turkey against Russia.
- The leaders of anti-Russian uprisings in Chechnya were impostors, and not true representatives of the aspirations of the common people. Their ultimate destiny, which they fully deserve, was a Russian prison.
- A protectorate for the Caucasus is an unreliable way to secure Russian interests in the region. The preferred form is direct control, with the region's inclusion in the realm.
- The Caucasian war is caused by the conflict between the interests of Russia as a great power (such as the geopolitical necessity of providing reliable communication between Transcaucasian possessions and the central provinces of Russia) and the traditional way of life of mountain people (which includes kidnapping for ransoms).
- Cruelty during the Caucasian war was commonplace, on all sides.
- The resettlement of mountain people to the Ottoman Empire was not so much the result of pressure from the czarist government, as of Turkish agitation.
- In integrating the Caucasus into the structure of the Russian Empire, Islam is to be respected, provided the Muslim clergy remain loyal.
- The familiar Bolshevik image of the Russian Empire as a "prison of peoples" was not only incorrect but blatantly slanderous. Russian imperial policies were different from those practiced by Western colonialists as well by Ottoman and Persian imperialists. Russians were not a privileged ethnic group within the

empire, and no Caucasian group has vanished. In fact, each group has had the chance to develop unimpeded.

- The collapse of the Russian Empire in 1917 was not from national repression, but a result of the weakening of centralized power and the support of autonomist-nationalists among Russian social democrats.
- In coming to power, Caucasian nationalists threw the region into the abyss of bloody civil wars. The Sovietization of the Caucasus by the Red Army ended ethnic conflicts and prevented armed expansion by Turkey and the West.
- The Soviet authorities made mistakes in national policies that created autonomous ethnic regions and infringed upon the rights of the local Russian population (Cossacks).
- Chechnya, in the structure of the Soviet Russian republic (RSFSR), was until World War II, a hotbed of armed criminality and insurrection movements, which the authorities had to fight with military means.
- During World War II, the threat to the rear of the Red Army by Chechen insurgents was real, but the responses of the Soviet leadership were inadequate. The deportation of Chechens and others was not just, and it was motivated by political, and not ethnic, considerations. The sentiments of the Russian people had no bearing on Stalin's decision.

This outline seeks to present objectively a view of a difficult and complex history. Both the positives and negatives of the empire, in both czarist and Soviet versions, are detailed. The key, of course, is the generally positive spin on the imperial experience. The reader is led to only one possible reasonable conclusion: the only solution to the problems of the Northern Caucasus—in this context, and with a slight widening of the argument one may talk of the entire Caucasus—is the strong governmental power and dominance of Russia in the region. Such a conclusion orients Russian politics to the methods of the past, and encourages Russian society to support a course that is increasingly inadequate given changing realities.

Like the Chechen campaigns, the crises in Central Asia have become a pretext for revising the history of the war in Afghanistan (1979–1989). In the early 1990s, the war was considered a shameful defeat of the

Soviet Union as well as a symbol of the mistaken, even criminal, foreign policy of Soviet Communist Party leadership.

In the assessment of General Makhmut Gareyev, the Soviet Union did not suffer a military defeat in Afghanistan: "Our forces, on orders from the government, entered the country in an organized manner and exited in an organized manner and did not run from it as the Americans did in Vietnam. There were no lost battles or operations, but it was not possible to win the war as a whole, mainly for political, not military, reasons."

The general's conclusion is that the mistake of leaving Afghanistan was worse than the alleged crime of sending forces into the country. As a result, Russia was deprived of an important buffer against Islamic extremism. Interestingly, this assessment leaves no place for the contribution of Soviet intervention to the rise and development of Islamic extremism.

The Army and Politics: The Civilian-Military Relationship

During the period of radical change in the country, the Soviet and then the Russian army was gradually but inevitably drawn into politics. Since 1989, the armed forces participated in political and interethnic conflicts in the Soviet borderlands. In August 1991 and September–October 1993, military forces were thrown into the power struggle in the country's capital. Radical regime changes, economic upheavals, the collapse of established values, the failure of the system of checks and balances, and the partial democratization of public life (through the introduction of the freedom of speech and the abolition of media censorship) threw the army into a completely new environment. As a result, a number of officers entered politics.

World War II gave the Soviet Union two generations of soldiers who had determined the face of the armed forces until the end of the 1970s. The youngest of the World War II veterans fought in Afghanistan, and some of those veterans died there. These soldiers were used to fighting the strongest military powers and coalitions of their time. Some thirty years after the end of the war, they of course left their leadership posts, making room for younger soldiers. By the 1990s, this rotation was complete. The generation that replaced World War II veterans was educated in conditions of local wars in a new period, the first of which was the ten-year war in Afghanistan.

The Afghan war (1979–1989) produced a group of officers who not only rose to military leadership but also became influential politicians. Among them were Boris Gromov, Pavel Grachev, Alexander Rutskoi, Alexander Lebed, and Ruslan Aushev.[95] Similarly, the Chechen war has become a new source of cadres, not only for the army, but also for the government. These men included Anatoly Kvashnin, Anatoly Kulikov, Viktor Kazantsev, Gennady Troshev, Vladimir Shamanov, Lev Rokhlin, Konstantin Pulikovsky, and Ivan Babichev. In this same league is Gen. Eduard Vorobyov, the former deputy commander of the Turkestan district and deputy commander of the Land Forces, who in 1994 refused to lead an ill-prepared operation in Chechnya and who subsequently became a prominent State Duma deputy.

The Communist Party's abdication and the dismantling of the Soviet Union happened extremely peacefully. Russia avoided the fate of both Romania and Yugoslavia. According to Yeltsin, however, until 1996 "a specter of impending civil war hung over Russia."[96] Violence, while occurring rarely, was always in the air. The militarization of politics as a result of the end of the Soviet Union occurred in parallel with the politicization of the army. Military might was viewed chiefly (and even exclusively) through the prism of political conflict. It was no accident that Pavel Grachev received the title of "best defense minister" from the first president of Russia. In December 1994, when Yeltsin decided to send forces to Chechnya, Grachev expressed his readiness to obey the commander-in-chief unquestioningly. His position as minister was wholly based on the disposition of the president to him. Remaining consistently loyal to Yeltsin, he provided a reliable rear guard for his patron. There was no more important task for the head of Russia's military department in that period.

If in the first two years the Russian leadership was nevertheless able to refrain from using violence in political conflicts, the shelling of the parliament building in Moscow on October 4, 1993, was an important turning point. Since the end of 1993, Russian intelligence services and the army have become secretly involved in an internal power struggle between various Chechen factions to manipulate developments in a controlled conflict.

During the first Chechen campaign, the military accused Russian politicians of treason. In the eyes of the military, periodic truces and negotiations with the separatists "stole victory from the army."[97] In

addition, several high-ranking officers publicly spoke out against negotiations and any compromise with the enemy. The Russian media dubbed
them a "party of war" despite the fact that in 1995 negotiations with
Maskhadov were led by Ministry of the Interior general Anatoly
Romanov. Negotiations seemed to be succeeding, and the effort was sustained even after Romanov was seriously wounded in an assassination
attempt. In the following year, it was General Lebed who signed the
Khasavyurt agreements.

Before the war in the Northern Caucasus, there were many military
men in the upper echelon of Russian politics. The Chechen war opened
the door more widely for them. After refusing to accept the Hero of Russia star from Yeltsin's hands, General Lev Rokhlin turned to the leading
left opposition for a short time. Relying on his position as Duma Defense Committee chair, he created a multitier organization of retired and
active-duty soldiers: the Movement in Support of the Army. Until
Rokhlin's murder in 1997, the Movement's progress was watched by the
Kremlin with growing unease.

Alexander Lebed, who came in third in the 1996 presidential elections and was appointed secretary of the Security Council in exchange
for his support for Yeltsin in the second round of elections, was immediately given the responsibility of Chechnya in the hope that he would
fail. Instead, he brought about a truce, which made him extremely popular. In the fall of 1996, as Yeltsin faced heart surgery, Lebed was considered a possible successor to the ailing president.

Lebed's rival, Interior Minister General Anatoly Kulikov, an old
Caucasus hand, rose to become vice premier. He was about to start regu-
lating economic relations when he was forced into retirement through
the efforts of Boris Berezovsky. Kulikov's successor, General Sergei
Stepashin, head of the Federal Counterintelligence Service before and
during the first Chechen campaign, became prime minister in spring
1999 and a candidate to succeed Yeltsin. Yeltsin later admitted that he
had been looking for an honest general to whom supreme power could
be transferred and found such a person in retired KGB colonel Vladimir
Putin, who passed his crucial political test during the second Chechen
campaign.

The second war, waged by Putin, opened the path to power for his
former colleagues from the intelligence services. Putin brought with him
Sergei Ivanov and Viktor Cherkesov. Ivanov became Security Council

secretary and later the first civilian defense minister. Cherkesov became the president's representative in northwest Russia and then head of the government's anti-drug committee. In general, intelligence and military personnel became key cadre reserves of the government. Of the seven presidential representatives in federal districts appointed in 2000, Pulikovsky and Kazantsev were Chechen veterans; of the five remaining, three were generals. Many military men were deputy plenipotentiary representatives. In 2000, Generals Boris Gromov, Vladimir Shamanov, and Vladimir Kulakov (of the FSB) and Admiral Yegorov were elected governors, and in 2001 Generals Manilov and Kulakov (the former head of training for the armed forces) became members of the Federation Council. This trend continued in the gubernatorial elections of 2002 (in the Smolensk region and in Ingushetia, for example).

Early in the second Chechen campaign, several generals of the fighting army publicly demonstrated independence from their so-called political masters. Mindful of the experience of 1994–1996, they did their utmost to keep the reins of operation in their hands. Generals Troshev and Shamanov publicly threatened to retire if political constraints were imposed on the military operation. Putin's timid attempt to announce an armistice in Chechnya a few days after accepting the powers of the presidency was openly sabotaged by the military command, and a bumbling personnel shuffle meant to transfer fractious generals ended up instead in confusion. In the end, acting president Putin was forced to admit publicly that "Russia does not have many generals like Troshev and Shamanov."

The military continued to claim that contradictory orders sent to forces in the first campaign had saved the Chechens from inevitable defeat. Many thought politicians who had ulterior motives had deliberately robbed them of victory. Everyone knew about the connections between Chechen rebels and such Kremlin-friendly "oligarchs" as Berezovsky. The tale of betrayal of the highest echelons of power became popular. In particular, surrendering Grozny to the Chechen rebels and then refusing to retake the city in August 1996 was considered "traitorous" by many in the army.[98]

In 1999, after acting cautiously at the start of the operation, the high command soon demanded authority for decisive action. Chief of the General Staff Kvashnin was able to secure a blank check from Putin and Yeltsin to take any steps necessary that would lead to the enemy's total defeat. The proposal by ex–prime ministers Primakov, Stepashin, and Kiriyenko and Moscow mayor Yuri Luzhkov to stop at the line of the Terek River, was rejected by the generals. The military was given a clear-cut task but no deadline. As a result, observers noted, the forces waged war "as it should be waged," using weapons absolutely superior to those of the Chechen rebels: aviation and artillery.[99]

This situation, which allowed the rapid achievement of the goal, presented the tough problem of the relation of means to ends in the war. Counting on raw force gave rise to a callousness toward victims that far exceeded even that of the first Chechen campaign. The brutally excessive so-called collateral damage was unequivocally explained as the product of the enemy's treachery. In his memoirs, Yeltsin totally absolves the Russian army of any responsibility for collateral damage.[100]

Most Russians shared this view. For them, the main thing was finally solving the Chechen problem, and not having to hear about it again. Initially leaning toward a solution by "expelling Chechnya from Russia," public opinion now swayed in the opposite direction, toward regaining control over the rebellious province by any means. To do so, the public counted fully on Putin and the military.

The second Chechen campaign marked a turning point in the public's attitude toward the armed forces. After the military dealt with the incursion into Dagestan by Basayev and Khattab, the army was once again regarded as the ultimate protector.[101] Moreover, the army was soon fully rehabilitated in the public's eyes from the failures of the first Chechen campaign.[102] Russian society tilted toward traditional values in matters of national security. Peace not guaranteed by military might was once again regarded as unreliable. Military power was celebrated for its conventional forces and not, as during the Cold War, for its missiles and nuclear arms. From 1996 to 2000, the number in favor of maintaining a large, powerful army at any cost increased significantly, while the number of those favoring a reduced military decreased noticeably.[103]

Still, Russian society as a whole was not ready to elevate the army interests above economic prosperity. The government, while increasing military spending, concentrated on economic reform. As a result, according to the military, funding levels reflected the belief that "if there's not a revolution, then make only a half turn toward the needs of the army."[104]

The Chechnya conflict has illuminated the extremely unsatisfactory level of control the Russian public has of its military organization. The political control of the military (subjective control) has weakened in comparison with the Soviet period, while processes for objective public control of the military and internal control (which appeared at the end of perestroika and the beginning of Russia's post-communist transformation) have not been developed.[105] For the moment, the public has stopped trying to control the military or to influence its organizational character and orientation. The only thing that continues to concern Russians is military casualties—notably only *Russian* casualties.

Military Casualties

In the nineteenth-century Caucasian war, as in other wars waged by the Russian Empire and then the Soviet Union, the lives of soldiers were not spared. The high command strove to achieve its goals at any price. The population was, in principle, ready to pay this price, considering casualties a necessary evil and placing all blame for them on the enemy. The public perception of losses changed during the war in Afghanistan. Recent publications about the human losses of the Soviet period, particularly during World War II, have made a great impression on Russian society. Thus, the problem of losses began to weigh on society's conscience and also began to be considered in government and military thinking. The military was forced to reassess its willingness to sustain many casualties, mindful not only of current public opinion but also of the decreasing pool of military recruits.

Russian military planners assessed the critical casualty level of their forces. The threshold value is considered to be 30 percent killed and wounded in large-scale operations against conventional forces, and between 12 percent and 15 percent in local wars like Chechnya. Casualities beyond that level, in their view, might spark antiwar demonstrations and lead to a political crisis. The optimum value was calculated to not exceed between 12–15 percent of personnel.[106] A special risk classification is being developed.[107]

In the first Chechen campaign, according to official data, around 4,300 Russian soldiers were killed, including 3,800 from the armed forces (with an average troop strength of the combined military forces in Chechnya of 70,000). In early 1996, the governor of the Nizhny Novgorod Oblast at the time, Boris Nemtsov, easily gathered a million signatures for a petition to end the war.

The campaign that began in 1999 was conducted under the slogan of minimizing casualties. From the beginning until the winter battles in Grozny, the number of casualties was indeed low. Nevertheless, according to the Russian military, more than 2,500 federal soldiers and more than 7,500 others were wounded in the first year of the second Chechen campaign. Chechen sources reported 15,000–20,000 "federals" killed during the same period (as well as the loss of 27 jet fighters, 40 helicopters, and more than 1,000 tanks and armored vehicles).[108]

The figures from the Chechen side were clearly inflated, but even if one were to use official data from the Russian Defense Ministry, the number of monthly casualties of federal forces stood at 250 killed for the period August 1999–July 2000. Compared with a similar period during the first war (December 1994–August 1996), the losses were lower, at 180 per month. The 1999–2000 campaign also turned out to be bloodier than in the peak year of the Afghan war in terms of losses.[109] Most casualties were sustained during the storming of Grozny. From the summer of 2000, the monthly losses decreased significantly. According to official data, from October 1, 1999, to December 23, 2002, 4,572 soldiers were killed, and 15,549 were wounded (the Ministry of Defense share is 2,750 dead and 6,569 wounded).

Russian public opinion is ambivalent. Although it is concerned about the constant flow of death notices, it seems to find the level of losses acceptable and still agrees with the authorities and the military command that if war were not being waged, there would be many more casualties. In general, Chechnya is considered to be a clear and present danger to Russian national security.

The losses of Russian forces in Central Asia are considerably less. During a decade-long deployment since 1992, around two hundred Russian soldiers died.[110] With the exception of the summer 1993 attack on the border security detachment when twenty-five soldiers died in battle, the losses did not provoke public outcry.

The first Chechen war took place against a backdrop of rapid social and economic differentiation in the Russian population. Furthermore, Russian military experts noted that in Russia, as in any poor country, the value placed on human life is lower than in the developed countries of the West. The issues of the value of human life and of socioeconomic compensation for the loss of life or health are on society's agenda.[111]

The Financial Cost of War and Reconstruction

The Chechen war has been, especially at its beginning, a considerable burden on Russia's weakened finances. In 1995, additional spending as a result of the war was estimated at $220 million.[112] In 1996, Chechnya swallowed 12 percent of the military budget.[113] On the whole, however, the war was within budget. Forces mainly used weaponry, matériel, and ammunition that had been manufactured during the Soviet period. Expenditures for "peace"—namely reconstruction—were much greater. The total economic damage from the first war was by some estimates $5.5 billion.[114]

A more important effect was that the second Chechen campaign brought about a redistribution of federal budget spending, favoring national defense. This happened in the year 2000. The 2001 budget (237.5 billion rubles, not including 30 billion rubles in military pensions) made up almost a fifth of federal expenses. Expenses for all power structures increased to one-third of Russia's budget. People in military circles noted with satisfaction that "the country's leadership began to strengthen the state, the military-industrial complex, and the work to achieve military reform."[115]

The beginning of the second Chechen campaign came during a profitable period of high oil prices. Moscow was able to spend 10 billion rubles ($350 million) on the war without much strain from August to December 1999 and in 2001. The period of peak of expenses (25 billion rubles, or just under $1 billion) came in 2000, when as much as 20 percent of the military budget went to the war. Expenses for reconstruction rose from 8 billion rubles in 2000 to 14.5 billion ($500 million) in 2001.[116]

Thus, the Chechen war did not ruin Russia's finances. Oil prices, which have stayed high since 1999, have provided the government with enough for substantial revenue. Yet, as Duma Defense Committee cochair Alexei Arbatov noted, Russia could wage only two local wars simultaneously under conditions of economic restructuring.[117]

The reconstruction of Chechnya will be much costlier, though. On the eve of the 2003 constitutional referendum, the Russian government promised to compensate Chechnya for the material damage caused to the population during the war. The total sum of compensation, however, some $20 billion, was too much to be paid out quickly. Damage compensation could be a useful tool for both the government and the Chechen population, as the former tries to pacify the republic and the latter seeks funding for rebuilding.

Russia's Military Allies

Until the mid-1990s, Moscow was unable to consolidate militarily the former republics of the Soviet Union, despite the Collective Security Treaty (CST) signed in May 1992. An alliance on the basis of a common past immediately showed itself to be an alliance without a future: there were too many differences in how that past was viewed in Moscow and in the capitals of the newly independent nations. An invitation to create an anti-Western union in the mid-1990s in answer to NATO expansion received a positive response from only Belarus. The only functioning military organization in the CIS in the 1990s was a joint anti-aircraft defense system, which was utterly useless in the new strategic environment. Not until the end of the decade did the real threats from the south help to create the necessary prerequisites for a new alignment.

The selection of Tashkent in 1992 for the signing of the CST reflected many changes: the end of military confrontation in Europe, Ukraine's rejection of any form of military or political integration with Russia, and armed conflicts in the South Caucasus. It also reflected the striving of Central Asian governments—against the backdrop of a civil war raging in Tajikistan—to enlist Russia's support in deciding national security issues. The significance of the agreement at the moment it was signed, however, should not be inflated. Its principal achievement was the allocation of the Soviet army and its weaponry. In retrospect, what proved to be extremely significant was the symbolic importance of where the treaty was signed.

When the civil war in Tajik reached its peak, Russia sought allies for a military operation to end the conflict. In 1993, CST forces (formally, "peacekeeping forces") were assembled in Tajikistan, consisting of Russian, Uzbek, Kazak, and Kyrgyz forces. A true military coalition did not develop, however, because of disagreements among the participants. Through the 1990s, Tajikistan remained the only military ally of Russia in Central Asia. Later, Kyrgyzstan, Kazakhstan, and even Uzbekistan, faced with the challenge of armed Islamists, also turned to Moscow for support.

By the end of the 1990s, Moscow had abandoned its ambitious but unrealistic plan to create regional coalition forces simultaneously in three strategic sectors: western (Eastern Europe), southern (the Caucasus), and southeastern (Central Asia). The southeast became the priority. This time, it was not a matter of lining up against a traditional foe, but positioning for battle against armed separatists, extremists, and international terrorists.

Since 1999, Moscow had been taking steps to create an antiterrorist coalition in Central Asia. Two coordinating antiterrorist centers were established, one under CIS in Moscow and the other under the Shanghai Cooperation Organization (Russia, China, Kazakhstan, Kyrgyzstan, Tajikistan, and Uzbekistan) in Bishkek, Kyrgyzstan's capital, which was also chosen as the headquarters for the CIS collective rapid-deployment forces. Gone was the early Russian urge to build huge, Warsaw Pact–like formations. The collective rapid deployment forces include just one battalion from each participating nation (a total of 1,500–1,700 men).[118] Moscow has also been trying to improve the coordination and information exchange among Council of CIS defense ministers, the antiterrorist center, and the council of the heads of CIS security services.[119] Interestingly, the Military Cooperation Coordination Staff, the last surviving structure of the discarded Joint Armed Forces of the CIS, was quietly buried.

When threats materialize, command and staff exercises become more frequent and better directed. The "Southern Shield of the Commonwealth" regulates military operations at Central Asia's borders, its main objective to keep rebels from reaching populated areas.[120] Hundreds of officers and cadets from Central Asian countries are undergoing military training in Russia. In five years, 24,000 Tajik soldiers have been trained in Russian border guard units deployed in Tajikistan.[121] Still, it remains a daunting task to build adequate military forces in Central Asia. Konstantin Totsky, the director of the Russian border service, and since 1993 Russia's chief military representative at NATO, opined that Tajikistan will be unable to guard its borders independently for ten to fifteen years.

The Russian military-political alliance with Central Asian countries has many deficiencies. Russia's allies in the region are weak, mostly authoritarian, states whose nation building is far from complete. The ruling elites routinely subordinate national interests to private and personal ones. Some have long since been clients of Moscow and benefit from such relations (including Tajikistan). Others, like Uzbekistan, are afraid of Moscow's hegemony. The armed forces of the new nations, built from the shards of the Soviet Army, are weak, ineffective, and corrupt. The command structure requires a radical overhaul, and the officer corps needs fundamental retraining. The irony, of course, is that Russia itself is hardly a model of successful transformation or modern military thinking. The budgets of Central Asian states for weapon modernization are extremely limited. Russia awarded grants to Tajikistan to buy Russian arms and matériel, which runs counter to its new principle of conducting exclusively commercial arms sales and is unwelcomed by weapon manufacturers. There is no choice, however. Russia regularly calls upon its allies to fulfill their obligations, at least in financing the antiterrorist center.[122]

Moreover, in frontline Tajikistan, the process of the post–civil war integration of government troops and the former Islamist opposition is difficult. The government in Dushanbe lacks control of a large part of the country, including the Tavildara region (where detachments of Juma Namangani's rebels were once based) and the Badakhshan highlands. Maintaining an army is burdensome for the formerly poorest republic of the Soviet Union, and its armed forces are constantly being reduced.[123]

The Kyrgyz army has twice (in 1999 and 2000) proved incapable of repelling attacks by rebels groups of five hundred. Even the Uzbek army, the strongest in the region, took several weeks in 2000 to defeat an incursion by Islamists, who managed to get within a hundred kilometers of the capital, Tashkent.

Table 1 provides some general data on the armed forces in Central Asian countries.

Throughout the mid- and late 1990s, Russia cultivated ties with the Afghan Northern Alliance. The irony is that the alliance was composed of former mujahideen who had fought against the Soviet army and who, after having been forced to leave, toppled the Moscow-installed regime of Najibullah. Among northerners, Moscow's favorite was the Tajik warlord Ahmad-Shah Massoud, assassinated by the Taliban in September 2001. Russia had hoped to maintain at least a buffer zone between its garrison in Tajikistan and the Taliban forces controlling most

Table 4.1   *The Armed Forces in Central Asia*

Country	Population (thousands)	GDP (PPP estimate) (billions)	Defense Expenditure (PPP estimate) (millions)	Armed Forces (in thousands of personnel)
Uzbekistan	24,100	$15.9	$615	59.1
Kazakhstan	15,000	14.5	504	64.0
Tajikistan	6,105	1.2	95	6.0
Kyrgyzstan	4,852	1.1	51	9.0
Turkmenistan	5,000	3.3	109	17.5

Source: *The Military Balance 2003–2004* (International Institute for Strategic Studies: Oxford University Press, 2003).

of Afghanistan.[124] Moscow had also hoped for a counteroffensive by the Northern Alliance and its retaking of Kabul.

In the fall of 2001, this did indeed become a reality, as a result of the United States' Operation Enduring Freedom. Russian government officials, from Putin downward, have frankly admitted that American intervention removed the most serious military threat to Russia and its CIS partners in the past decade. The Russians cooperated with the United States in helping the Northern Alliance achieve victory, and then refrained from engaging in a power play against the new Kabul-based government under Hamid Karzai. Russia even agreed to provide a military unit to the NATO-led peacekeeping force in Afghanistan. (General Totsky's Tajik experience will be useful here.) With the situation in Afghanistan and neighboring Pakistan still fluid and the defeated but not fully eliminated Taliban raising its head, Afghanistan has become a new field for Russia's security cooperation with the United States and NATO.

Summary

The traditional inclination of the Russian elites to continue to play the role of a great power on the expanses of Eurasia led them to adopt a posture of defense in all directions. The extreme expense of such a security system is unlikely to be realized. More important, the failure to distinguish between strategic directions would logically emphasize the Western direction as a function of United States–NATO military might.

Russian supporters of the de Gaulle concept take it literally, discounting French NATO membership. This is not an oversight. Maintaining a stand-off with the West while eschewing direct confrontation satisfies influential military and political circles. They know they would lose power if the threat from the West were confined to history books, where it has rightly belonged since the end of the Cold War. Similarly, the desire for a scaled-down version of the Warsaw Pact within the CIS is based on a traditional security mentality that cannot imagine a great power without a retinue of satellites.

The first and second Chechen campaigns have spurred a reorganization of the Russian armed forces, such as improving military structures. The second campaign led to an increased interest of the elites in Russia's military forces, which led to significant increases in military spending. Yet, neither new organizational impulses nor new funds brought about meaningful military reform. If one were to analyze the results of the two Chechen campaigns using the methods of Russian military experts[125] the following conclusions could be drawn:

In terms of achieving political goals, the first campaign ended in abject failure. The second gave rise to the illusion of efficiency of a largely military solution to the real problem of Russian national security in the southern sector. Protracting the war, however, leads to a desire for a political solution to end the conflict or to an acceptance that Chechnya, for the long term, remains an area of guerilla activity and counterinsurgency operations.

The morale of Russian forces during the first campaign evidenced the profound degradation of military organization in the country. In the second campaign, authorities tried to use the psychological factor (defense from aggression and subsequent defeat of the enemy) to raise the prestige of the army and to justify the Kremlin's policies in the eyes of the public.

More than a change in public perception is necessary, however. Unless fundamental change takes place in the structure and policy of the Russian military organization, the psychological climate in the forces in the Northern Caucasus and the armed forces as a whole will continue to deteriorate. One complication to ending the conflict is that the Chechen war continues to be a profitable enterprise for many participants on all sides.

The first and second Chechen campaigns resulted in thousands of Russian military casualties. Still, according to public opinion, these have remained significantly below critical levels. Yet the draft system and the practice of sending police units into Chechnya from throughout Russia makes a local conflict a national problem. Continuing losses, without a clear prospect of a peace settlement, engender a war weariness that may overwhelm the country's tolerance for war.

Russian federal forces completed the task set before them in the second campaign, once the political leadership gave them a blank check. By contrast, the level of incompetent intervention from the political leadership in military operations during the first campaign was such that the Kremlin must take most of the responsibility for its failure. Nevertheless, military force can accomplish only so much. A failure to reach a political settlement in Chechnya will weigh heavily on President Putin's record.

The costs of waging the Chechen war in the first and second campaigns remained feasible for the federal budget, but war-related reconstruction requirements clearly exceed available capabilities. Worst of all, the informal commercial relationships in and related to Chechnya have eroded the morale of the military and enhanced corruption in Russia generally.

The 1994–1996 Chechen campaign became the first war in Russia's history to be televised. Those images were key in producing the public's negative attitude toward Russia's military machine. The second campaign, however, partially restored the public's regard for the army and was the most important instrument of the superficial consolidation of political power in Russia. Still, the government's increasingly rigid information policy may cause the public's blanket mistrust of government-provided information to resurface, helping to create a credibility gap.

6

International Ramifications

The Chechen conflict emerged from the general confusion and withdrawal of Russia from the former Soviet periphery in the early 1990s, and the efforts of other forces to fill the vacuum. The Chechen war, along with the broader war on terrorism and other politico-economic trends, has altered the landscape along Russia' entire southern periphery. This chapter discusses how the military campaigns in Chechnya and politico-military developments in Central Asia, including Afghanistan, helped shape a new approach in Moscow toward the south, and ultimately facilitated Russia's security policy rapprochement with the West.

The principal challenge for Moscow is stabilizing the still weak post-Soviet states, while finding an acceptable *modus vivendi* with the increasingly turbulent Muslim world beyond the former Soviet territory. Other factors complicate Russia's task, from the 2003 Iraq war and its effects, to the Israeli-Palestinian situation, to the developments in and around Iran. Although the United States, Russia, and the European Union profess great commonality of their fundamental interests in the region, significant differences among them will remain. If one adds China, which has already become a player in the region, as well as Japan and India, which have both recently paid more attention to Inner Asia, a fabric of sometimes conflicting interests emerges. A new and full-fledged "Great Game" around the Caspian basin is unlikely to resume, but instead a rather complex model of competition and cooperation, with Russia as a key participant.

The Genesis of Moscow's "Southern" Strategy

Following the collapse of the Soviet Union, developments south of the border have proceeded at a fast pace. After several clumsy attempts to bring Chechnya back into the federation, in 1996 Russia suffered a humiliating defeat and was forced to retreat from what it viewed as a local conflict. The subtitle of Anatol Lieven's book on Chechnya is *A Tombstone of Russian Power*. Inside Russia, however, the first campaign in Chechnya and the fighting in Tajikistan were still not viewed in an international context but as isolated third-rate local conflicts. After the first campaign, as Anatol Lieven wrote, "Chechnya has become a tombstone of Russian power. That is a powerful symbol of the passing of imperial glory. The Soviet Union was, in a sense, a continuation of the czarist statehood tradition." Russia lost in Chechnya and won in Tajikistan, but the stakes in both cases were believed to be low. The Russian public and government were again about to ignore the difficult southern front. By the late 1990s, however, the stakes rose quickly.

In September 1996, a month after federal forces had surrendered Grozny to the Chechen rebels, Afghan Taliban rebels took Kabul and within two years controlled 90 percent of the country. At that time, Moscow was as concerned about the Afghan Taliban as the West had been concerned about Iranian fundamentalists in the early 1980s.

There were also other potential, but less immediate problems in the south. Although the conflict in Tajikistan was resolved through the good offices of Moscow and Tehran in 1997, the new threat to Central Asian stability emanating from Afghanistan seemed to be much more powerful. The Russian ambassador to Tajikistan believed that the Islamists and their allies intended to create a new entity, the Greater Islamic Caliphate, comprising the areas around the Uzbeki cities of Samarkand and Bukhara, as well as the Ferghana Valley. He warned, "If religious radicals strengthen their positions in Central Asia, a 'holy war' might create a Muslim state on the Russian territory as well."[1]

Although it was the most immediate and menacing danger, Afghanistan was not the only source of a serious threat from the south. The 1992–1995 war in Bosnia had contributed to the rise of an Islamic factor in the Balkans. The subsequent Albanian crisis in 1997–1998 had much more serious implications. In 1998–1999 the crisis in neighboring Kosovo resulted in NATO intervention and turned the former Yugoslav province into "Europe's principal breeding ground of terrorism and crime,"[2] as the Russian foreign minister put it. In the spring of 2001, Kosovo became the base for a military action waged by ethnic Albanians against the Slavic government of the former Yugoslav Republic of Macedonia. In the summer of 2001, NATO and the Macedonian government agreed on a compromise solution under which NATO troops were deployed in the country, but peace remains fragile.

For the public in the West, the story of the Balkans was essentially about Serbian expansionism, but for the Russian government and much of the public, the most serious threat came from Islamists, who Russia believed the United States short-sightedly supported. In 2001, President Putin repeatedly compared the Macedonian situation to that in Chechnya, and Macedonian Albanian rebels to Chechen terrorists. (To make the analogy complete, note that the Macedonian authorities in Skopje, like Moscow, sometimes contributed to the intensification, rather than settlement, of the conflict.) Some in the Russian leadership believed the threat had assumed transcontinental proportions. At the beginning of the turn of the twenty-first century an Islamic extremist strategic triangle emerged that comprised Afghanistan, the North Caucasus, and Kosovo.[3]

Since the late 1990s Moscow has been concerned about international terrorism. In 1996 President Yeltsin participated in the first antiterrorist summit in Sharm el-Sheikh, Egypt, but his presence there was more symbolic than substantive. In Russia, Middle Eastern terrorism had traditionally been seen as an integral part of the region's political process and military confrontation; the wave of terror that swept Algeria after the army stepped in to prevent Islamists from winning the elections was seen as a local development. When the Islamic leader Nedjmeddin Erbakan became Turkey's prime minister, Moscow's concern over his rise to power was no greater than the concern over the romantic pan-Turkists or conservative geopoliticians from the Turkish General Staff. Even Basayev's raid on Budennovsk, or Raduyev's on Kizlyar, could not shake this deeply rooted belief. Osama bin Laden changed Moscow's views on the region.

The 1998 bombings of U.S. embassies in Kenya and Tanzania and the resulting U.S. counterstrikes against targets in Afghanistan and Sudan demonstrated that the regional "front line" from the Western Mediterranean to Southeast Asia had profoundly changed. Superpower struggle for the region was replaced by the radicals' struggle against the West, Israel, Russia, and their allies. It was on the Taliban issue that Russia and the United States found themselves for the first time on the same side of the new front line. While reacting sharply to the U.S.–U.K. air raids against Iraq in 1998 (Operation Desert Fox), Moscow stayed calm when it came to American missile attacks against targets in Afghanistan.

The series of Indian and Pakistani nuclear tests—another highlight of 1998—did more than stress Moscow and Washington's shared interest in containing nuclear proliferation. The real problem was the nature of the regime that had acquired weapons of mass destruction. From Moscow's perspective, Pakistan, not India, was the concern. The real threat was not an "Islamic bomb," but a large and internally unstable Islamic country (with a population slightly exceeding that of Russia) having nuclear weapons. At a later point, when the second intifada started in Palestine after the Arab-Israeli peace process failed in 2000, Russians found it more natural to identify with Israelis, many of whom spoke Russian, than with Arabs. In Moscow's view, the issue of Israel's nuclear capability had ceased to be a problem.

In this context, the second military campaign in Chechnya, which began in August 1999, contrasted sharply with the first campaign. When Chechen radicals sought to interfere in Dagestan, Russia demonstrated both its willingness and ability to retaliate militarily on a reasonably massive scale. After an Islamist incursion in Kyrgyzstan several weeks later, the Russian leadership linked the Chechen and Afghan threats. It now appeared as if Russia faced a challenge along its entire southern periphery. Not only did Russia use force, it also pursued a more coherent policy, one with considerable implications for Moscow's relations with the southern CIS countries, other Muslim states, the West, China, and India.

Separatists, Terrorists, and Relations with CIS Countries

Most important, the conflicts in Chechnya and Central Asia confirmed that the former Soviet Union was history. The 1979–1989 war in Afghanistan affected Belarus as much as it did Tajikistan. Conversely, the campaigns in Chechnya became momentous developments in Russia and the South Caucasian countries (chiefly Georgia and Azerbaijan). Instability in Afghanistan and outbreaks of Islamic extremism are a concern for both the Central Asian countries and Russia. For other CIS countries, these situations are increasingly external and therefore less directly relevant. This further erodes any basis of common interest among the CIS countries.

The first campaign in Chechnya obviously weakened Russian influence in the CIS, primarily in the Caucasus region. In the early years of independence, the ruling elites in Georgia and Azerbaijan feared a repetition of the events of 1918–1921, when Moscow restored its control over the Transcaucasian region after a brief pause caused by the civil war in Russia. In doing so, Moscow combined military methods (the Eleventh Red Army's advance) with political ones (the actions of local Bolsheviks against the "bourgeois" governments). Seventy years later, the elites saw a parallel in the Russian army's engagement in active peace-making, supporting both Abkhazians against Georgia and Karabakh-Armenians against Azerbaijan. Moscow's military presence in the region contrasted sharply with the weakness of the national armies. Russian security services were routinely accused of hatching conspiracies. Russia provided a safe haven for an ousted president (Azerbaijan's Ayaz Mutalibov) and less fortunate contenders who were being kept in reserve as potential leaders (Azerbaijan's Suret Gusseynov and Georgia's Igor Georgadze, for example). At that point, South Caucasian elites tended to overestimate the opportunities available to Russia, and thus they demonized Russian policies. This attitude was partly sincere and partly tactical: having Russia as an enemy served to consolidate the new states, if (initially) chiefly at the elite level.

The first war in Chechnya, however, demonstrated to the Caucasus as well as to other countries (Ukraine, the Baltic States, Poland, and other Central European states) that restoration of the Soviet Union by military action was not feasible. Ultimately, Moscow lacked both political will and military might. Not only did independent Ichkeria continue to exist during 1994–1996 with Moscow's de facto acquiescence but it also succeeded, like Abkhazia and Karabakh before it, in defending its independence in a direct military conflict with the federal center. This served as a material guarantee against Russian military intervention in Georgia and Azerbaijan. As a result, Tbilisi and Baku were obviously relieved, despite armed separatism having taken an upper hand in Chechnya and the many discomforts and dangers brought about by their geographical position next to Chechnya.

As a result, the CIS—in 1993 considered the forerunner of a new Eurasian federal state (just as in 1921–1922 the military and diplomatic union of the Soviet republics paved the way for the creation of the Soviet Union)—could no longer be seen as an efficient instrument of reintegration. From 1994 to 1996, CIS countries effectively refused to support Moscow in its debate with the West over NATO enlargement. The peacekeeping coalition in Tajikistan had effectively fallen apart by 1996. Uzbekistan, Kazakhstan, and Kyrgyzstan had withdrawn their troops from the combined force, leaving Russia the sole peacekeeper in the region. The bilateral alliance of Moscow and Dushanbe generated concern and suspicion in Uzbekistan over Russia's policy objectives in the region. The 1998 attempt by Uzbekistan to become a third member of the alliance against the Islamists failed because of intergovernmental differences with Tajikistan and Uzbekistan's lingering suspicions about Russian intentions.

Inside the CIS, an association of Georgia, Ukraine, Azerbaijan, and Moldova (GUAM) was formed in the mid-1990s to counterbalance Moscow. In early 1999 Uzbekistan joined, and the alliance was remaned to become GUUAM. Its members declared their intention to actively develop military and political ties with the United States and NATO, a position the West supported. In 1997, shortly before Russia and NATO had signed the Founding Act on Mutual Relations, Cooperation, and Security, Ukraine signed the Charter on Distinctive Partnership with NATO. Georgia declared its desire to join NATO. Azerbaijan opened a discussion on whether U.S. or Turkish military bases should be allowed on its territory. NATO contingents began to take part regularly in military exercises in Ukraine, including the Crimea and the Black Sea (Sea Breeze) and Central Asia (Centrasbat).

While the United States sought to prepare its new partners to repel future threats, especially those jeopardizing pipeline security, its main objective was to strengthen and propagate geopolitical pluralism in the post-Soviet realm. This meant countering Moscow's presumed trend toward re-imperialization by strengthening the new states' independence from Russia. Though not all these developments resulted directly from Moscow's defeat in the first Chechen campaign, these became possible because of Russia's political and military weakness, which the first campaign in Chechnya highlighted so graphically.

Bear in mind that during the Yeltsin presidency Russian foreign policy was not only decentralized, but also partially privatized. Feliks Stashevsky, the Russian ambassador to Georgia from 1996 to 2000, described the situation as follows: "No foreign ministry could have possibly controlled the activities of various ministries, agencies, subjects of the federation, and high-ranking bureaucrats"[4]—each of which pursued corporate or personal objectives. Similarly, the Kremlin lost control of the situation. With state actors (who often acted separately and against each other), private actors emerged in the foreign policy arena. These private actors represented business cartels and often competed with one another by manipulating the state machine. Boris Berezovsky, during 1997–1998 the deputy secretary of the Russian Federation Security Council in charge of Chechnya, openly lobbied for the interests of the companies he controlled. Criminal groups played an enormously important role.

The second campaign in Chechnya and rebel attacks in Central Asia brought about dramatic changes in the situation on both sides of the Caspian. Vladimir Putin rejected Boris Yeltsin's policy of a fake integration of the post-Soviet realm and embarked on a course of tough advocacy and expansion of national interests in specific countries and regions. Russia's withdrawal in December 2002 from the 1992 Bishkek accords on visa-free travel within the CIS was a momentous, although initially symbolic, decision. Russia was the first to install checkpoints on its border with Kazakhstan.[5] There, as well in the Stavropol and Krasnodar territories, where the local population has lived for centuries in the Russian heartland, people suddenly found themselves on the front line of conflict and instability. In 2001 Moscow demanded that CIS countries support its general political course and threatened that failure to do so would cost them their "privileges" from Soviet times, including concessional debt repayments, free travel, and employment. Many responded positively.

Policy vis-à-vis the Caucasian states seriously changed. With Putin at the helm, Yeltsin's generally condescending attitude to Georgia and Azerbaijan's pro-Western leaning was replaced with harsh reprisals. Andrei Nikolayev's words clearly illustrated the Russian government's long-restrained annoyance: "Having admitted their helplessness, they [Georgia and Azerbaijan] looked for sponsors not only in the economic sphere, but also in the areas of security and defense." According to the ex-general turned Duma member, the former Soviet republics were "giving the Caucasus away" to the Americans and their allies.[6]

The second campaign in Chechnya became a catalyst for political conclusions. According to Feliks Stashevsky, "Georgian neutrality in Chechen affairs, which initially had been openly well disposed toward Chechen rebels" helped Moscow to "adjust" its policy with regard to Tbilisi.[7] The Russian leadership was enraged by Tbilisi's refusal to allow Russian border guards to control both sides of the Russian-Georgian border in Chechnya, as it had in 1995–1996. The Georgian government even tolerated losing control of the Pankisi Gorge, at the Chechen border, where, according to Russian government sources, between 1,500–2,000 Chechen rebels and refugees had found shelter.[8]

The introduction in 2000 of a visa regime on the Russian-Georgian border, with the exclusion of the breakaway states of Abkhazia and South Ossetia as an added humiliation for Tbilisi, became the ultimate symbol of the policy adjustment. The exclusions were meant to pressure the Georgian authorities to accept a Russian proposal for a joint counterterrorist operation against the Chechen groups in the Pankisi Gorge. In fact, Russian pressure further alienated most Georgian politicians. The Russian company Itera simultaneously demanded that Georgia repay its debts for natural gas supplies. As a result, Russian-Georgian relations deteriorated sharply.[9] The Georgian leadership used every opportunity to demonstrate its intention to become more closely associated with the United States and Turkey and to join NATO. Georgia insisted that Russia withdraw its military bases from Georgian territory. Russia retaliated by threatening especially painful countermeasures. In 2000–2001, the scenario of Russian troops crossing the Georgian border to crush Chechen rebel camps, which would have certainly triggered a harsh reaction from Washington, was the main threat. Shortly thereafter, Russia was further provoked by Ruslan Gelayev's raid from Pankisi through Western Georgia to attack Russian military bases in Abkhazia.[10] In the fall of 2001, Moscow directly accused Tbilisi of using Chechen rebel groups to resolve the Abkhazian problem. A year later, Putin personally issued an ultimatum to President Shevardnadze: Tbilisi must clamp down on the Chechens in Pankisi or face the consequences of Russian military action. Shevardnadze finally obliged, but the Georgian counterterrorist operation failed to find terrorists in Pankisi. Moscow was unimpressed, claiming the rebels had been tipped off. Tensions between Moscow and Tbilisi continued.

Since the start of the first campaign in Chechnya, the Russian government has seen Azerbaijan as a safe haven for Chechen rebels and as a site for various Islamic charity foundations to set up paramilitary camps for the rebels. In 1995, Russia restricted passenger and cargo traffic across the Russian-Azerbaijani border. Although this move created numerous difficulties, its only real effect was to cause an increase in corruption among officials on both sides of the border.

In 1999, Moscow applied more immediate pressure on Azerbaijan, similar to the tactics it had used in relations with Georgia. This "family quarrel," however, produced totally different results from the one with Georgia. President Haydar Aliyev, concerned over the succession of power in his own family and disappointed by the lack of ability or willingness by the United States to ensure such a succession, decided to meet Moscow halfway to demonstrate his loyalty. In its turn, the Russian leadership "highly appreciated the understanding of, and efficient measures undertaken by, the government of Azerbaijan aimed at preventing the proliferation of international terrorism in the Transcaucasian region."[11]

In January 2001, President Putin paid a state visit to Baku, the first visit by a Kremlin leader to Azerbaijan since Leonid Brezhnev in 1982 (Haydar Aliyev played host on both occasions). In 2002, Aliyev made several visits to Moscow and Saint Petersburg. Notwithstanding lingering differences between Moscow and Baku, the rapprochement on Chechnya and the status of the Caspian Sea contributed positively to a better climate in Russian-Azerbaijani relations. In addition, Baku respected Russia's security interests in relation to the Ghabala radar facility, a component of the Russian early warning system.

Thus, whereas the first campaign in Chechnya undermined Russian positions in the region, the second campaign helped to strengthen them. Moscow's regional strategy had begun to take shape. Affirming its political position as the fourth Caucasian power, in 2000–2001 Moscow attempted to create an integrated (in effect, closed) system of regional security within the so-called Greater Caucasus, incorporating the Russian North Caucasus, South Caucasus, and the adjacent areas of the Black and Caucasus Seas. The authors of this concept believed that Turkey and Iran were only situated beside the Greater Caucasus, whereas the United States and European Union countries were external forces.[12] As part of this approach, Moscow's Caspian policy was based on the premise that all regional problems must be resolved by the Caspian states without external interference. That meant without the United States, European Union, or Turkey being involved. Thus, the idea was that Russia should become the only power with "a legitimate presence" in the Caucasus as well as the entire post-Soviet south.

Having officially declared a policy to combat international terrorism (with reference to Chechnya) two years before September 2001, Russia relied on its military-political alliance with Armenia, developed an asymmetrical partnership with Azerbaijan, and pursued a hard-line policy vis-à-vis Georgia, forcing Tbilisi to respect Russian geopolitical and strategic interests in the region. Integrating the lessons of Afghanistan and enforcing the cooperation of neighboring countries were meant to rule out a repetition of a Chechen situation. Initially, Moscow was determined to prevent NATO countries from establishing a permanent presence in the Greater Caucasus area and to limit the new independent states' military cooperation with the West. Upsetting plans to build oil and gas pipelines that would bypass Russia was an important economic policy objective. Russia's stronger positions in the CIS enabled Moscow to expect a more favorable disposition of commercial interests from Almaty (Kazakhstan) and Ashgabat (Turkmenistan). To remain competitive, Moscow tried hard to isolate Chechen rebels physically and eliminate their supply channels. Seeking to strengthen its hand as an oil-transit country, Russia rerouted the Baku-Novorossiysk pipeline so that it bypassed Chechen territory.

As it had with peacekeeping efforts in the early 1990s, Moscow sought to use cooperation in combating international terrorism to consolidate the military and political cooperation of CIS countries with Moscow. During the civil war in Tajikistan, collective peacekeeping force members did not cooperate, and its mission ended in 1997–1998. The Collective Security Treaty, which had never worked owing to sharply differing perceptions of external threats, was collapsing: in April 1999 Azerbaijan, Georgia, and Uzbekistan refused to prolong their membership. The second campaign in Chechnya helped to reverse this trend.

The Islamic challenge alarmed post-Soviet regimes in Central Asia. Realizing only too well that they lacked the resources necessary to guarantee their own survival, the ruling elites concluded by 1999 that the United States was not a reliable source of assistance in an emergency. Regardless of any need for Caspian oil, until September 2001 the United States had not rated Central Asia high enough on its scale of priorities to justify the use of force. In these circumstances, the post-Soviet regimes decided that Moscow was the only possible source of real military assistance.

During the ten years since the breakup of the Soviet Union, post-Soviet political elites became confident that Moscow was not seeking to restore the Soviet Union. If the first campaign in Chechnya had been waged under antiseparatist slogans, then it might have helped avoid a dangerous crisis in relations between Moscow and Kiev over the Crimea. After Yuri Meshkov was elected Crimean president in January 1994, the confrontation between the governments of Ukraine and its Autonomous Republic of the Crimea escalated. Moscow's stance was a key factor. By the fall of 1994, when Moscow's attention was increasingly diverted to Chechnya, it had become clear that Russia would not get involved in an internal Ukrainian conflict. A Russian-Ukrainian treaty was finally signed in 1997 and ratified by the Russian parliament two years later. It marked a point of no return. Ukrainian independence was at last accepted by the Russian ruling elite and the public. In the mid-1990s, Russia stopped providing direct support to Abkhazia and Moldova's breakaway Trans-Dniester Republic, without, however, severing ties with those two entities. Russian diplomacy had finally embraced the concept of a "common state" in tackling ethnic issues.

This evolution of Moscow's policies enabled the ruling elites in CIS countries to assume a pragmatic position: if Russia was not going to encroach on their independence (and, therefore, on the ruling elites' positions), then cooperation with Russia was not only risk-free but necessary when used as a tool to buttress post-Soviet regimes.

In exchange for having its interests respected, Moscow abandoned even symbolic attempts to nudge the Central Asian regimes toward democracy. Trying to present itself as a more accommodating partner in the context of combating international terrorism as compared with the "overscrupulous" West, Moscow turned a blind eye to both the suppression of opposition in Central Asia and the violations of human rights of Russian ethnic minorities in Central Asian states. (The only exception, in 2003, was Turkmenistan, which takes no part in antiterrorist coalitions.)

This quiet position contrasted sharply with continuous public pressure from Moscow on Latvia and Estonia on their treatment of Slavic minorities. Russian authorities do not regard OSCE activities in the region as especially important. Moscow has not been averse to tolerating authoritarian and despotic regimes within the post-Soviet territory, and this stance coincided with the unprecedented hardening of all Central Asian regimes. The conventional wisdom is that such regimes are easier and more efficient to work with. (Ironically, in the context of antiterrorist operations, the United States displays a similar approach to the problem with regard to Uzbekistan, Egypt, Saudi Arabia, Pakistan, and some other countries.)

Even before the second campaign in Chechnya had begun, Russia sought to reorient CIS military and political cooperation under the Collective Security Treaty toward combating international terrorism. Such attempts, however, immediately proved to be a failure. As noted, in 1998, Russia, Uzbekistan, and Tajikistan entered into a trilateral alignment "to combat religious extremism." The alignment, however, survived for only a few months. Its disintegration was triggered by Colonel Mahmud Khudoyberdiev's mutiny in Northern Tajikistan and the resulting mutual accusations from both Tashkent and Dushanbe (indeed, justified) of sponsoring subversive forces within the territories of the two countries. In the same year Kyrgyzstan succeeded in having Russian border guard troops withdrawn from its territory.

It was only after February 1999, when Islamists exploded several powerful bombs in downtown Tashkent, that the Uzbekistan leadership decided to renew security cooperation with Moscow. In 1999, several CIS countries concluded the Treaty of Cooperation in Combating Terrorism and in 2000 established an antiterrorist center. The Council of Heads of Antiterrorist Services comprising prosecutors-general, ministers of internal affairs, heads of security services, and tax police chiefs, was organized. Kyrgyzstan requested Moscow's assistance in defending its borders—only a year after requesting their removal. In December 1999, Putin, as the head of Russia's government, signed a bilateral treaty in Tashkent on military and technological cooperation. The Southern Shield of the Commonwealth joint military exercises became annual events. Neither Uzbekistan nor even Kyrgyzstan, however, ever asked Moscow to send in Russian troops or establish permanent military bases on their respective territories.

Until the fall of the Taliban, Central Asian governments saw Afghanistan as well as the "Ferghana Triangle" (named for the Ferghana Valley at the juncture of the Uzbekistan, Kyrgyzstan, and Tajikistan borders) as the source of a strategic threat. During the Sovietization period in Turkestan, the Ferghana Valley was the main center of anti-Communist resistance. Local ruling elites suspected that they were pawns in the new game of the great powers, which saw "eliminating the threat of international terrorism" in terms of strengthening their own "imperial" security. As a result, the newly independent states feared their sovereignty would be tightly constricted. The militarization of individual countries and their dependence on external forces increased. In this context, until the fall of 2001, Russia as a power in decline (compared with a progressively stronger China) was perceived as a lesser threat, and therefore a more preferable partner, when American troops were first deployed in Central Asia.[13] The United States' financial, economic, and political opportunities cannot, of course, be rivaled, making it a lesser threat.

Still, the accelerated militarization of the region has created additional, although perhaps temporary, opportunities for Russia to enhance its influence. The armed forces of the post-Soviet republics are, in fact, remnants of the Soviet army. They are organized according to the Soviet model, armed with Soviet-made weapons. They serve, train, and fight using Soviet manuals. (The Russian language is widely used in all of them.) From the start of the first war in Chechnya to the intensification of tensions in Central Asia (1995–1999), Uzbekistan has increased its military expenditures by 137 percent, Azerbaijan by 73 percent, Turkmenistan by 71 percent, and Armenia by 45 percent. Georgia and Kazakhstan are the only countries whose military expenditures were reduced.[14] After 1999, military expenses continued to grow.

The countries of the CIS do not have sufficient resources to buy state-of-the-art weapon systems. In early 2001, Moscow changed its approach to arms trading from one used throughout the first ten years following the breakup of the Soviet Union, and it decided to apply concessional terms to arms sales to signatories of the Collective Security Treaty. Russia thus tried to limit as much as possible U.S. and Turkish military involvement in the South Caucasus and Central Asia. The situation changed sharply after the United States launched a counterterrorist operation in Afghanistan. While the United States has tried to create a modern Afghan army, it has also stepped up military cooperation with post-Soviet countries in the region, primarily Uzbekistan and Georgia. In those countries, therefore, the Soviet military tradition is unlikely to continue in the twenty-first century.

Nontraditional Threats

Drug trafficking plays a considerable role in Moscow's relations with southern neighbors. The drug flow to Russia from the southern borders began during the war in Afghanistan. The breakup of the Soviet Union, civil wars in Afghanistan and Tajikistan, and conflicts in the North Caucasus have imparted a powerful impetus to the development of the drug trade. Russian officials sometimes argue that drugs have become the silent weapon of Islamic extremists in their struggle against the "infidels"—the best means of exterminating their number one enemy, namely, Russians."[15]

Both Afghanistan and Tajikistan have economies that are nearly totally dependent on drug production and transit. In Kyrgyzstan, the ancient city of Osh has become the most important hub of the so-called northern route of drug trafficking. According to various estimates, every fourth resident of the Ferghana Valley is involved in drug trafficking.[16] Afghan Taliban, Uzbeki Islamists, and "nonintegrated" Tajik opposition forces have been regularly accused of producing and trafficking drugs. However, this is not a full list. The Northern Alliance (Moscow's ally in Afghanistan), powerful groups within the Tajikistan and Kyrgyzstan leadership, and finally, the Russian military have been directly or indirectly involved in the drug business.

The health of the nation has ultimately been undermined. Russia finds herself allied with regimes that are linked to local drug barons. The Russian power structures have been corrupted from within. Local authorities can do little, even if they wanted to: the incessant wars and conflicts create a favorable and secure situation for making exorbitant profits.[17]

Drug contraband is closely linked to illegal arms trading. In fact, the money earned by selling drugs in Russia is sometimes spent in Russia or Ukraine to buy weapons for Islamists. The Chechen conflict acted as a catalyst for the skyrocketing growth of trafficking in both drugs and illegal arms.

Armed conflicts and instability in the Caucasus and Central Asia have resulted in floods of internally displaced people, refugees, and forced migrants from the CIS countries to Russia. The northward exodus of Russian and Russian-speaking populations is a fact. In the extreme case of Chechnya, only several thousand of three hundred thousand Russians (in 1989) remain. In Tajikistan, less than a hundred thousand remain out of a 1991 population of four hundred thousand. The Russian population share fell sharply in Kazakhstan and Kyrgyzstan (to 32 percent and 15 percent, respectively). This resulted in a waning Russian cultural tradition and Russian language education and, consequently (at least in the short term), the increased influence of traditional local communities and institutions.

Yet people of Caucasian and Central Asian extraction are flooding the cities of the Russian Republic. According to widely accepted estimates, at the turn of the twenty-first century there were about two million Azerbaijanis, up to one million Georgians, and hundreds of thousands of Tajiks in Russia. Most of these people are illegal migrants in retail trade, construction, and other jobs. For the past decade, Russia's population has decreased by 700,000 to 750,000 each year, despite this immigration. Still, the idea of complementary pairing of Russia and Central Asia as embodied in the "people for land" formula (the project of resettling people from Central Asian countries to sparsely populated areas in Russia), has few, if any, supporters in Russia.[18] The unregulated legal status and economic plight of most immigrants from the post-Soviet south has forced some of them into organized crime, which in turn leads to a backlash among Russian Slavs. In some regions, particularly Kuban, local authorities advocate deportations of illegal immigrants (not only Muslims but Christian Armenians as well). One justification for both police brutality and the quotidian anti-Semitism of ordinary Russians is the argument that "Russia is in a state of war."[19] These prejudices have far-reaching implications for Russia's relations with her neighbors to the south.

Despite Moscow's attempts to keep CIS countries within its geopolitical orbit, Central Asian republics have largely ignored the OSCE membership they inherited from the Soviet Union and are becoming increasingly integrated into the Greater Middle East. Even before the September 11 attacks in the United States, this region was becoming more vital to for international stability and security in the twenty-first century. Rapid population growth, a widening gap in development among countries, brewing internal controversies and conflicts, and stronger interstate competition have added to the volatility of the situation. A tremendous problem by itself, terrorism also reflects the fundamental difficulties of modernization. Of special significance are the futures of Turkey and Iran, which, like Russia, are traditionally imperial countries. The futures of Pakistan and Saudi Arabia remain highly uncertain. In this broader context, the wars in Chechnya as well as crises in Central Asian have a direct bearing on Russia's role among the nations south of the old Soviet border.

With the war in Chechnya continuing and rebels stirring sporadic unrest in Central Asia, Russia is at pains to redefine her national interests in the Caucasus and Central Asian region. The Putin leadership is seeking, pragmatically, to realize Russia's competitive advantages over weaker neighboring countries. It is not about resuming "traditional Russian expansion," but about controlling security when local order is crumbling and securing Russia's national, primarily commercial, interests in the region. In other words, while pursuing a predominantly defensive security policy in the southeast, Russia is clearly implementing an offensive economic strategy.

It is important, however, that the Russian leadership not overplay its hand. Moscow continues to be restricted economically, financially, politically, and even militarily. Projecting force even within the nearest periphery is going to remain difficult for a long time.

Islamists are also known for their pragmatism, as borne out by Tajikistan in the late 1990s and Iran. It is possible that leaders of other Islamic movements will decide that preserving normal relations with Russia is more important than the potential benefits from associating with radical movements. Thus, in the long view, Russia might not have to fight Islamic regimes, but to cooperate with them. Once the Russian authorities reject the quest for an illusory victory, they may one day conclude that the best policy is to cooperate with moderate Islamist circles, maintain a dialogue with the radicals, isolate the extremists, and ensure that agreements are honored. Such a strategy cannot succeed unless Russia establishes sustainable relations with the major players in the Muslim world, which would also give Moscow new partners against radical groups.

Chechnya and Moscow's Relations with the Core of the Muslim World

Russian elites remain divided on the Muslim world's importance to Russia's foreign policy. For most Russian nationalists, aligning with the Muslim world to oppose Western domination is an attractive strategy for restoring Russia's role as a great power. Throughout the 1990s, politicians and analysts belonging to the imperial-nationalist camp, as well as prominent mainstream officials, called for an alliance with Iran, Iraq, and Libya as part of the multipolar world strategy. This camp is the meeting place of the three demons from the Russian past: great power policies, anti-Americanism, and anti-Semitism. This camp last tried to mobilize before and during the 2003 Iraq war. Yet the war in Chechnya and conflicts in Central Asia have dealt a powerful blow to these chauvinistic sentiments, inherited from Soviet times and especially widespread since the collapse of the Soviet Union. No one can ignore that rebels are closely allied with Arab extremist organizations, which see the United States and Israel as their primary enemies.

Another strain of nationalists joins with most Westernizers in concluding that Russia is on the front line in the war between the West and the East. (They disagree, of course, on whether Russia should be with the West or try to remain neutral in this war.) In the mid-1990s, there was speculation about an expansionist "Islamic bloc" striving for dominance in the Near and Middle East and trying to obtain nuclear capability, as reflected in this sample of media statements: "Amid so much pain and despite excessive internal differences, an Islamic empire is being born before our eyes"; "We have heard calls for the restoration of the Islamic empire from Russia to China before"; and "[Islamists] will sweep us away." The sense of weakness, if not doom, is generated by both geopolitical and demographic forecasts. Due to negative growth, Russias' population, which stood at 148 million in 1991, fell to 145 million by 2002, despite massive immigration. Pessimistic forecasts show the population slumping below 100 million by 2050. The alarmists' conclusion is gloomy: as the Russian Slavic population dies out, it will be replaced by growing populations in Muslim Caucasian societies. Their expansion into the labor force has already begun: migrants from the south are flooding the Stavropol and Krasnodar Krais, Astrakhan, and Orenburg oblasts. Of Moscow's eleven million inhabitants, some two million are Muslim.

Igor Kon, a prominent sociologist, warns, "Tomorrow's Moscow is today's London or Paris multiplied by yesterday's Beirut and Kabul."[20]

Alarmist sentiments have also appeared in the military. For added credibility, the newly perceived threats are sometimes dressed in familiar clothes. Thus, in the late 1990s some military analysts apparently believed that the Islamic Big Nine (Bangladesh, Egypt, Indonesia, Iran, Iraq, Malaysia, Nigeria, Pakistan, and Turkey) was a precursor of a "Muslim NATO." This group of military analysts has made alarming conclusions. "The passionate upsurge of Islam," says a publication of the Military History Institute under the Ministry of Defense, is already influencing Russia through events in the North Caucasus. In the longer run, these wars may even "destroy Russia."[21] The security services have their own bugbear: the so-called Islamic caliphate that international terrorist organizations purportedly plan to extend to the Caucasus, Central Asia, and the Volga region.

Flanked by these more extreme views, the Russian political leadership is fairly traditional in its *Realpolitik*. With Chechnya behind the lines and Central Asia in front of them, it engages in complex geopolitical maneuvering, especially regarding Russia's traditional regional counterparts such as Turkey, Iran, and Pakistan. The draft National Security Concept and Military Doctrine of Russia, prepared by the Russian Foreign Ministry in April 1992, said that "rivalry between Iran and Turkey" is to be exploited in order to prevent the emergence of coalitions against Russia.[22] Because working against international organizations of Islamic radicals is a new activity, it would be appropriate to analyze the Chechen factor's influence on relations between Russia and some key regional powers.

Turkey: An Eternal Adversary?

The Chechen war has become a key and largely negative factor (especially throughout the 1990s) in the new Russian-Turkish relationship. Moscow has been unhappy with Ankara about the following issues:

1. Many politicians in Moscow are sure that since the breakup of the Soviet Union, Turkey has struggled to take revenge for the

defeats it suffered at the hands of the Russian Empire in the eighteenth and nineteenth centuries. Closely tied to Azerbaijan, Turkey has penetrated both Central Asia and Georgia politically, militarily, and economically, and has isolated Armenia, the only ally Russia still has in the region. Turkey is also active inside Russia, including the North Caucasus and Volga regions. Many Russian analysts believe that Ankara is following a "pan-Turkic" policy.[23] Consequently, some Russian elites believe Turkey's strategic objective is to weaken Russia and eventually dislodge it from the post-Soviet south: an objective Chechen separatism is instrumental in promoting.

2. Turkey is the United States' leading geopolitical partner and agent acting in Washington's interests in the Greater Middle East, including the Caspian region and the entire post-Soviet territory. Chechnya is a pawn in this strategy.

3. Turkish authorities are known to be lenient toward Chechen rebels. Using the protection afforded them by highly placed Turkish officials, rebel leaders (Movladi Udugov, the Ichkerian propaganda chief, for example) engage in political and propaganda activities, rest, and receive medical treatment in Turkey. Turkey is suspected of having sheltered training camps for Chechen rebels. For a time it was believed Turkish territory was used by rebels and terrorists as a bridgehead to penetrate the North Caucasus,[24] as well as a corridor for redeploying forces to other fronts (such as Afghanistan).[25]

4. Some Russian military figures have expressed a "private" opinion that Turkish General Staff officers were not only actively involved in intelligence operations in the North Caucasus, but also helped rebels to prepare specific combat operations against Russian troops. Turkish volunteers are rumored to have fought in Chechen rebel groups.

5. There are about eighty North Caucasian diaspora organizations operating in Turkey, providing financial support to the rebels.

6. Chechen terrorists have repeatedly carried out terrorist attacks on Turkish soil. In January 1996, they hijacked the Avrasiya sea ferry; in March 2001, they hijacked a Russian plane on the Moscow-Istanbul route; in April 2001, they took control of a hotel in

Istanbul. These incidents have created the impression in Russia that Turkey has been a safe haven for would-be Chechen terrorists.

7. The self-declared Turkish Republic of Northern Cyprus has recognized the independence of Chechnya.

This list shows the Chechen factor has contributed considerably to the strengthening of traditionalist geopolitical thinking among the ruling elites in Moscow. Thus, Turkey is an eternal adversary, and a relationship with Turkey is at best a zero-sum game.

Economic Ties and Common Challenges Causing Role Shift

Remarkably, despite the campaigns in Chechnya and resulting suspicion and enmity, in the 1990s Russia and Turkey became major economic partners. This new economic relationship was symbolized by the Blue Stream project to transport Russian natural gas to Turkey by pipelines across the Black Sea bottom; this made Turkey be one of the largest importers of Russian natural gas. Moreover, a "popular" dimension has been added to the bilateral trade and communication, thanks to numerous private Russian cross-border traders ("shuttle traders," as they are known in Russia). More important, Turkey has replaced the Crimea and Caucasus as the favorite holiday destination of Russia's nascent middle class. Finally, the struggling Russian defense industry and the General Staff, which lobbies on behalf of defense industry interests, see in the Turkish armed forces a lucrative potential client. Thus, economic interests are slowly but surely gaining ground in replacing geopolitical considerations.

As for the actions of Islamists, Russia cannot fail to notice the Turkish government's determination often manifested in tough measures in combating Wahhabi, fundamentalist, and other radical influences. The Turkish ruling circles are chiefly concerned over local Islamic radicals, calling for the Islamization of Turkish society. When the Islamic Salvation Party headed by Nejmeddin Erbakan (who traditionally sympathized with Islamic radicals fighting in the North Caucasus) came to power in 1995, a wave of panic swept the pro-Western sections of Turkish society.

Soon, the army pressured Erbakan to step down as prime minister. The arrival in office in 2002 of the Islamist Welfare Party produced noticeably fewer fears.

Moreover, Turkish authorities even feel an obligation to combat the growth of religious radicalism in the region. This is one of the responsibilities of Diyanet, a Turkish agency acting as a ministry of religious affairs, which provides all kinds of assistance, including financial, to the Religious Muslim Office in Dagestan, the principal opponent of Wahhabism in the south of Russia. Bin Laden's terrorists are sworn enemies of the Turkish government.

Finally, while sharply criticizing the Russian army's operations in Chechnya, the Turkish government is intolerant of manifestations of separatism at home. An obvious connection exists between the problems of Kurdish and Chechen separatism. An independent Chechnya is an example for advocates of Kurdish independence and vice versa. An equally obvious analogy is between the military operation in the North Caucasus and Turkish army operations in the Kurdish-populated areas of eastern Anatolia in the 1980s and 1990s. The European Union and the Council of Europe have similarly criticized both operations, quoting the examples cited here as evidence of Russia and Turkey being insufficiently civilized.

It is therefore not surprising that Moscow's silence on the Kurdish problem encouraged Ankara's restrained position on the Chechen issue. Whenever Moscow decides the Turkish government has forgotten this convenient link, it steps up informal contacts between Russian officials and Kurdish representatives in Syria. The opposite has happened as well. In particular, in 1996 Russia refused to grant political refuge to Abdallah Ocalan, the leader of the Kurdish Workers' Party. He was, however, allowed to enter the Russian Federation under personal guarantees of Vladimir Zhirinovsky, the head of the nationalist Liberal Democratic Party of Russia (LDPR). Soon after he had been expelled from Russia, Ocalan faced the Turkish court and Kurdish resistance withered away.

The Chechen conflict has never been an important tool for Turkey in making its Russian policy. After the terrorist attacks in the United States and the subsequent military campaign in Afghanistan, where several Chechens were identified as Taliban helpers, Turkey altogether "rejected the years-old policy of tolerance with regard to the Chechen rebels."[26]

Iran: An Important Regional Partner

In the early 1990s, Russian Foreign Minister Andrei Kozyrev viewed fundamentalist Iran as the main threat to Russia's southern flank. These fears were dispelled, however, even before the first war in Chechnya started, largely owing to the shared position of Moscow and Teheran on the importance of conflict settlement in Afghanistan, as well as the Iranian policy of noninterference in the Caucasian conflicts. Moscow's subsequent revision of foreign policy in the mid-1990s, which adopted the multipolar world concept, further enhanced the importance of relations between Russia and Iran. Those relations were based on Russian arms and technology sales, as well as Russia's involvement in the implementation of Iranian civilian nuclear program. The rapprochement between the two countries was symbolized in the mid-1990s by Teheran's support for Moscow's position on NATO enlargement, and on Moscow's readiness to ignore American protests over the construction of a nuclear power plant in Bushehr.

The second campaign in Chechnya did not in any way affect the pragmatic cooperation between Russia and Iran. Moreover, the second campaign untied the hands of Russian politicians advocating even closer ties with Iran. The interests of the Russian military, military-industrial sector, and nuclear industry came to the fore. In the top echelons of power in Russia, the "Iranian lobby" actively promoted the prospect of going into the Iranian arms market, estimated to be worth $2–$7 billion a year.[27] In the fall of 2000, these forces pressed Moscow to denounce the 1995 agreement with the United States on curtailing Russian-Iranian military cooperation. The December 2000 visit to Iran of then minister of defense Igor Sergeyev was presented by the military as a breakthrough that enabled Iranian president Khatami to visit Moscow in 2001.

Numerous contacts with Iran have convinced Russian diplomats and the military that in the case of Iran, religious fundamentalism at home does not translate into an expansionist foreign policy. Moscow realizes that Shiite-dominated Iran cannot count on the support of the predominantly Sunni North Caucasus, where a large Shiite population (30 percent to 50 percent of the country's population) is found only in Azerbaijan, whose relations with Iran are lukewarm at best. The Russian General Staff regards Iranian military doctrine at least regarding Iran's north, as a defensive policy. Official Moscow is not greatly concerned over the Iranian missile program. Russian political circles are convinced that Teheran is "capable of demonstrating responsibility" and will "refrain from proliferating missile technologies."

Russia's quiet assessment of Iran's international role, which differs markedly from American and Israeli assessments, is largely based on Russian-Iranian contacts during the Chechen and Central Asian conflicts. One might say that, unlike the face it shows the United States and Israel, Iran's "better half" is turned toward Russia. As the presiding country in the Organization for the Islamic Conference, Iran essentially supported Moscow's policy toward Chechnya. In 1997, Moscow and Teheran cooperated to end the civil war in Tajikistan, and for many years they provided military, technological, and material support to the Taliban's nemesis, Ahmad Shah Massoud. Based on these facts, Russian officials have concluded that "without Iran, few problems can be resolved in the North Caucasus" and that "without Iran, the Russian strategy would be impossible to pursue" in Central Asia, Afghanistan, or the Middle East.[28]

According to an American analyst, "Moscow's vulnerability on the Chechen issue" is a primary motive behind the Russian-Iranian partnership.[29] It is believed as long as Russia is involved in the conflict in Chechnya, Moscow will continue to have a stake in stable relations with Iran. Being pragmatic, Iranians in turn need Russia as a counterbalance to the United States and as a source for combat equipment and modern technologies. Iran will therefore expediently ignore the fact that in Chechnya Russian soldiers are fighting Muslim fighters. One could agree with this American assessment in principle, although the key factors of bilateral relations include the commonality of interests in Central Asia, especially in Afghanistan, as well as within the Russia–Iran–Turkey regional triangle.

Meanwhile, Russian-Iranian differences (for instance, on the Caspian status issue) remain and grow deeper. Moscow has been forced to adjust its position in light of the intensification of Iranian-Azerbaijani tensions in the summer of 2001 and the possibility of armed clashes between the two countries. Denying Russian support for Baku in its relations with its southern neighbor would mean leaving Azerbaijan only the choice of turning for help to Turkey and the United States. That would certainly be inconsistent with the Russian strategy of avoiding the involvement of external forces in the Caucasus. Close observers of Middle Eastern developments have become increasingly convinced that for Russia, Iran is a temporary partner and not an ally. In the future, economic considerations may well make Iran turn to the United States and become closer to European Union countries.

Initially, the U.S.-led counterterrorist operation in Afghanistan led to some warming of Iranian-American relations, a development that concerned certain political quarters in Russia. Once Iran finally emerges from isolation, Russia might lose an important client and partner. Stakeholders in Moscow believe this prospect is a good argument for developing cooperation with Iran before it is too late.

Afghanistan: A Bone of Contention? Seat of Tension? Buffer Zone?

The second campaign in Chechnya and especially conflicts in Central Asia led to a more active Russian policy vis-à-vis Afghanistan. After a short pause from 1992 to 1995, Russia once again found itself involved, albeit indirectly, in the civil war in that country. Viewing the Taliban successes as a threat to its national interests in Central Asia, Moscow entered into an alliance with its former sworn enemies, the Afghan mujahideen. Since the mid-1990s Russia provided military assistance to the Northern Alliance; allowed Akhmad Shah Massoud to deploy his bases on the territory of Tajikistan, Moscow's ally; initiated anti-Taliban sanctions in the United Nations; and in 2000 even threatened Kabul with missile strikes against Chechen rebel camps in Afghanistan.

Aslan Maskhadov and other separatist leaders strove to win the international recognition of Chechnya. They opened Chechen political and commercial offices anywhere they could. They offered to sign "intergovernmental" and other agreements at an "official level." Meantime, whenever they traveled abroad, Maskhadov and his lieutenants still had to show Russian passports. During every visit (as to Georgia in 1997), the Chechen leader stressed he was "arriving as the president of the independent Chechen Republic."[30]

The Taliban regime, which never won international recognition, was the only government to recognize the independence of Chechnya. In

2000 (and for the first time in its diplomatic practice) Moscow stated the principle of immediately severing diplomatic relations with any country recognizing Chechen independence. In the 1950s and 1960s, the West German government used the same principle regarding countries that established diplomatic relations with East Germany. China is using the same principle today in connection with Taiwan.

The Taliban regime was the only source of assistance to Islamic separatists in the North Caucasus from another state. In fact, the amount of that assistance was modest. In the late 1990s, Taliban leader Mullah Omar invited his main enemy, Ahmad Shah Massoud, to conclude a ceasefire so they could together help the Chechens. Massoud ignored the invitation, and the Taliban had to act on its own. The assistance was limited chiefly to military training of small groups of Chechens. Remarkably, official Kabul pretended not to notice even that meager assistance. Waqil Ahmad Mutawaqil, who was the Taliban's foreign minister, insisted Afghanistan was providing moral support to Chechens, but not economic or military assistance.[31]

By "moral support," the Taliban government meant its early 2000 call to the Muslim world to declare jihad on Russia to force Moscow to end its military operation in Chechnya. The call coincided with Maskhadov's intensive search for a country in which the Chechen government in exile could have its headquarters. Naturally, a call for a holy war from a regime that enjoyed little popularity in the Middle East could not possibly be a turning point in the Muslim world's attitude to Russia. Nonetheless, the Taliban's support of the Chechen resistance served to strengthen the regime's sought-after image as the most radical Islamic government— further confirmation of which was its destruction in early 2001 of the ancient Buddhist monuments in Bamian.

To further enhance this image, the Taliban regime was interested in supporting other Islamic radicals. Chechen separatists, who fought under Islamic slogans, offered a good opportunity to demonstrate the Taliban regime's international influence. Bin Laden participated in the Taliban's financial assistance to the Chechens. The Saudi terrorist is said to have been in Chechnya several times and met with local Wahhabis. He also received Chechen emissaries in Afghanistan. One such meeting allegedly took place in Kandahar at the end of the winter of 2000. Not all Islamic radicals, however, support claims of bin Laden's close ties with

Chechen separatists and Islamists. For instance, the leader of the well-known extremist group Ansar Ash-Shari'a (Followers of Shari'a), Abu Khamza of Egypt, told a Russian journalist that he doubted "bin Laden's sending fighters or assistance to Chechnya."[32] Taliban assistance to Chechens may have been confined chiefly to diplomatic recognition of Chechnya and sheltering bin Laden and the international terrorist organization he heads.

Mutual, demonstrated recognition between the Islamic Emirate of Afghanistan and the separatist Chechen Republic of Ichkeria was important for both parties. The Taliban regime was interested in continued Chechen resistance, while Chechen separatists appreciated the international support base represented by a state that, although never recognized internationally, was nonetheless feared by its neighbors. Notably, two countries that officially recognized the Taliban regime—Saudi Arabia and the United Arab Emirates—provided moral and material assistance to Chechnya.[33]

General Omar Murtazaliyev, a Daghestani who served in the Soviet army in Afghanistan in the 1980s, offered his own interpretation of the link between the Taliban regime and Chechen separatists. He believes that one of the reasons of the conflicts in Chechnya and Dagestan is "Taliban revenge for the [Soviet] invasion in Afghanistan. . . . Today's Talibs are children who lost their parents after the April 1978 revolution. They were taken to Pakistan under the pretext that they should attend religious schools."[34] The direct connection here may not be evident, but General Murtazaliyev has rightly sensed the issue binding Afghan and Chechen resistance: a sense of common insult to those who resisted the Soviet invasion under the Islamic flag in the 1980s and to those who became the hostages and victims of the war of independence in the 1990s. Both movements were brought to life by an external influence, and both chose holy war as their ideology. Both movements have also demonstrated an extraordinary commitment to jihad.

The Arab World and the Islamic Conference

As a result of its military operation in Chechnya, Moscow risked isolation from the Arab world for the first time since the Soviet Union sent troops to Afghanistan, when in a January 1980 United Nations (UN) General Assembly vote, only eighteen countries supported Moscow's invasion of Afghanistan. Avoiding a repeat of isolation was partly why, during the first campaign, Moscow periodically made offers for a ceasefire and negotiations with the rebels, risking the displeasure of the military. Yevgeny Primakov, then the director of the Foreign Intelligence Service, tried to convince Arab leaders not to support separatism in Chechnya.[35] The majority of Arab leaders were not interested in destabilizing Russia, and they would hardly find it appropriate to use Islam to strengthen their positions in the North Caucasus. After the breakup of the Soviet Union, many Arab countries were still interested in Russia as a political ally and economic partner. A weak Russia torn by ethnic and religious conflict would cause them great concern. Primakov therefore succeeded in his goal. After the second campaign in Chechnya had begun, Moscow tried to persuade Arab leaders to adhere to the same policy.

A single position on Chechnya in the Arab world was impossible anyway because the Arab world itself was internally fragmented. While Egypt, Saddam's Iraq, and Syria initially supported Russia, condemnation came from Persian Gulf countries, including Saudi Arabia and Libya. Qatar and the United Arab Emirates were the only countries to receive Chechen representatives at the official level. Not a single Arab country ever recognized Chechen independence, and their rulers consistently voiced support of Russia's territorial integrity. Even Jordan, with its fifteen-thousand strong and influential Chechen community, has repeatedly made diplomatic statements that the "Hashemite kingdom opposes terrorism and at all times refrains from interfering in the affairs of other countries."[36]

The Islamic Conference, an organization commanding much authority in the Muslim world, chose to distance itself from the conflict in Chechnya. In 1999, Iranian foreign minister Kamal Kharrazi, who chaired the Islamic Conference, stressed the organization had no intention of becoming an intermediary between Moscow and Chechnya and that the Chechen conflict was an internal affair of the Russian Federation.[37] When they met in 2000 in Kuala Lumpur, foreign ministers of Islamic Conference member states issued a fairly neutral resolution on Chechnya. On a visit to Malaysia in 2003, President Putin voiced Russia's intention to join the Islamic Conference as an observer.

Chechen separatists have never taken for granted the Islamic world's support of their struggle for independence; President Maskhadov, Basayev, and other prominent Chechen separatists have said so more than once. The former acting president of Chechnya (1996–1997), Zelimkhan Yandarbiyev, was probably the only person who believed from the start that external support was effective, a position perhaps caused by Yandarbiyev's being responsible for mobilizing international aid. At one point, though, Yandarbiyev tired of trying to convince Muslim states to stand with Chechnya and admitted bitterly the "rulers of Islamic countries have joined the United States and Israel in their support of Moscow so that an Islamic state could not be created in the North Caucasus."[38] After the international antiterrorist operation began, the flow of assistance from the Arab world dried up completely.

Thus, the Muslim world's reaction to the Soviet invasion in Afghanistan in 1979 is incompatible to their response to the Chechen war. Chechen separatists receive support not from governments but from various radical Muslim organizations and movements, both national and international. The real extent of such support is often exaggerated, for obvious reasons, by both the separatists and Russian military and security services.

Though largely restrained on Chechnya, Arab governments, however, have proved unable (or unwilling) to stop the recruitment of volunteers to fight in the North Caucasus. According to official Russian data, about 900 Arab fighters were killed and 500—700 continued to fight in Chechnya in for two years (from fall 1999 to fall 2001).[39] In contrast, more than 15,000 Arab mujahideen, for example, fought in Afghanistan, many times the number of all the Muslim volunteers who have ever fought in Chechnya.

Once the second Chechen campaign began, Russian security services began to pay more attention to the activities of various international radical Islamic organizations and to the intelligence agencies of some conservative Arab monarchies, primarily Saudi Arabia, the United Arab Emirates, and Kuwait. In Saudi Arabia, Wahhabism is the official religious ideology, whereas outside the kingdom it is "an aggressive extremist movement,"[40] as Yevgeny Primakov defined it as director of the Foreign Intelligence Service.

For the ultraconservative Saudi monarchy, providing financial and political support to Wahhabis outside the country is a judgment of the cultures of non-Wahhabist Muslim nations as iniquitous. Analysts from the Russian counterintelligence service (FSB) believe that the ultimate objective of Wahhabis is to create "statelike entities of the Islamic type as part of the 'World Islamic Caliphate'"[41] in Central Asia and the Muslim-populated areas of Russia. Faced with this challenge, in the 1990s Moscow opened a new counterintelligence front based on materials accumulated during the war in Afghanistan.

Security agencies, however, often equate religious fundamentalism with political radicalism, and cultural Islamization with intelligence gathering and subversive activities. This indiscriminate approach not only undermines the operational efficiency of Russian government agencies, but also creates a reaction of growing mutual distrust between Russia's Islamic communities and the state.

Though condemning the operations of Russian troops in Chechnya, however, Saudi authorities harshly treated Chechen terrorists who hijacked a Russian jet and flew it to Saudi Arabia. Saudi antiterrorist troops stormed the plane, and the hijackers were sentenced to long terms in Saudi prisons.

The crisis in Chechnya and developments in Central Asia have added to Moscow's suspicions about the role that Pakistan, and particularly Pakistani special services, have played in sponsoring extremists and terrorists. Pakistani intelligence was accused of financing Chechen field commander Ruslan Gelayev.[42] In a sense, this was a repeat of the 1980s Pakistani role as the logistical base of the Afghan resistance to Russian troops. This assessment of Islamabad's activities boosted Moscow's further political rapprochement with Delhi, which began in the second half of the 1990s after a prolonged period of stagnation in bilateral affairs. At the end of 2001, however, the logic of fighting terrorism forced the Russian leadership to publicly support Pakistani president Pervez Musharraf, who aligned his country resolutely with the international coalition. In 2002, Musharraf paid the first visit of a Pakistani head of state to Moscow in thirty years.

The growing mutual understanding and cooperation between Russia and Israel are the most interesting consequences of the two Chechen campaigns, especially the second one. The increasing closeness of Moscow and Tel Aviv's attitudes to Albanian separatism and related NATO actions first became evident during the Kosovo crisis. Another factor is that the second war in Chechnya and the second intifada coincided; when they found themselves in difficult circumstances, Shamil Basayev and the leaders of terrorist Palestinian organizations publicly supported one another against Israel and Russia, respectively. In speaking of foreign mercenaries fighting in Chechnya, Russian officers often impolitically and bluntly refer to them as Arabs.

Thus, a sense of a common threat appears both in Russia and Israel: the threat of extremism and terrorism feeding on the ideas of radical Islam. Another tie between the two nations is that more than one million recent immigrants from Russia and the former Soviet Union live in Israel: 20 percent of the nation's total population. Many maintain close ties with Russia. Leading Russian television stations have resident correspondents in Israel, and after each terrorist attack there is no shortage of eyewitnesses ready to be interviewed using their most vernacular Russian by ORT, RTR, or NTV. Despite lingering and sometimes intense anti-Semitism in Russia among the Russian elite, pro-Arab sentiments can hardly prevail because of the notable similarity of the Chechen conflict and the conflict between Israel and Palestine.

President Putin's contacts with Israeli leadership and politicians (especially the right wing) have occurred more frequently and are more cordial than were those under his predecessor. The security services of the two countries are cooperating.[43] Since the time of Pavel Grachev, the Russian military has openly admired the special operations of their Israeli colleagues and, in a broader context, of the military organization of the Jewish state. Nevertheless, the significance of this new trend in Russian politics should not be overestimated. To affirm its weakened positions in the Middle East, Moscow occasionally tries to maintain a balance between its new relations with Israel and the old Soviet tradition of supporting Arabs. In this context, Russia sometimes criticizes Israel for a "disproportionate use of force," even though Russian operations in Chechnya are much less selective.

Thus, the developments in Chechnya and Central Asia have caused Moscow to reconsider its traditional policy of supporting Arabs in their disputes with the United States and Israel. In the fall of 2001, the Russian government decided to once again show solidarity with the Organization of Petroleum Exporting Countries (OPEC) on reducing oil production to support oil prices, which resulted in a further price increase. That action, however, was seen as counterproductive by some leading Russian businessmen. In particular, Mikhail Khodorkovsky, the head of the oil company YUKOS, called for a Russian alliance with the West against Arab sheikhs. In 2002, Russia changed its policy and declared its intention to create energy partnerships with the United States and the European Union, whereby Moscow would sustain energy supplies at reasonable prices in exchange for Western investments in the Russian fuel and energy sectors.

Relations with the West

President Yeltsin wrote in his memoirs: "As soon as the operation in Chechnya began [in 1999], I immediately realized the moment of truth in our relations with Western countries had finally come. Now the West was going to bring some really serious pressure to bear on us!"[44] Relations with the West, already strained over the NATO intervention in Kosovo, soured again three or four months after the June 1999 "conciliatory" G–8 summit in Cologne. The first Russian president recalled that at the December 1999 OSCE session in Istanbul "Western countries were preparing a really tough statement on Chechnya. . . . Effectively, a new round of the isolation of Russia had begun. This development had to be prevented by any means."[45] The Russian reaction came in the form of the key phrase that Yeltsin claims he inserted in his speech, ignoring the protestations of his more cautious Foreign Ministry: "No one has the right to criticize us for Chechnya." The ensuing showdown with the West was presented as "Moscow's important international victory."

Instead, it was the crisis in Kosovo that marked the beginning of a short but painful period of Moscow's "geopolitical solitude."[46] The European Union session in Helsinki and OSCE summit in Istanbul, which were held as the second war in Chechnya raged on, registered an isolation unprecedented in post-Soviet Russia. In fact, Belarus and Tajikistan were the only countries to fully support Russia on Chechnya. The situation changed in Moscow's favor in early 2000. An energetic new president emerging in the Kremlin was an important factor driving that trend. Yet much more important factors were defeating key rebel forces, forcing the rebels to retreat into the mountains, and taking Grozny by Russian troops. Since mid-2000, the Chechen problem has become a secondary, and then tertiary, priority on the Moscow-Western agenda. It remains a nagging issue, nevertheless, one most clearly manifested in Russia's relations with the European Union and OSCE.

Since the era of nineteenth-century historian and philosopher Nikolai Danilevsky,[47] many Russians remain convinced Europe refuses to accept Russia's "civilizing role" in the Caucasus and only reluctantly accepts that role in Central Asia, despite the fact that the cruelty of the imperial conquests of Western European matched the cruelty of Russian conquests. In the 1990s this attitude toward Europe intensified with the frank sympathy for Chechen separatists in the countries of Eastern and Central Europe. During the first campaign in Chechnya, a Chechen information center with an affiliated radio station, Free Caucasus, operated in Poland with a branch in Lithuania. These circumstances, as well the symbolic renaming of streets to pay tribute to Johar Dudayev, contributed to Russia's distrust of Poland and the Baltic States. In Ukraine, the war in Chechnya brought about increased enmity toward Russia by such nationalist organizations as UNA–UNSO.

Conversely, the activation of anti-Russian forces added to the friction between Moscow and capitals of former satellite countries in Central and Eastern Europe, which were seeking closer integration with, and into, the West. Arguments in favor of such integration included the unpredictability of post-Soviet Russia, of which the war in Chechnya was a perfect example. In Moscow, policy makers concluded that the "demons of the past"—that is, anti-Russian forces—had raised their heads in Central and Eastern European capitals. No one in Moscow had the slightest inclination to talk to these demons.

Moscow accused European politicians of having a double standard. Moscow complained that the Russian military operation in Chechnya was perceived differently from Spain's treatment of Basque separatists, Britain's fight against Irish Republican Arms terrorists, and France's efforts to rid Corsica of proindependence troublemakers. Even the Turkish army's missions in Kurdistan in the 1980s and 1990s, the Russians claimed, were looked upon more kindly by Europe. Thus, because of the Chechen war, Russia's formerly positive attitude toward Europe was replaced by barely concealed annoyance with the behavior of the "near West." Many Russian politicians believed that the Council of Europe's tough stand on Chechnya was politicized. Many—from Zhirinovsky to Dmitri Rogozin (the chair of the Duma foreign affairs committee)—made harsh and sometimes insulting statements about European parliamentarians. The Russian military was strongly opposed to the Council of Europe's parliamentary assembly (PACE) monitoring of missions in the North Caucasus. European parliamentarians were told publicly by Russian generals to mind their own business.[48] The top brass clearly wanted to send the message that they would not allow the Chechen issue to be internationalized.

Yet the harsh criticism of PACE from Russian politicians and military helped the Russian public learn more about the human rights watchdog organization that Russia had joined, with some pomp, in 1996. In 2000 the Kremlin was seriously concerned about Russia's possible expulsion from PACE and the Council of Europe itself and therefore had to make an effort to soothe its European critics.

Because of human rights issues in Chechnya, officials in Russia revised their attitude toward the Organization for Security Cooperation in Europe, one of Moscow's long-time foreign policy favorites. In 1995 the Russian government agreed to the presence in Grozny of an OSCE mission, which tried to act as an intermediary between the federal authorities and Chechen rebels. Four years later Russia effectively refused to grant OSCE access to the area where the counterterrorist operation was being conducted. OSCE therefore soon acquired a reputation in the Russian foreign ministry of being a pro-Western organization whose interests were limited to developments in the Balkans and the CIS. This attitude was reflected in a 2000 official foreign policy concept paper.[49] The organization was touted as the flagship achievement of Moscow's diplomacy in the 1970s and 1980s and in the early 1990s was proposed by Russia to be the overarching pan-European organization (eclipsing NATO, the European Union, and the CIS. Today it has slipped low on Moscow's priority list. Chechnya all but killed it.

As the 2003 war in Iraq has demonstrated, Moscow continues to regard the United Nations as the foundation for the "creation of a stable, just, and democratic world order." Yet criticism over Chechnya has also affected Russia's attitude toward the United Nations. Even the usually soft-spoken Vladimir Kalamanov, then President Putin's envoy in charge of monitoring human rights violations in Chechnya, made little effort to conceal his annoyance with UN criticisms: "When [the world community] always acts as judge, it becomes tiring." Referring to the primacy of national sovereignty, the Russian government plainly refuses to accept the possibility of an international investigation of war crimes in

Chechnya.[50] Having signed the Statute of the International Criminal Court, Russia has balked at ratifying it, clearly with Chechnya in mind. Moscow also blames the International Committee of the Red Cross, whose staff has been working in the North Caucasus since 1993, of a "one-sided politicized approach." Thus, Chechnya has exposed the limits of Russia's often trumpeted multilateralism.

At his 2001 meetings with the President Bush in Lubljana and French President Chirac in Moscow, Vladimir Putin asked his foreign counterparts the supposedly tough question: "What would you do if separatists gained control in Texas or terrorists landed in the south of France?" The transparent analogy, however, failed to produce the desired effect. American and European leaders did not dispute Russian sovereignty or territorial integrity. Rather, they objected to the methods used by the Russian government forces.

True, the attitudes of Western governments to the conflict in Chechnya have been ambiguous. During the first campaign, the Clinton administration was fairly lenient toward "Mr. Yeltsin's war." When Bill Clinton came to Moscow in May 1995 to participate in World War II Victory Day celebrations, he went so far as to liken Yeltsin's antiseparatist stand with that of Abraham Lincoln during the American Civil War. Four years later, in an atmosphere of widespread disillusionment with Russia's "transition," the same administration openly condemned the disproportionate use of force by the Russian troops during the so-called counterterrorist operation.

The second Chechen campaign immediately followed NATO's military intervention in Yugoslavia, which brought about the most acute crisis in Russian-Western relations since the end of the Cold War. To a large extent, the Chechen campaign itself was a reaction to NATO's air war in the Balkans and the alliance's new strategic concept. It was seen by many in Russia as a preemptive move designed to rule out the possibility of military intervention by the United States and its NATO allies anywhere in the Caucasus, such as Abkhazia.[51] It was also a reflex action aimed at showing the West that Russia was not defeatist and was capable of using force when need be.

Members of the Russian political elite have traditionally viewed American policies in the Caucasus and Central Asia in the context of the struggle for spheres of influence and control over energy resources. Zbigniew Brzezinski's statement that he who controls communications controls the region was fully embraced in Russia even by those who had never read him.[52] The Kremlin and President Yeltsin personally were strongly concerned because some Clinton administration officials claimed that the United States had "vital interests" in the Caucasus and the Caspian region. This strengthened old suspicions that the United States was interested in continuing instability in Chechnya in order to remove Russia as a competitor in the fight for Caspian oil transportation contracts. The "fight for oil" was thus elevated to the level of a major geopolitical confrontation, with Washington's goal being undiluted American hegemony in the region.

In the late summer and fall of 1999, as it faced armed incursions into Daghestan and apartment house bombings in Moscow, the Russian leadership was most unhappy with Washington's refusal to form a united front against international terrorism. Far from joining Russia, the United States and other Western governments and peoples were discussing reports of corruption in the top echelons of power in Russia. The Clinton administration, accused by Republicans of having mismanaged Russia, turned a cold shoulder to Moscow. American diplomats were instructed to hold working-level contacts with Maskhadov and his representatives. This, in turn, strengthened the arm of Moscow's hardliners.[53]

Speaking in November 1999 before Prime Minister Putin, Defense Minister Igor Sergeyev concluded that the "United States [is] interested in a continuous smoldering of the conflict," which would leave Russia weakened and enable full American control over the North Caucasus.[54] The minister's words reflected the unwritten military and political doctrine that had emerged from the defense establishment. It could be called a two-fronts doctrine because it posited the existence of two simultaneous threats: the principal one from the West (exemplified by NATO's Kosovo model), and an auxiliary threat in the south (Chechnya and Afghanistan). Both threats were considered linked by a Western policy aimed at further constraining Russia. In early September 2001, a week before the terrorist attacks against New York and Washington, the Russian Air Defense Force and Russian allies under the Collective Security Treaty engaged in an exercise that simulated a coordinated invasion of the CIS from the West (by NATO) and the south (by the Taliban).

Since the mid-1990s, independent Russian analysts have noted that the private organizations supporting Chechen rebels are located in countries that are the traditional clients of the United States in the Middle

East: Saudi Arabia, the United Arab Emirates, Pakistan, Yemen, Jordan, and Turkey. The Russian government was particularly suspicious of the initial support by the United States of the Taliban movement. Russian officials, who remembered that in the early 1990s the United States supported the Bosnian Muslims, were particularly concerned about the U.S. embrace of the Kosovo Liberation Army and the National Liberation Army of Macedonia, which the U.S. government had originally classified as terrorist organizations. Together, this generated Russian distrust of the true commitment of the United States to the antiterrorist struggle and generated speculation about Washington's "hidden agenda." In the late 1990s, geopolitically minded Russian analysts had the following vision of this covert strategy:

Washington's minor objective was to cut Moscow off from the Persian Gulf. The Taliban were to be used as the principal tool of a strategy that was to divert Moscow's attention from Iraq, Iran, and the Balkans by forcing it to concentrate on increasingly vulnerable Central Asia. The Taliban are a creature of Pakistan, an American ally. From the start Americans saw the Taliban as the only force capable of consolidating Afghanistan and creating conditions that would enable the export of Turkmen natural gas to Pakistan. The liquidation of the Russian monopoly of the pipelines from Central Asia was the prerequisite for installing pro-American regimes across the region. Using Central Asia as a bridgehead, the United States could then apply pressure not just on Russia, but also on China, Iran, and India. Russia stood to lose more than its positions in the south. The next step would be penetration by American agents into the Russian Federation's Muslim republics and territories (including the main oil-producing regions of Tatarstan and Tyumen) assisting them in achieving independence and dealing the final blow to Russia's territorial integrity. This was the major objective. The only reason the plan was not implemented was that the Taliban failed to observe its commitments to Pakistan and the United States and went out of control.[55]

These fantasies, never publicly stated by Russian officials, were nevertheless typical and widespread within the foreign and security policy community. The habit of thinking in terms of a zero-sum game remains strong in Russia. The Chechen war, superimposed on intense competition for Caspian oil, further strengthened anti-American sentiments within Russian ruling circles.

Anti-Americanism also fed neo-Eurasianism, a marginal school of thought whose best-known representative is the Russian philosopher Alexander Dugin.[56] In developing "a common Eurasian concept of anti-Americanism," Dugin suggested alliances built on the principle of a "common enemy." As a "natural opponent of Atlanticism," the Islamic world is a welcome Russian ally, he insisted. This vision assumes that an orientation to Iran (with the Moscow-Teheran axis as the foundation of the Eurasian geopolitical project and much-needed counterweight to the U.S.–Turkish alliance) and Saddam's Iraq ("a left-wing Arab regime") would help Moscow gain access to the southern seas.[57]

These geophilosophical speculations, though absurd, are consonant with the pragmatic interests of the Russian business community—especially those profiting in Iran from arms and nuclear transactions and in Saddam's Iraq—as well as the interests of the political and mass media structures close to such business circles. Since about 2000, Dugin, a once-obscure figure now cultivated by nationalists and militarists, has also been taken up by senior members of the Kremlin administration, which holds Dugin and his "Eurasianist party" in reserve.

In the context of the wars in Chechnya and conflicts in Central Asia, however, the neo-Eurasianist project is unconvincing. Realizing this, those advocating an alliance with the Islamic world against the United States advance the following idea: Washington consistently uses the Islamic factor against Russia. According to Russian politician and businessman Martin Shakkum, "the skilled hand" of the United States "guides the potential for aggression of radical Islamic regimes" against Russia."[58] Some high-ranking military officers seem to agree with Shakkum. General Makhmut Gareyev believes that

> the "Islamic factor" is a dangerous fiend in the hands of global policy makers. . . . The "Islamic threat" is a trap for this country designed to heighten tensions in the Russian Federation and worsen Russia's relations with the CIS states. The most important lesson from the development in Afghanistan and the Caucasus is that one must finally disperse this smokescreen to see what lurks behind international terrorism, extremism, and separatism. It is time to identify the source of the real threat, in the face of which Russia and all other countries and peoples ready to challenge that threat and protect their independence must join forces.[59]

Some observers in Central Asia tend to agree. One observer believes that "drawing Russia into the fight [against international terrorism] gives the West both time and opportunity to strengthen its own security."[60]

Although the "source of the real threat" to Russia was not mentioned directly, the allusion is clear. With the end of the 1990s the specter of a new opposition bloc emerged in the Greater Middle East. The United States, Turkey, GUUAM countries, and Israel lined up on one side, while Russia, Iran, Armenia, Syria, and Greece lined up on the other.[61] In 1999, the Russian military became concerned over the enlargement of the U.S. Army Central Command (CENTCOM) zone of responsibility to include Central Asia. CENTCOM's commander, Gen. Tommy Franks, said that in the military arena, U.S. relations with Central Asian states would be determined not only by the extremist threat from Afghanistan, but also by the nature of the states' relations with Russia. In both cases, the objective was to assist the new countries in preserving their independence, sovereignty, and territorial integrity.[62] In its turn, Moscow was convinced that "imported advisers" were pursuing their own objectives rather than helping to create security systems in the new countries.[63]

Most Russian observers believed that these objectives were to support "dislodging" Russia from the Caspian region and replacing Russian influence with that of the West. Radical circles went even further. In their view, "The war for world domination, for monopolism" had already begun. That war's "theaters of operations" included the area of NATO enlargement, conflict zones in the former Yugoslavia, and Iraq. Thus, Russia was implicitly the target of a new war for monopolism. Once again, Russia, according to that distorted Russocentric view, was facing a life or death dilemma. Although the United States had triumphed, the Cold War was far from over.[64]

Among Russia's security, foreign policy, and military elites, the traditional geopolitical world outlook was strengthened by skepticism regarding Western views of Moscow's policies in Central Asia and the Caucasus (including Chechnya). The new Western image of Russia was of a revanchist state seeking to use its military superiority over weak and defenseless neighbors to regain dominance and control their resources. This perspective led logically to a U.S. policy toward opposing Russian hegemonistic ambitions.[65] American encouragement of a "geopolitical pluralism" in the former Soviet south was perceived in Moscow as unabashedly anti-Russian.

Marginalized in the early 1990s, the "neo-Eurasianists" had become by the end of the decade a strategic reserve of the ruling elite. They never had an opportunity, however, to implement Russian foreign policy. Following the second campaign in Chechnya, Moscow began to feel more confident and more comfortable in its relations with the United States. Potentially large oil deposits were discovered in the Russian sector of the Caspian, while elsewhere in the Caspian new oil discoveries were finally tapering.[66] Kazakhstan, Azerbaijan, and even Turkmenistan showed a readiness to take Russian economic and geopolitical interests into account. Further, while Central Asia and the Caucasus came to occupy a visible yet modest place in the foreign policy and economic interests of the United States, Washington, shortly before September 11, ruled out direct U.S. interference in Central Asian crises and saw value in preserving the Russian presence in the region.

By 2000, a new configuration of forces emerged in reaction to the Islamic extremist challenge, turning traditional geopolitical arrangements upside down. The United States, Russia, Turkey, and Israel, as well as China and even Iran, discovered common interests. American policy makers had to admit that Russia was able to be a pillar of regional stability. The closeness of Russian and American interests in Afghanistan resulted in the institualization of the U.S.-Russian partnership in 1999 in the form of a bilateral ad hoc working group at the deputy foreign minister level. Reports of the U.S. Special Forces planning an operation against Osama bin Laden from the territory of Tajikistan, a Moscow ally, came as early as August 2001. Finally, after the September 11 terrorist attacks in the United States, the international coalition against terrorism became a reality.

The Chechen war has been the principal factor in helping to create the first Moscow-Washington military and political alliance since 1945. Combating international terrorism became the formally accepted foundation of the alliance. The Russian leadership found an opportunity not only to fit the war in Chechnya into the context of the U.S.-led international efforts against terrorism, but also to insist that Moscow had identified the threat and began combating it long before the West had.

In the past, the Soviet Union condemned the U.S. policy of "international terrorism" (for example, its 1986 air raid against Libya), but was lenient regarding terrorist attacks as long as they were not aimed against the USSR or its clients. Meanwhile, Soviet instructors trained saboteurs and terrorists for special missions at the "anti-imperialist front." Since the second half of the 1990s, however, terrorism became a prominent reality in Russia. Shamil Basayev's raid on Budennovsk in 1995 and Salman Raduyev's on Kizlyar in 1996 sent the country into a state of shock. The apartment building explosions in Moscow, Kaspiysk, and Volgodonsk in the fall of 1999 generated broad public support for the second campaign in Chechnya, officially referred to as a counterterrorist operation.

The Putin administration at various levels advocated the need to struggle against terrorism, which it called the main threat to international security at the turn of the twenty-first century. To make its case on Chechnya, the Kremlin pointed to the presence among Chechen rebels of foreign, mainly Arab and Afghan, "warriors of jihad." It also drew parallels between the situations in the North Caucasus and Central Asia, and more broadly with those in the Balkans and the Middle East. Since 1999, Russia has been an active participant in the discussion of the terrorism problem in the United Nations and G–8 arenas. In 2001, it joined the Council of Europe's European Convention on Fighting Terrorism, which assigns criminal responsibility to those financing terrorist activities.

Terrorist attacks against the United States in 2001 became a powerful catalyst for Russian-American rapprochement. By pointing out that terrorists were moving from Afghanistan to Chechnya to fight Russian troops, and from Chechnya to Afghanistan "to kill Americans," President Putin agreed to both the unprecedented cooperation of Russian and U.S. special services against a common enemy and the U.S. presence in Central Asia.[67] He also referred to the activities of Russian troops in Chechnya as "a ground operation against international terrorism in the North Caucasus." The United States reciprocated by toning down its criticism of the methods Russia used in carrying out that operation.

Putin spoke of a common struggle against terrorism and of the shared positive results. He announced an ultra-ambitious and almost unattainable objective: "to eradicate, eliminate, and liquidate terrorism, not only in Afghanistan but in the whole world" so that our peoples may "feel more secure." "A new quality of relations with the United States" was to come from this policy.[68] A strategic choice was made toward an "alliance with the Alliance" (NATO) based on shared decision making on several issues as part of the Russia-NATO Council established in May 2002. In broad terms, this commitment survived a bitter disagreement between Moscow and Washington over Iraq in early 2003.

Chechnya, Central Asia, and China

China is the only major power whose relations with Russia were wholly strengthened after the two campaigns in Chechnya and developments in Central Asia. Beijing unambiguously supported Moscow's policy on the Chechen issue and made a step toward quasi-allied relations in Central Asia.

From point of view of the Chinese leadership, the conflict in Chechnya is, first and foremost, about preserving territorial integrity. China faces similar problems in its own periphery, in particular in Tibet. But the main analogy the Chinese leadership sees when it looks at Chechnya is with Taiwan. The sovereignty issue is related to another principle, that of the legality of the unlimited use of force to restore territorial integrity. By verbally supporting Moscow's use of force against Chechen separatists, Beijing is counting on Russia's practical assistance should a conflict break out over Taiwan. Chinese arms procurement in Russia is chiefly to strengthen the People's Liberation Army against Taiwan. For Beijing it is extremely important that Moscow should continue to supply it with weapons and spare parts.

Insisting that the use of effectively unlimited force in "restoring the homeland," China, like Russia in Chechnya, adamantly rejects interference from foreign states in its internal affairs. The main objective is to resist efforts by the United States and its allies to implement principles of international humanitarian law that limit the sovereignty of individual states. In this context, Chechnya has a mainly symbolic significance. The armed conflict in the North Caucasus is of a local nature, its spillover effect is highly unlikely, and direct interference by big powers can easily be excluded as a possibility. Conversely, a conflict between mainland China and Taiwan, should it ever happen, would be highly likely to become a regional conflict and, in the worst-case scenario, could lead to a direct clash between China and the United States.

Incursions by armed rebels into Kyrgyzstan and Uzbekistan in 1999 and 2000 alarmed China because the radical Islamic forces behind the incursions also support Muslim separatists in the Xinjiang-Uygur autonomous region of China (also known as Eastern Turkestan). Although Chinese security services and army units have spent years trying to eradicate separatist sentiments in the region, no definitive success has yet been achieved. Destabilization in Central Asia, to say nothing of Islamic radicals coming to power there, would make that success impossible to achieve. To prevent this scenario from occurring, Beijing is ready to reject its traditional policy of isolationism and embark on a policy of close cooperation with neighboring countries.

The intensification of the situation in Central Asia has brought two principal results. First, Russia and China have entered into a quasi alliance to prevent further destabilization in the region. The Shanghai Forum was created in 1996 by neighboring countries on both sides of the former Soviet-Chinese border with the goal of settling border disputes and building mutual confidence. It has gradually transformed itself into a regional association with its own institutions (including annual summits) and mechanisms. In 2001, the Forum was renamed the Shanghai Cooperation Organization (SCO), and in 2002 the SCO charter was adopted.

Second, although Russia and China are SCO informal leaders with parity, the organization's activities effectively promote China's involvement in Central Asian problems and boost Beijing's regional role. China insists that the SCO be institutionalized as soon as possible and is examining opportunities for its involvement in various antiterrorist exercises and operations in the former Soviet republics. From a long-term or even medium-term perspective, the Shanghai process leads to the gradual, "friendly" replacement of Russian influence in Central Asia with that of China. The achievement of this objective is more difficult since the United States emerged as a regional Central Asian power alongside Russia and China in the fall of 2001.

The war in Chechnya and crises in Central Asia have highlighted the most vulnerable and most dangerous regional axis of Russia's foreign and security policy. Despite NATO's two-stage enlargement and the Balkan crises being managed by the West, Russia's Western strategic axis is becoming increasingly stable. In the East, Russia's relations with China are based on a balance of interests, which are likely to remain sustainable for at least the next fifteen years. By contrast, along the southern axis Russia has had to deal with multiple crises and major challenges. The federation has tried to contain threats of separatism, extremism, and terrorism occurring simultaneously along its far frontiers (Afghanistan) as well as within its "security area" (Tajikistan, other CIS countries, and even within sovereign territory (Chechnya, Daghestan, other North Caucasian republics, and, as a precaution, the Volga regions).

Conflicts and general instability in the south have demonstrated that the weakness of both the newly independent states and the Russian Federation is the chief source of security problems. All former Soviet republics have become sovereign states. Yet they all remain weak states, and some might be described as failing states. Unable to cope with the challenge of political Islam, Central Asian regimes represent a problem for Moscow. Merely supporting its nominal allies could bring Russia into conflict with the discontented populations—with the risk that the unrest will spread northward into Russia's Muslim regions.

In this situation, it should make sense to the Russian leadership to nudge Central Asian autocrats toward broadening their social, political, and ideological support base by expanding popular participation in the government. Conversely, attempts to preserve the status quo by predominantly military and military-police methods should be seen as a losing, and dangerous, strategy. This, however, is not the thinking of the Putin administration and is not Russia's policy. The Kremlin entertains few, if any illusions, about its Central Asian partners, but it remains wedded to the status quo.

7

Chechnya and the Laws of War

by Anatol Lieven

The suffering of the Chechen population at the hands of the Russian armed forces in Chechnya since October 1999 has severely damaged Russia's international standing as well as the goals of the Russian operation. It has created numerous new recruits for Chechen militants, even among people who before the Russian military intervention loathed the militants and their aims. The suffering has made a negotiated end to the conflict much more elusive, and has undermined the possibility of fruitful diplomatic mediation by outside parties. It has also gravely complicated Russia's efforts at closer relations with western Europe as well as its attempts to exploit the deep anxieties that Europeans feel about U.S. policies; and of course it has also undermined Russia's standing in the Muslim world.

The Abuse of Civilians

Some of the suffering in Chechnya has been an unavoidable part of urban and antipartisan warfare. Similar atrocities against civilians have unfortunately been carried out by almost all the armies involved in this kind of operations, including leading Western ones. The U.S. armed forces in Afghanistan have not yet carried out serious abuses against civilians—but then, they have done only a fraction of the fighting and suffered few casualties compared with Russian casualties. One reason for this is that much of the fighting on the ground has been the work of local Afghan allies of the United States, which have committed numerous atrocities.

As of June 2003 U.S. forces in Iraq had on several occasions opened fire into crowds, incidents that were described as massacres by some of the Arab media. This description was an exaggeration, as were accounts of torture and other abuses by U.S. troops. In Iraq too, however, U.S. casualties so far have been small: less than a tenth of credibly reported Iraqi civilian casualties. It remains to be seen how the U.S. army will behave if it finds itself in a long-running guerrilla and terrorist war with a steady stream of American deaths.

Some of the Western criticism directed at Russia has therefore been both unfair and ignorant of military realities, and some indeed has been motivated not by goodwill toward the Chechens or real concern for human rights, but only by malignant hatred of Russia. Until the terrorist attacks of September 11 against the United States, many Western critics and organizations showed indifference to the atrocities committed by the Chechen militants and their international Islamist allies. When the West did take notice, their judgments were sometimes marred a double standard concerning atrocities by Russian troops and those by Western allies like Turkey and Israel.

That said, however, the disastrous extent of abuses by Russian troops in Chechnya must also be fully recognized. The evidence of them is simply overwhelming. Above all, atrocities have taken place in the course of sweeps by Russian troops looking for suspected militants. As documented by Human Rights Watch, the Russian NGO Memorial, and numerous Russian and international human rights organizations, extortion, beatings, kidnapping for ransom under the guise of arrest, and not infrequently, murder and rape have been the hallmarks of these operations. The Human Rights Watch report on Russia and Chechnya, for example, examines particular sweeps and numerous eyewitness accounts.[1]

Meanwhile there have been strong suspicions that the actual militants have on occasions paid the Russian troops involved to escape; or that fearing a fight, the soldiers have taken care to proceed so slowly with their operations that the militants were able to slip away. In the previous war of 1994–96, I saw evidence of this kind of thing with my own eyes; and it would certainly help explain how after four years of fighting, and despite the small size of Chechnya and the presence of tens of thousands of Russian troops, the armed resistance remains very active and many of its chief leaders still at large.

While some atrocities were ordered by the high command, a great many were the result of military demoralization and a lack of discipline, albeit gravely worsened by indifference, callousness, and the tacit complicity of senior officers. While torture as part of interrogations might be seen as part of a rational strategy, acts of rape, kidnapping, and looting by soldiers form no part of official strategy or goals. They are instead a symptom of the same rotten conditions of the Russian army which produced massive corruption and the phenomenon of *dyedovshchina* ("grandaddyism"), the savage bullying of younger soldiers by their "comrades," which over the years has claimed the lives of almost as many Russian soldiers as have the two Chechen wars.

The extent and effect of the problem of human rights abuses were recognized by the Russian authorities themselves under heavy pressure from pro-Russian Chechen authorities. Thus, in March 2002, Order No. 80 of the commander of Federal Forces in Chechnya, Lt. Gen. Vladimir Moltenskoi, declared that illegal actions by soldiers

> annihilate the efforts of commanders to enforce security, law and order, and favorable conditions for restoring social and economic life; boost the anti-Russian mood; and give the leaders of the illegal armed units additional opportunities to bring new members and supporters into their ranks.

According to this order, sweeps should take place only on the personal order of the commanding general. The soldiers involved are not to wear masks, and the license plates of their vehicles are to be legible. The names of those arrested are to be given immediately to the local administration as well as to the superiors of the soldiers.

However, given previous experience, observers were understandably skeptical about both the will and the ability of Russian commanders to enforce these rules. As other international examples have shown, the tight control of soldiers in the field is never easy. For Russian soldiers to respect human rights, the new rules would have to be part of truly comprehensive military reform that would also replace the partially conscript army by a fully professional one, and levels of pay which would allow the armed forces to attract a far higher class of recruit than at present. It would also require really ruthless actions against corrupt officers, up to the highest level—for without this it will be impossible to get ordinary soldiers to respect their superiors or feel pride in their service.

Russia's Legal Right to War against Chechnya

Despite much Western and even Russian writing on this subject, according to any traditional or universally accepted version of the laws of war, Russia's legal right to prosecute this war is incontestable. Since the onset of thinking about the laws of war, such laws have been divided into the *jus ad bellum* (the right, or lack of it, to make war) and the *jus in bello* (the rules governing the conduct of war). Regarding *jus ad bellum*: Chechnya is an internationally recognized part of Russia's territory in rebellion against its sovereign. Throughout history and all over the world today, states have reacted to armed secession with armed repression. By contrast, the number of cases in which a territory has separated peacefully from its sovereign state is extremely small. For example, in the great majority of cases (and invariably where its own territory or its own allies have been involved), the United States has backed the existing internationally recognized sovereign: the Kurdish revolt against Turkey being only one example.

Moreover, when Russia yielded de facto self-rule in Chechnya in 1996, the government there proved incapable of controlling its own territory. The result was a great wave of kidnapping and other forms of criminality directed at Russian citizens in the North Caucasus and the establishment on Chechen soil of forces publicly dedicated to the prosecution of a religious war against Russia and to carving away further pieces of Russian territory. Leaving aside the unproven issue of Chechen-based terrorism, prior to the second war, it is uncontested that this movement led to a large-scale armed incursion, in August 1999, from Chechnya into the Russian autonomous republic of Dagestan, and that in the subsequent fighting 270 Russian soldiers and several hundred Dagestani policemen and civilians lost their lives.

Legally, therefore, Russia certainly had the right to retaliate, as the United States has repeatedly done with armed force in independent states in Central America, when it has felt threatened by domestic developments and especially by criminal behavior in these countries (Panama being only the most recent example). On the only occasion when U.S.

territory was directly attacked as a result of civil war in a neighboring state (Pancho Villa's raid on Columbus in March 1916), the immediate U.S. response was counter-invasion, on a vastly larger scale.

But of course, legality and morality are not the same, nor are morality and past U.S. international practice. Morally, the issue of Russia's latest intervention in Chechnya is less clear. Much of the pathological behavior emanating from Chechnya between 1996 and 1999 can be seen as a direct result of the unnecessary and even criminal Russian armed intervention of December 1994, and the bloody and destructive war that followed.

Not only was that intervention a great deal less justifiable than that of 1999, but the memory of the futile bloodshed of 1994–1996 and the ferocity of the Chechen resistance should have given the Russian leadership pause before embarking again on a war in Chechnya. Warfare, and especially anti-partisan warfare, is inherently savage. Before you engage in it, you have a moral obligation to be very sure indeed that all other policies have been exhausted, and that there is no better alternative.

Hence the force of the criticism, for example, concerning the American use of atomic bombs against Japanese cities in August 1945, when Japan was, in effect, already defeated. The use of nuclear weapons would in any case cause grave moral qualms. Yet these would have been far fewer had bombs existed and been dropped on Germany or Japan in 1942, when victory was still in the balance and when tens of millions of other lives would have been saved by an Axis surrender. The gravest doubts concerning the morality of the obliteration of Hiroshima and Nagasaki relate to the fact that it was probably unnecessary, or at least wholly incommensurate with the result to be gained.

As Thomas Aquinas affirmed, there must also be a reasonable hope of achieving the goal of a war. As with the United States in Vietnam, Russia's leadership clearly failed to think adequately about whether the suppression of Chechen anti-Russian activities was achievable with the strategies adopted. The results of the war to date have been at best highly inadequate from the point of view of Russian national interests and goals. On the positive side, the radical Islamic threat has been curbed, Chechen-based kidnapping and banditry greatly reduced, and Russia's military prestige somewhat restored from its nadir in 1996. However, thanks in large part to the atrocities committed by Russian troops against the Chechen population, Russia has become bogged down in a brutal partisan struggle with no end in sight; the threat of terrorism has actually increased; and the Russian-backed Chechen authorities have failed to consolidate their authority and, in many cases, even to save their own lives.

All this was entirely predictable, given the experience not only of 1994–1996, but of many similar conflicts around the world. The Putin administration should therefore have made a much more determined and earnest attempt to pursue other strategies before deciding on full-scale armed intervention (for example, some combination of an occupation of Chechnya, north of the Terek River, with extra carrots and sticks directed at the Maskhadov regime to persuade him to crack down on the extremists).

This said, if Moscow had pursued such policies, and after a reasonable time they had clearly failed to work (if major Chechen-based armed attacks on Russia had continued), then it must also be recognized that Russia would have had the full moral *and* legal right to go to war in Chechnya, as would any organized state in Russia's position. And it must also be recognized that, unfortunately, even a legally and morally justified war of this kind would probably involve massive civilian suffering and numerous human rights abuses, especially if the state concerned simply does not possess and cannot acquire the latest U.S.-style military technology.

It is extremely important that Russian commentary on Chechnya should combine honest reporting and the stern condemnation of military atrocities, with recognition of these harsh truths. For one of the most disturbing aspects of the Russian public discussion of this war has been the way it has reflected an old and extremely dangerous division between elements of the Russian liberal intelligentsia, on the one hand, and "state supporting" groups on the other. In the process, it has tended to bring out the worst features of both sides.

This divide is of course present to some extent in all Western societies. It corresponds to the distinction drawn by Max Weber between a *Gesinnungsethik,* an ethic based on principle and sentiment, and a *Verantwortungsethik,* an ethic based on a sense of responsibility for the consequences of actions and policies.

In Russia, however, the historic absence of democracy, first under the tsars and then under the Communists, meant that this divide became huge and extremely dangerous. Largely safe from outside criticism and investigation, the state forces were able to define their personal and class interests and those of the state as identical, a situation that bred oppression, corruption, extortion, and reckless policies. The history of the Soviet and Russian armed forces over the past two generations is the best possible illustration of this, with the first Chechen War of 1994-96 as the most glaring example of all. The Russian liberal intelligentsia, however, has also suffered from its historical lack of a share in power. Denied political responsibility, both under Tsarism and in recent years it has shown a strong tendency toward political irresponsibility. Wild accusations are often hurled at the state, and positions taken without regard to their likely impact on Russian interests and Russia's future.

War Crimes

This brings me to the question of the *jus in bello* with regard to Chechnya, and what is a war crime and what is not, because the approaches to this issue by both Russian and Western intellectuals have often been extremely confused. And as promoted by Western governments, this confusion could pose a future risk to the actual growth of relative humaneness in the conduct of war. This is because, like any other law, the laws of war have to bear some practical relation to the actual field they are meant to regulate. If they cease to be applicable, practically, by soldiers in concrete situations, they will become not laws but a form of scholastic theology, practiced by a priestly caste of international lawyers; perhaps formally beautiful, but with no reference to actual, human activity.

The collapse of communism as an ideological force has created the genuine possibility of the universal establishment of Western humanitarian values—the first time in history that such a development is possible. But even with communism gone, this is inevitably going to be a slow, incremental process. And above all, these values have to be seen by other societies as genuinely universal and equal in their application—not a crude and cynical tool adopted by U.S. politicians to weaken rival states. It should be remembered that in the nineteenth century European and North American imperial powers also declared that they were spreading what were then called "civilized" values to lesser breeds all over the world. Unfortunately, the manifest colonial greed, aggrandizement, ruthlessness, and hypocrisy that attended these "civilizing missions" fatally compromised them in the eyes of other peoples and helped to produce pathological backlashes against the West and, in some cases, even against modernity in general.

In any conflict, war crimes can be divided into two general categories. The first is deliberate war crimes, ordered by the leaders of a state or of a state-run military campaign. They include organized torture to extract information, extrajudicial executions, and systematic methods of terrorizing the population; and so on. The second category involves spontaneous crimes committed by soldiers without or against orders and for the sake of personal revenge or gratification: murder, rape, looting, and so on.

Clearly, these categories may often overlap. In the past, generals like Wellington, after the capture of Badajoz in 1811, or (reportedly) French Marshal Alphonse Juin, after the fall of Cassino in 1944, may give their troops the "right of pillage," entailing mass rape and looting, as a reward for courage and to improve morale. This was also true on occasion of the Russian imperial army in the nineteenth century during campaigns in the Caucasus and, on a much larger scale, of the Soviet Army in Germany in 1944–1945. In Bosnia, mass rape was evidently sanctioned by the Bosnian Serb high command as a way of terrorizing, demoralizing, and driving out Bosnian Muslims. Any policy of officially ordered mass reprisals against a civilian population will give ample room for ordinary soldiers to satisfy lust, anger, revenge, and greed.

Nonetheless, the difference between these two categories does need to be remembered. Because they are usually directed against the general population, spontaneous crimes by soldiers usually weaken the cause they are fighting for and only generate more recruits for the other side. A classic instance may be seen in the "arrests" of Chechens at Russian military checkpoints. There is ample evidence to suggest that in a great many cases—perhaps even a majority—the Russian soldiers making the arrests did not suspect those arrested of partisan activities. The intention is simply that their families should pay ransoms for their release. In effect, this has become a kidnapping racket, certainly not ordered from above and contrary to every Russian goal and interest in Chechnya.

Such crimes by soldiers are often the result of demoralization and a lack of discipline that weakens their cause and may also be directed against their own officers and noncommissioned officers. As with the Russian troops in Chechnya, spontaneous atrocities by U.S. troops against Vietnamese civilians were matched by a strong tendency to murder ("frag") unpopular officers and noncommissioned officers, something that will obviously give pause to any officer or noncommissioned officer who tries to prevent attacks on the civilian population.

As in Vietnam and Chechnya, when a majority of the soldiers are extremely unwilling to fight hard and are unhappy with their commanders and economic position, strong disciplinary actions are likely to result in soldiers ceasing to fight altogether, with the result that the war is lost. This is a dilemma that every state, and indeed every political class, also faces with regard to domestic police forces. If excessive abuses are allowed, the rule of law will be undermined, whole classes pushed toward criminality or violent protest, and the state ultimately weakened. Crack down too hard, however, and the police will cease to work seriously against crime, with potentially terrible consequences for their critics. New York City has seen episodes of this kind. As a result, even many Western liberals are cautious when it comes to alienating the force that, in the end, protects their lives and property. Although the state bears the ultimate moral responsibility for abuses committed by its servants, one must remember that in practical terms, this problem is a complicated one.

It may also be that the individual soldiers (or police) committing crimes may have previously distinguished themselves for courage and ferocity in combat. Unfortunately, because of their training and the personality type that joins such forces, elite troops like the British paratroops are often distinguished by ruthlessness toward civilians and violence in their personal lives. In these circumstances, a fighting officer—not a staff officer at headquarters, let alone a civilian lawyer—will face acute moral and emotional dilemmas, not readily understandable by those who have not experienced combat and comradeship in combat.

When it comes to crimes in Chechnya deliberately ordered by the Russian state, more clarity of thinking, again, is needed. What have been described by Russian liberal intellectuals, and by the Western media and politicians as war crimes can be divided into three categories.

The first comprises actions universally recognized as crimes and treated as such since the beginning of the formulation of modern laws of war in the later nineteenth century: torture, massacre, and extrajudicial execution. Almost all states involved in antipartisan warfare have committed such crimes to some extent. Equally, however, since 1945 at least, all states have denied it and sought to cover up their crimes. No modern state (with the exception of certain maniacal Communist states) has ever declared torture and massacre to be its official policy.

The French forces in Algeria conducted a major torture campaign, as recently revealed by Gen. Paul Aussaresses, that was not only ordered by the French high command in Algeria but was condoned by the French justice minister (and later president) François Mitterrand. The French, however, have never admitted this official policy, and when General Aussaresses made a statement in April 2001, French officials were forced to pretend to be shocked and amazed.

There is ample evidence of the extensive use of torture in Chechnya and of many extrajudicial executions. The latter, as in Algeria perhaps, were intended in part to cover up evidence of particularly savage torture. Human Rights Watch has gathered details suggesting that 853 illegal executions had taken place by February 2001. At least one verified mass grave has been located close to a Russian detention camp. Extensive killing of civilians have taken place during military sweeps, though they do not yet amount to a systematic program of massacres, as took place in Bosnia. (As of spring 2001, Human Rights Watch had documented three massacres, with a total figure of around 130 killed.)

The second category consists of actions not previously considered crimes by Western governments but that are, nonetheless, gradually coming to be considered crimes as a result of moral consensus and informal convention. These include the bombing of populated areas away from the immediate fighting and the use of especially destructive and unpleasant weapons like napalm and "vacuum bombs." Such strategies and weapons have been employed openly and on a massive scale by Western armed forces. In World War II, in Korea, and, to a more limited extent in Vietnam, the systematic destruction of civilian populations by aerial bombardment was a central part of U.S. strategy. Both U.S. and French forces used napalm extensively during antipartisan operations, with horrible results. The United States has used "thermobaric" weapons against al-Qaeda and Taliban cave complexes in Afghanistan, making nonsense of some previous statements by U.S. commentators concerning the inherent immorality of such weapons. Yet a strong sentiment still exists against their use in heavily populated areas, and it is in this that one can see a change in public opinion over the past thirty years leading to a new set of attitudes and even of behavior.

The third category concerns actions that have been widely described as war crimes but that cannot, in fact, be so described—at least, not without both indulging in massive hypocrisy and rendering the whole concept of war crimes absurd. Above all, this relates to the bombardment of defended towns and cities, most notably of Grozny itself, which was defended to the bitter end by separatist forces both in 1995 and in 1999–2000 and was attacked by separatists in March and August 1996.

Clearly, if one side in a war decides to entrench itself in a town, that town will be attacked, whether or not it contains civilians, and a large proportion of those civilians will be killed. Unfortunately, despite advanced technology-development programs by the U.S. military, to this day there is no effective way of storming a bitterly defended city without destroying much of it in the process—not, at least, if massive casualties among one's own troops are to be avoided. In the U.S. assault on Manila in the winter of 1944–1945, General Douglas MacArthur initially tried to avoid the use of artillery and air bombardment in order to spare the civilian population, but he soon abandoned this as U.S. casualties began to mount. The same was true later in Seoul, Hue, and elsewhere.

During the extrication of the U.S. Rangers from Mogadishu in October 1993, U.S. firepower claimed the lives of up to fifty Somalis, mostly civilians, for every U.S. soldier killed. Not to have used such firepower would have constituted a betrayal of the U.S. soldiers involved, and while international lawyers might make or accept an argument for not using this destructive option, commanders cannot do so. Realistically, and even ethically, the first duty of commanders is to pursue victory, and the second is to protect the lives of their troops. Once battle is joined, it may be possible to persuade soldiers to avoid legally and traditionally recognized war crimes. Commanders will never deliberately sacrifice the lives of their own people for the sake of a vague and contradictory moral principle.

Of course, the attacking side might try to allow the civilian population to leave the city before it is attacked. The Russians did, indeed, warn the population of Grozny to do so, but they certainly should have done more to create safe corridors of escape for them. Western criticism should have focused on this failure and on the Russian military's refusal to allow the International Committee of the Red Cross to play a stronger role. Instead, however, too much Western criticism treated even the Russian warning to the population as a crime, which is ridiculous.

Nonetheless, a traditional means does exist for averting the destruction of cities: it is for the side on the defensive to declare the town concerned an "open city" and to promise not to station troops there or prevent the other side from entering. If such an agreement is made, then, if the other side bombards that city, it is guilty of a war crime. Otherwise, however, to accuse the attacking side of committing a crime in its use of heavy firepower, is to declare war itself a crime.

This has, indeed, been the underlying approach of many Russian liberal intellectuals and members of the Western nongovernmental organization world. Hating war and its inevitable cruelties, they tend to forget that the intention of war-crimes legislation is not to end war but to regulate it. Ending war may be possible some day, but it is certainly not possible now. In any case, the whole question of the *jus ad bellum* is, as I have pointed out, covered by a different set of international laws, traditions, and conventions. In any conflict, for those who hate war as such will be added those who, for whatever reason, hate this particular war or, more commonly, take sides and hope for victory, in the process condemning all the actions of the opposition as "crimes." This has been evident in some Western approaches to the Chechen conflict, as it has been in the previous approach of many left-wing Europeans and Americans to U.S. wars of which they disapproved. The association of Russian critics with such anti-Russian positions has naturally tended to discredit them in the eyes of many Russians.

Antipartisan Warfare

As has often been pointed out, there is something inherently illogical about attempts to regulate the conduct of war, given war's naturally violent and seemingly anarchic nature. The Latin maxim "In war, the laws are silent" expresses this view or, more colloquially, "All's fair in love and war." Nonetheless, in the one hundred years and more since modern international legislation on war crimes began to be discussed and drawn up, considerable progress has been made when it comes to the treatment of uniformed soldiers.

In World War II, the generally civilized German treatment of prisoners from the Western allies—compared with the bestial inhumanity displayed toward Soviet prisoners of war—was mainly a result of Nazi racial attitudes. But it also reflected the fact that the Western powers and the Germans had both signed the Geneva Convention, while the Soviet Union had not. The Germans had the same racial hatred for the Poles as for the Russians, but thanks to Poland's signature of the convention, prisoners of war from the Polish army were treated far better than those from the Red Army. It was otherwise, of course, with the German treatment of prisoners from the Polish underground forces, who, from 1939 to 1944, were usually tortured and shot or sent to concentration camps.

This brings us to the central problem of war crime legislation and thinking: the question of partisan and antipartisan warfare. When the European powers began thinking seriously about internationally agreed-upon treaties on war crimes toward the end of the nineteenth century, the universally recognized approach to partisans was explicit: if caught out of uniform with weapons in hand or where they had obviously been engaged in fighting, they could be executed on the spot without trial.

This approach was somewhat complicated by the European (and American) involvement in operations against "native" peoples, whose fighters often did not wear regular uniforms. On the whole, Western forces respected their enemies as warriors and did not simply massacre prisoners; but the decision whether to do so was very much in the hands of the local commander and his troops. Where—as so often on the American frontier and during the revolt of 1857 in India—the other side had itself been guilty of atrocities, massacre by the purportedly civilized forces was the frequent result and never, as far as I am aware, received official punishment.

The essential moral problem of partisan warfare hinges precisely on the fact that the most basic partisan or guerrilla strategy consists of hiding amid the civilian population: at best, to use it as a shield; at worst, to try actively to provoke anticivilian atrocities by the other side in order to stir up more hatred in the population. Combined with this strategy is the attempt, in all circumstances, to kill "enemy" civilians as well as soldiers while trying to disguise your men as civilians and, increasingly, to choose heavily populated areas as your sphere of operation. All of these approaches have been followed by the Chechen militants and their allies.

One possible response to the problem of civilian casualties in antipartisan operations is to try to deport noncombatants from the contested area and concentrate them in other areas under secure guard, in

"protected hamlets" (the U.S. term during the Vietnam War). This supposedly saves civilian lives while also "draining the water in which the
guerrillas swim," to adapt Mao Tse-tung's famous dictum. That was a
policy followed by the French in Algeria and by the Americans in Vietnam. It has not yet been adopted by the Russians in Chechnya, though
the creation of large numbers of refugees has something of the same
effect. This sometimes works when it comes to achieving victory against
the partisans. Is it more merciful? The usual result is that, rather than
being killed by bombs, shells, and marauding soldiers, the deported die
of malnutrition and disease in an equivalent of "protected hamlets," (the
Vietnam War description) even as their women become prostitutes for
the occupying forces.

But where, as in Chechnya, partisan attacks are erupting from the
midst of the civilian population, preventing attacks on civilians by the
antipartisan forces is obviously going to be extremely difficult. Soldiers
may have a certain respect and even strange affection for the soldiers on
the other side, who are undergoing the same risks and hardships as they.
They may even prefer them to their own civilians sitting safely and com-
fortably at home.

This respect will, however, nearly always be restricted to recogniz-
able soldiers. The eminent British military historian John Keegan has
discovered that in many wars, soldiers are much more likely to spare the
life of an enemy from their own fighting arm and, conversely, to kill a
prisoner from another fighting arm. Infantry sympathize with infantry
but hate cavalry or armored troops, and so on. World War I memoirs of
Verdun recall that the infantry on both sides reserved their greatest hatred for the artillery, which was pounding them from a distance—a hatred that extended even to their own artillery. Of course, captured enemy infantry were also sometimes killed, but on average they still stood
a much better chance than captured gunners.

This attitude fully shows the difficulty of inducing regular troops to
respect irregular partisans, as well as the civilian population that shel-
ters them. The willingness of soldiers to take prisoners from among enemy soldiers and to treat them decently also depends critically on a belief in reciprocity: that they themselves will be treated the same way if
captured. Given the nature of partisan warfare, it would be impossible
for a partisan force to give such assurances even if it wanted to. In fact,
the usual practice of guerrillas is to take few prisoners and to treat those

they do take abominably. Both approaches have been characteristic of the Chechen partisans, and the international mujahideen—who were also fighting there—have announced publicly the execution of prisoners and attempted to justify it under Islamic law.

Finally, antipartisan operations inevitably embody major elements of policing and therefore lead to the typical crimes of policemen—but this is policing in exceptionally brutal, dangerous, and squalid conditions, with far less supervision from commanders, far less regulation by clear rules, and usually conducted by men who by their training and psychology are hopelessly unfitted to be policemen. In these circumstances, some use of physical force against prisoners and civilians is inevitable, although of course the extent of its severity depends on the character and policies of the states involved, the morality of the commanders, and the discipline of their troops. It will also depend, however, on the success of the partisans in killing those troops and thereby provoking them into taking revenge.

The above remarks are not intended to lay down any exact set of intellectual and moral approaches concerning the war in Chechnya or indeed warfare in general, but only to suggest that these approaches should be a good deal more nuanced than has often been the case. Genuine Russian military crimes in Chechnya must be condemned—and these have been legion. However, we also need to be much clearer about what is and is not a crime. No legal, moral, or intellectual approach to war crimes will stand for long if it essentially treats all soldiers as criminals and ignores the harsh realities of their profession.

This is of the greatest importance as far as Russians themselves are concerned. For on the one hand, as stated, getting a grip on abuses by troops in Chechnya, and punishing those who is not only a moral imperative for the Russian state. It is also a key part of efforts to restore wider discipline and order within the armed forces. And this in turn is central to the absolutely essential task of reforming and modernizing the armed forces so that they can successfully fight Russia's wars in future.

But it must also be remembered that they will have to *fight* those wars, and often, fight them on the ground. Russia is not the U.S., Canada, or Western Europe. It is not protected by seas. It is a land empire, with land borders, some of them bordering on areas of extreme instability. Afghanistan and Iraq are separated from the U.S. by thousands of miles of ocean and the territory of U.S. allies. They are at Russia's backdoor. Russia therefore does not possess the American ability to send small expeditionary forces to fight overseas wars in far off countries, and then pull them out again when the short-term objective seems to have been achieved. Especially when fighting on its own territory, Russia also cannot use local native auxiliaries to nearly the extent that they have been employed by the United States (admittedly with mixed success) in Afghanistan and elsewhere.

Nor does Russia possess the West European option of restricting its truly effective armed forces to tiny groups of special forces backed up by airpower, while the armies as a whole (it is presumed) will never have to fight at all, but at most are intended for largely nonviolent peacekeeping missions. Danes and Swedes can afford armies most of whose troops are in effect no more than state-subsidized backpackers; Russia cannot. Finally, given the severe budgetary constraints on Russia, Russia will not be able to produce large numbers of "smart" bombs and missiles, thereby greatly reducing the need for fighting on the ground.

So while Russians may see themselves as Europeans, and hope to be treated as such, their army for the foreseeable future will bear more resemblance to that of India, in the challenges it faces and the internal forms which follow from those challenges. It will have to be prepared to fight and die—as Russian soldiers have fought and died in Chechnya, to an extent inconceivable to most Western armed forces, and in the face of courageous, skilled, ferocious, and implacable enemies. While criticism of the Russian soldiers must therefore be searching, it must also be tempered by respect—above all from their fellow countrymen.

8

Conclusion

A decade and a half after the beginning of Gorbachev's perestroika, Russia is still much closer to the beginning, rather than the end, of its transformation process. Compared with countries of Central and Eastern Europe, or even countries of the former Soviet Union, the task of Russian society is complicated by the fact that its economic, political, and social transformation is linked to a transition from imperial—or more accurately, post-imperial—status to a new modus vivendi with the world.

The path toward the reconstruction of a Eurasian empire (under whatever name) is finally closed. The resignation of Yeltsin did not result in imperial revenge. As Russia's second president, Putin is clearly a national leader, not an imperial one. The main goal of his administration is modernization of the country, and from that perspective, an empire seems both inefficient and archaic.

Yet Russia has not fully completed its exit from the imperial stage. The elites as well as the majority of the country's population have found it easier to reconcile themselves with the loss of the entire Ukraine, including the Crimea and Sevastopol, than to reintegrate the North Caucasus in a new fashion. Alongside the problems of ethnic republics within the Russian Federation, the regional policy agenda continues to include problems of the once colonized periphery: the northern areas, the far east area, and Siberia.

The affirmation of Russia as a federation is a tortuous process. In the 1990s, the Soviet totalitarian central model of the state was replaced with conditions not dissimilar to feudal fragmentation. Then the pendulum swung in the opposite direction, and the system of national governance was partially recentralized.

The so-called Putin stabilization may well become an incubation phase for the establishment of new state and social structures. The Kremlin's current preference is for a more united, if not unitary, Russia. While such an outcome will be tempered by the interests of regional elites, it is far less likely that a "Russia of the regions" will emerge. Striking an optimal balance between centralization and decentralization within the Russian Federation will crucially depend on the success of economic reforms and their social and political consequences. The maturing of democracy in Russia depends directly on the main actor of democracy—the property owner and taxpayer—coming into being.

In this broad context, Russia's rapprochement with the West after the attacks of September 11 is only nominally a foreign policy move. It reflects the country's internal needs, and it also demands that habitual though outdated attitudes and ambitions be rejected. From this standpoint, the historic significance of changes in Russian foreign policy in the fall of 2001 is that Russia unilaterally brought to an end its hopeless and devastating geopolitical competition with the United States.

While its relations with the West, primarily Europe, are of an increasingly internal nature ("integration through transformation"), Russia's future position in Asia will be determined by the development prospects of far western Russian territory and Siberia. At the beginning of the twenty-first century, the south, loosely defined as the Caucasus, Central Asia, and the Greater Middle East, offers Russia a fundamentally different set of challenges and opportunities. The south includes not only Russia's closest periphery, but partially a chain of enclaves within the Russian territory from the North Caucasus to the Volga region.

Here, as well as in other directions, the challenges and threats of the twenty-first century are different from those of the nineteenth and twentieth centuries. The Great Game of the great powers has lost its rationale. It is no longer possible to control the peripheral and buffer areas according to the old czarist, Soviet, or Anglo-Indian model. Yet under conditions of economic, financial, and information globalization, formal sovereignty is not an obstacle for those who possess soft power. With the rules of the new game in place, the sum of wins and losses is not necessarily zero.

No state can possibly benefit from the difficulties of modernization in Muslim, primarily Arab, societies. The weakness of new states, which once invited domination and stimulated a struggle for spheres of influence, has turned into a source of threat not only for neighbors, but also for the international community. The commonality of threats leads to the emergence of new and broad coalitions. The objective, however, is not only to cope successfully with external threats, but also to eradicate them. In its turn, this is possible only through the transformation of traditional societies—by modernization, democratization, and the inclusion in global processes—into entities more important that mere sources of raw materials.

The exploration for power and energy resources in the Greater Caspian region and their transport to international markets could, in principle, create material conditions for a second wave of modernizing societies in the countries of the South Caucasus and Central Asia. This is further facilitated by the openness of these countries to the United States, Russia, and European Union countries, as well as Asian states (China and Japan). As for relations between Russia and Western countries, energy has become one of the most important binding links of interdependence.

The success of efforts to combine Islam, modernization, and democracy in Iraq, Palestine, and Iran can have tremendous consequences for the entire Middle East. Democratization that rests on indigenous cultural, social, and political foundations is the most important force of modernization in the region. Predictable and responsible political regimes emerging in Baghdad, East Jerusalem, and Teheran could become the centerpieces of regional stability.

How sustainable the Russian state will be in the early years of the twenty-first century will largely depend on the extent and conditions of integration of the growing Muslim minority into Russian civil society. The processes of the further Islamization of some ethnic groups in Russia and of the Muslim renaissance will continue. Moreover, they will develop in parallel with similar processes in Central Asian countries and in an unbreakable link with the development of the core of today's Muslim world.

This creates at least two challenges for Moscow. The first is the challenge of multiculturalism. The second is the need to harmonize Muslim cultural autonomy with the European development model that Russia aspires to. In a sense, little Chechnya is a microcosm of all or almost all these problems. Russia will not become a modern, successful, democratic country until it unties the Chechen knot—or, conversely, not until efficient reforms produce a positive influence in Russia on the prospects of untying it.

One should not entertain illusions. The continuing war in Chechnya will be a barrier, organically as well as factually, to Russia as it moves closer to Europe. The example of Turkey's acceptance into NATO despite the unresolved Kurdish problem is not a convincing one: back in 1952, the decision was made in the context of the Cold War and Stalin's persistent pressure on the Turks. It was geopolitics pure and simple. It would be more useful and instructive for Russians to study the experience of Turkish relations with the European Union.

The prospects of settling the Chechen problem remain foggy. After 2000, the situation in Chechnya stalemated. Despite incessant acts of sabotage and the mounting death toll, this time the Russian government will not withdraw troops from Chechnya. There will be no repetition of the Khasav-Yurt peace accords. Nor will efforts to impose a peace model made in Moscow on the Chechens bring about the desired results. On the Kremlin's initiative, a referendum was held in February 2003 to adopt a republican constitution and to hold elections under the Russian army's control. Representative bodies of power can be formed with Moscow-loyal Chechens, but doing so will not legitimize the new regime in the eyes of the Chechen population. Instead, it will be necessary to engage all influential members of the Chechen elite to forge a consensus. A key objective is to make the Chechen elite responsible for the republic in the eyes their own people. Determining the nature and forms of future relations between the Russian Federation and Chechnya is a matter for the next stage. In Russia's true interests, the most important thing is to ensure national security. This goal can be attained only in cooperation with *all* Chechens.

Notes

Chapter One

1. Throughout this book we refer to the Chechen conflict as a war, a single phenomenon broken into two phases or campaigns. The "first war" is understood to be the period between 1994–1996. The "second war" began in August 1999 with the invasion of Dagestan.
2. For an excellent compendium of recently declassified Soviet diplomatic documents on the Middle East covering the period between 1947 and 1967, see V. Naumkin et al., *Blizhnevostochy konflikt, iz dokumentov arkhiva vneshney politiki RF, 1947–1967* (Moscow: International Democracy Foundation, 2003).
3. The Ingush-Ossetian conflict in the fall of 1992 was quickly suppressed by federal troops. Before the Chechen war, Russian Federation forces had not fought on its territory.
4. Z. Brzezinski, *The Grand Chessboard* (New York: Basic Books, 1997), p. 123.
5. A. Nikolayev, "Bol'shoy Kavkaz: Strategiya Rossii," *Krasnaya zvezda*, January 5, 2001.

Chapter Two

1. D. Furman, "Samyi trudnyi narod dlya Rossii" [The most troublemaking people for Russia] in *Chechnya i Rossiya: obstchestva i gosudarstva* [Chechnya and Russia: societies and states] (Moscow, 1999), pp. 7–8.
2. Interview with M. Vachagaev, "Ja blagodaren sudbe za etot urok" [I'm grateful to the fate for this lesson], *Nezavisimaya gazeta*, February 19, 2000.

3. *Rossiya i Chechnya (1990–1997): Dokumenty svidetelstvuyut* [Russia and Chechnya (1990–1997): Documents give evidence] (Moscow, 1997), p. 19–20.

4. *Sbornik ukazov prezidenta Chechenskoy respubliki s noyabrya 1991 g. po 30 iyunya 1992 g.* [A collection of decrees by the president of the Chechen republic from November 1991 to June 30, 1992] (Grozny, 1992), p. 4.

5. About the agreement between Moscow and Grozny on the transfer of a part of the Soviet arsenal in the territory of the republic to the Chechens, see chapter 5.

6. See *Sbornik ukazov prezidenta Chechenskoy respubliki s 1 iyulya 1992 g. po 31 dekabrya 1992 g.* [A collection of decrees by the president of the Chechen republic from July 1, 1992, to December 31, 1992] (Grozny, 1993).

7. *Suverenny Tatarstan: Dokumenty. Materialy. Hronika.* [Sovereign Tatarstan: Documents. Materials. Chronicle.] (Moscow, 1998) vol. 1., p. 59.

8. *Chechenskiy krizis* [Chechen crisis] (Moscow: Center for Complex Social Research, 1995), vol. 8, p. 7.

9. A. Lieven, "Voyna v Chechne i upadok Rossiyskogo mogustshestva" [Chechen war and the decries of the Russian power] in *Chechnya i Rossiya: obstchestva i gosudarstva* [Chechnya and Russia: societies and states] (Moscow, 1999), p. 272.

10. V. Bobrovnikov, "Abreki i gosudarstvo: kultura nasiliya na Kavkaze" [Abreki (mountain fighters) and the state: the culture of violence in Caucasus], *Vestnik evrazii*, no. 1, vol. 8, (2000) p. 42.

11. L. Shevtsova, *Regim Borisa Yeltsina* [Boris Yeltsin's regime] (Moscow: Carnegie Moscow Center, 1999), pp. 229–231.

12. Ibid., p. 240.

13. Alexander Lebed was one of the more colorful figures of Russian politics in the mid-to-late 1990s. As commander of the Fourteenth Army in Moldova's Dniester region, he used force to suspend a conflict between Moldova and its breakaway region. Discharged from military service for his independent character, he became a staunch advocate of the restoration of the prestige of the Russian state and its armed forces. His salient feature was surprising flexibility and respect for the enemy on the battlefield, which was demonstrated in his approach to the Chechen war. Elected governor of Krasnoyarsk in Siberia in 1998, he died in a plane crash in 2002.

14. Several versions of Dudayev's death exist. Some attribute it to a brilliant Russian covert operation, others to inter-Chechen fights. It is interesting to note that no senior government official in Russia was given any award after Dudayev's death. The Chechens are telling the legend that Dudayev is alive, but paralyzed in a wheelchair and thus reluctant to meet anyone.

15. *Krasnaya zvezda*, August 14, 1996.

16. M. McFaul and N. Petrov, eds., *Politicheskiy almanah Rossii 1997* [Russia's political almanac] (Moscow: Carnegie Moscow Center, 1998); *Sotsialnopoliticheskie portrety regionov: Kn.1* [Sociopolitical portraits of regions: book 1], p. 304.

17. V. Akaev, "Chechnya: Vozmozhen li afgansky variant?" [Chechnya: is the Afghan variant possible?] in *Centralnaya Asia i Kavkaz* [Central Asia and Caucasus] (Lulea, Sweden, 1999), no. 1, vol. 2, p. 148.

18. A. Saidov, "Tayna vtorzhenya (o nachale voennyh deystviy na Kavkaze v avguste 1999)" [The mystery of the intrusion (about the beginning of the military actions in the North Caucasus in August 1999)] manuscript, p. 80.

19. M. Yusupov, "Politicheskaya neopredelionnost" [Political uncertainty], *Set' etnologicheskogo monitoringa I rannego preduprezhdenya konflictov* [Network for the ethnologic monitoring and conflicts' early prevention] September–October 2000, p. 41.

20. "Aslan Maskhadov Dovolen rezultatami vstrechi s Borisom Yeltsinym," [Aslan Maskhadov is content by the results of meeting with Boris Yeltsin], *Nezavisimaya gazeta*, August 19, 1997.

21. Volsky maintained an attempt on the life of Oleg Lobov, the presidential envoy to Chechnya, was linked to the missing money.

22. A. Arbatov, "Dengi mogut ischeznut' v 'chernoy dyre'" [The money can disappear in a "black hole"], *Izvestia*, March 20, 2001.

23. V. Zmeiushenko, "Chechnya epohi vozrozhdenia" [Chechnya of a renaissance epoch], *Profil*, January 22, 2001.

24. V. Batuev, "Chechne razgoraetsia novy skandal" [A new scandal flame up in Chechnya], *Vremya MN*, May 11, 2001.

25. "Ya ne uydu s etogo posta, esli menya ne vynudyat" [I will not leave this post, only if I wouldn't be forced to], *Kommersant-Vlast*, November 14, 2000, p. 27.

26. Some sources insist Ilyasov was involved in commercial activities while head of Stavropol provincial government, which was a reason for his sacking. The formal reason was ineffective work of his government team. He was later put in charge of an energy company that supplied electricity to Chechnya.

27. V. Baranets, "Voyska uhodiat iz Chechni: chto dalshe?" [The army retired from Chechnya: what's next?], *Komsomolskaya pravda*, February 6, 2001.

28. "Segodnya armiya v Chechne ushla na vtoroy plan, i eto pravilno" [The army in Chechnya retired to the second plan, and it's correct], *Rossiyskaya gazeta*, March 28, 2001.

29. Gazeta.ru, January 19, 2001.

30. I. Maksakov, "Mnozhestvo planov dlya odnoy problemy" [Numerous plans for one problem], *NG-regiony*, February 13, 2001.

Chapter Three

1. According to polls conducted by the Independent Research Center (ROMIR). E. Pain, "Vtoraya chechenskaya voyna i eyo posledstviya" [Second Chechen war and its consequences] in Nikolai Petrov, ed., *Regiony Rossii v 1999 g.: ezhegodnoye prilozhenie k "politicheskomu almanahu Rossii"* [Annual application to the "Russia's political almanac"] (Moscow: Carnegie Moscow Center, 2001), p. 281.

2. E. L. Elbakyan, *S.V. Medvedko, Sotsialny portret sovremennogo rossiyskogo veruyustshego: Obstshye cherty, Zakonodatelstvo o svobode sovesti i pravoprimenitelnaya praktika v sfere ego deyatelnosti* [Social portrait of a modern Russian believer: Common traits] (Moscow, 2001), pp. 164–165.

3. Centr kompleksnykh sotsialnikh issledovaniy i marketinga [General Project Center for complex social research and marketing], "Rossiya v tret'em tysyacheletii" [Russia in a third millennium] (Moscow: Center for Complex Social Research, 1995); Chechenskiy krizis [Chechen crisis], vol. 8, p. 52.

4. *Izvestia,* September 13, 1994.

5. E. I. Bashkirova, "Russia's 1999–2000 Elections in the Light of Public Opinion" in *Russian Presidential Election 2000,* Y. Fedorov and B. Nygren, eds., (Stockholm, 2000), p. 95.

6. *Stavropolskye gubernskye vedomosti,* July 6, 1995.

7. More than 50 percent of Cossacks believed this. T. Tabalina, *Kazaki: drama vozrozhdeniya* [Cossacks: the drama of the renascence] (Moscow, 1999), p. 143.

8. "Pogasit' ogon' vrazhdy na Kavkaze" [To liquidate the flame of an enmity in Caucasus], *Kavkazskaya zdravnitsa* [Kislovodsk], January 18, 1995.

9. *Chechenskaya tragedia* [Chechen tragedy], (Moscow, 1995), vol. 2, p. 111.

10. "Regionalnye vozhdi vozvrastshayutsia" [Regional leaders' return], *Nezavisimaya gazeta,* November 28, 2001.

11. V. Dyatlov, "Kavkaztsy v Irkutske: konfliktogennaya diaspora" [The Caucasians in Irkutsk: a diaspora prompt to conflict] in G. Vitkovskaya and A. Malashenko, eds., *Neterpimost' v Rossii: Starye i novye fobii* [Intolerance in Russia: old and new foes] (Moscow: Carnegie Moscow Center, 1999), p. 113.

12. V. A. Tishkov, *Obstshestvo v vooruzhennom konflikte: Etnografia chechenskoy voyny* [The society in the armed conflict: Ethnographie of the Chechen war] (Moscow: Nauka, 2001), p. 180.

13. V. A. Tishkov, "Itogi starogo I perspektivy novogo desiatiletia" [The results of a past & the perspectives of a new decade] in *Mezhetnicheskie otnoshenia i konflikty v postsovetskih gosudarstvah: Set' etnologicheskogo monitoringa I rannego preduprezhdenia konfliktov, Ezhegodny doklad 1999* [Interethnical relations and

the conflicts in the post-Soviet states, Network of the ethnological monitoring and conflicts' early prevention: Annual report] (Moscow, 2000), p. 12.

14. See for example, such progovernment publications as *Kriminalnyy rezhim: Chechnya* [Criminal regime: Chechnya] (Moscow, 1995) and the *Govorukhin Commission Report* (Moscow, 1995), which provide credible evidence about the plight of the ethnic Russian population.

15. This was the title of an article in the *Moscow News* (February 4–11, 1996) by A. Krutov that talked about a clash in Saratov between Ingush students and local officer cadets.

16. The media routinely report on sometimes blood-chilling crimes perpetrated by Chechen veterans.

17. On the role of Islam, see chapter 1.

18. *Epokha Yeltsina* [Yeltsin's epoch] (Moscow: Vagrius, 2001), p. 591.

19. See Kaziev Sh. Imam Shamil (Moscow, 2001), pp. 227–228.

20. M. Lermontov, *Sobranie sochineniy v 4-kh tomakh* [Collected works in 4 volumes] (Leningrad, 1981), vol. 4. p. 422.

21. Y. Gordin, "Kavkaz: zemlya i gory" [Caucasus: the land and the mountains], *Zvezda*, 2000, p. 335.

22. The historian Yakov Gordin, who maintains that Russia and the Caucasus simply cannot do otherwise than live together, notes that nevertheless, Chechnya presents a very special problem.

23. See for example, S. Turialay, "Russkie rabyni dlya 'voyna islama'" [Russian women slaves for the "Muslim-fighter"], *Komsomolskaya pravda*, November 29, 2001.

24. The bar owner has pasted a notice at the entrance: "To prevent conflict situations from arising, we do not serve people of the Caucasus nationality." Found at http://TCP.rbc.ru on November 29, 2001.

Chapter Four

1. N. F. Bugay, "Sovremennye mezhetnicheskie problemy v Severokavkazskom regione" [The modern interethnic problems in the Russian North Caucasus region] in *Rossiyskoy federatsii problemy naselenia i rynkov truda Rossii i kavkazskogo regiona: Materialy Mezhdunarodnoy nauchnoy konferentsii 14–17 sentyabrya 1998* [The problems of population and labor markets in Russia and the Caucasus region: The Materials of the Scientific Conference, September 14–17, 1998] (Moscow: Stavropol, 1998), p. 97.

2. This issue was much discussed by the founders of the pro-Kremlin "Eurasia" movement, including Talgat Tajuddin, the head of the Central Muslim Administration.

3. H. Jamal, "Bolshie kavkazskie igry Turkskiy mir" [Great Caucasian games], *Turkskiy mir*, 1998, nos. 3–4, p. 18.
4. J. Dudayev and Y. Zarakhovich, "Terms of War and Peace," *Time*, March 4, 1996.
5. See A. Malashenko, *Chto hotiat i chto mogut imenuemye wahhabitami* [What they want and what they can, so called "wahhabits"] in *Islamskie orientiry Severnogo Kavkaza* [Islamic landmarks of the North Caucasus] (Moscow: Carnegie Moscow Center, 2001), ch. 5, pp. 137–164.
6. O. Roy, *L'Echec de l'Islam politique*, (Paris: Du Seuil, 1992), p. 245.
7. M. Brill Olcott and N. Udalova, *Narkotrafik na velikom shelkovom puti: bezopasnost' v Centralnoy Azii* [Drug trafficking on the great silk road: the security environment in Central Asia] (Moscow: Carnegie Moscow Center, 2000), working paper #2, p. 5, available at www.carnegie.ru/en/pubs/workpapers/48568.htm.
8. I. *Rotar, Nezavisimaya gazeta*, September 12, 1998.
9. L. Beres, "Geroinovaya voyna kommersant" [Heroin war], *Kommersant-Vlast*, July 24, 1998.
10. Y. Yegorov, "Trebuetsya zeleniy tsvet" [The green color is needed], *Nezavisimaya gazeta*, July 26, 2000.
11. A. Klochkov, "Wahhabitskiy polumesiats kommersant" [Wahhabi crescent], *Kommersant-Vlast*, August 24, 1999, p. 19.
12. A. Baranov and A. Surikov, "Wahhabity kak kontseptualnaya ugroza" [Wahhabis as the conceptual threat], *Pravda*, February 5, 1998.
13. G. Murklinskaya, "Islamskaya 'voltova duga' Rossii dagestanskaya" [Islamic tension of Russia], *Dagestanskaya Pravda*, August 15, 2000.
14. See S. Kurginian, M. Mamikonian, and M. Podkopaeva, "Chetverty Rim ili vtoraya Orda?" [Fourth Rome or second orda?], *Zavtra*, 1998, no. 3.
15. A classic example is the story of the so-called Kadar zone in Dagestan. Islamic radicals (Wahhabis), once dominant in the villages Karamakhi, Chabanmakhi, and Kadar, were defeated by federal forces in an operation against invading Chechen rebels led by Shamil Basayev. Eyewitness accounts of the fighting in the area are highly controversial.
16. *NG-religia*, April 24, 1997.
17. S. M. Abubakarov, "Ne teriat' veru v budustshee" [Do not lose the faith in future] in *Islam v Rossii: traditsii i perspektivy*, p. 116.
18. A. Dzadziev, "Kongress narodov Chechni i Dagestana" [The Congress of the peoples of Chechnya and Dagestan] in *Set' etnologicheskogo monitoringa i rannego preduprezhdenia konfliktov* [Network of ethnological monitoring and early prevention of conflicts], (June 1998), p. 19.
19. *Hejira* has sacred meaning in Islam. The Prophet Mohammad had to flee from Mecca to Medina, under pressure from the infidels.

20. I. Maksakov, "Estsho odin general stal politikom" [One more general became a politician], *Nezavisimaya gazeta*, December 29, 1998. In June 1997, Alexei Malashenko took part in a roundtable where an attempt was made to form a Muslim union of Russia. General Vladimir Semenov, a Muslim, who was a guest of honor, spoke against the use of religion in politics.

21. I. Dobayev, "Islamskiy radikalizm v kontekste problemy voenno-politicheskoy bezopasnosti na Severnom Kavkaze" [Islamic radicalism in context of a problem of military-political security in the North Caucasus], *Nauchnaya mysl' Kavkaza*, 1999, no. 1, pp. 54–58.

22. Y. Snegiriov, "Jihad podoshel k granitsam" [Jihad approach to the boards of Dagestan], *Dagestana Izvestia*, February 10, 1998.

23. I. Maksakov, "Sootnoshenie islamskih dvizheniy Dagestana" [Correlation of the Islamic movements of Dagestan], *NG-religia*, March 18, 1998.

24. H. Shogenov, "Priverzhentsy wahhabizma nahodiatsia pod kontrolem" [The followers of Wahhabism are under control], *Gazeta Yuga*, June 22, 2000.

25. H. V. Dzutsev and A. I. Pershits, "Wahhabity na Severnom Kavkaze: Religia, politika, sotsialnaya praktika" [Wahhabits in the North Caucasus: Religion, politics, social practice], *Vestnik RAN*, 1998. vol. 68 no. 12, p. 116.

26. Z. Malbahova, "Novye musulmane" [New muslims], *Gazeta Yuga*, April 13, 2000.

27. D. V. Makarov, *Ofitsialny i neofitsialny islam v Dagestane* [Official and unofficial Islam in Dagestan] (Moscow, 2000), p. 30.

28. In that republic, heathen renaissance, rather than the struggle against Wahhabis, is the prime concern.

29. H. Shogenov, "Priverzhentsy wahhabizma nahodiatsia pod kontrolem" [The followers of Wahhabism are under control], *Gazeta Yuga*, June 22, 2000.

30. *Kavkazskaya konfederatsiya* [Caucasian confederation] (Grozny, 1998), no. 6, p. 1.

31. L. Hoperskaya, "S'ezd narodov Ingushetii" [The Congress of the Peoples of Ingushetia] in *Set' etnologicheskogo monitoringa i rannego preduprezhdenia konfliktov* [Network of ethnological monitoring and early prevention of conflicts] (March–April 2001), p. 22.

32. E. Skakunov, "Prigorodny rayon: Uregulirovanie—v ramkah federalnogo tsentra" [Suburbs: Settlement within the frameworks of the federal center], *Nezavisimaya gazeta*, July 31, 1997.

33. R. Abdulatipov, "On the Fundamentals of the State Nationalities Policy of the Russian Federation in the North Caucasus," report submitted at a North Caucasus Regional Conference, (Yessentuki, January 29, 1999).

34. "Itogoviy document Mezhdunarodnoy islamskoy konferentsii 'Rol' musulman v vozrozhdenii Rossii'" [The final document of the international

Islamic conference "Muslims' role in Russia's renascence"], *Religia i pravo,* June 6, 1999, no. 3.

35. A. Malashenko, "Musulmane i gosudarstva ot Kaspiya do Issyk-Kulia" [Muslims and the states from Caspian Sea to Issyk-kul'], *Sodruzhestvo NG,* 1998, no. 6.

36. M. Bondarenko, "Otkuda i ch'ey vy krovy?" [Where are you from and who are you related to?], *NG-regiony,* 1998, no. 16.

37. President Putin's interview with the Malaysian media, broadcast by ORT television on August 4, 2003.

38. K. Polyakov, *Vliyanie vneshnego faktora na radikalizatsiyu islama v Rossii v 90-ye gody XX veka (na primere arabskih stran)* [The influence of the exterior factor on the radicalization of Islam in Russia in 1990 (on the Arabian States' example)], manuscript, (Moscow, 2001), p. 10.

39. See "Propagandistskiy listok 'Islamskoy pomoshi'" [Agitation paper of "Islamic Relief"], *Gazeta Yuga,* July 13, 2000.

40. "Arabskie strany prodolzhayut okazyvat' pomostsh boevikam v Chechne" [Arabian states continue to provide the help to the fighters in Chechnya], *Severniy Kavkaz,* January 2, 2000.

41. K. Polyakov, pp. 17–19.

42. V. Ostrovnoy, "Spisok Shamilia" [Shamil's list], *Moskovsky Komsomolets,* May 24, 2001.

43. "Korol' Fahd pomog chechenskim bezhentsam" [King Fahd helped the Chechen rebels], *Kommersant,* April 21, 2000.

44. E. Lefko and V. Paukov, "'Voiny allaha' vybirayut Kavkaz" ["Allah fighters" choosing Caucasus], *Nezavisimaya gazeta,* August 30, 1999.

45. See O. Blotskiy, "Chechnya: Ohota boevikov-wahhabitov za deputatami" [Chechnya: Fighter-wahhabis' hunt for the deputies], *Rossiya i musulmanskiy mir,* 1999, no. 7 (85).

46. "Obuchalsia v chechenskom lagere" [Trained in the Chechen Camp], *Gazeta Yuga,* August 24, 2000.

47. A. Polyakova, "Wahhabizm v importnoy upakovke" [Wahabism in the import packing], *NG-Stsenarii,* 1998, no. 5.

48. Personal communication, A. Malashenko, 2000.

49. O. Guseynov, "V Chechne voevali dva-tri desiatka grazhdan KBR" [Two, three dozens of KBR citizens fought in Chechnya], *Gazeta Yuga,* July 29, 2000.

50. S. Mel'kov, "Voinstvuyushie musulmane nedostupny ponimaniyu" [Militant Muslims cannot be understood], *Nezavisimoe voennoe obozrenie,* January 16, 1998.

51. V. Voronov, "Djinn na djipe" [Genie on a jeep], *Novoe vremia,* 2000, no. 43 (99), p. 13.

52. E. Krutikov, "Aslan Maskhadov nachal bor'bu s kosmopolitizmom" [Aslan Maskhadov began the fight with the cosmopolitanism], *Segodnia*, July 21, 1998.

53. A. Boroday, "Ichkeria do moria?" [Ichkeria to the sea?], *Zavtra*, 1999, no. 33, p. 298.

54. S. A. Mel'kov, *Transformatsiya voennoy politiki Rossii pod vliyaniem islamskogo faktora* [Transformation of Russia's military policy under the influence of the Islamic factor], manuscript, (Moscow, 2001), p. 21.

55. *Svobodnaya Gruziya* (Tbilisi), November 5, 1999.

56. A. Koychev, "Faktor religii v Ferganskoy doline" [Religion Factor in Fergana valley], *Tsentral'naya Aziya: politika i ekonomika* (Almaty), January 2001, no. 1, p. 29.

57. A. Klochkov, "Wahhabitskiy polumesiats" [Wahhabit crescent], *Kommersant-Vlast*, August 24, 1999.

58. G. Murklinskaya, "Islamskaya 'voltova duga' Rossii dagestanskaya" [Islamic tension of Russia], *Dagestanskaya Pravda*, August 15, 2000.

59. A. Gadjizade, "Otnosheniya s Tegeranom obostryayutsia" [The relations with Tegheran become sharp], *Nezavisimaya gazeta*, May 4, 2001.

60. T. Ansari, "Bin Laden razvorachivaet reklamnuyu kompaniyu," [Bin Laden open the publicity campaign], *Ekho* [Baku], June 30, 2001.

Chapter Five

1. The Chechen wars were the subject of several studies, including: N. N. Novichkov, V. Y. Snegovsky, A. G. Sokolov, and V. Y. Shvarev, *Russian Armed Forces in the Chechen Conflict: Analysis, Results, Conclusions* (Paris: Kholveg; Infoglobe; Trivola, 1995).

2. The Russian military prefers to talk of military-civilian relations.

3. Nevertheless, General Troshev insists in his memoirs that as early as October 1994, the Northern Caucasus Command knew about the impending campaign in Chechnya. See G. Troshev, *Moya voyna* [My War: One General's Chechen Diary] (Moscow: Vagrius, 2001), p. 9.

4. B. Yeltsin, *Prezidentskii marafon* [Presidential marathon] (Moscow: AST, 2000), p. 68.

5. Y. Primakov, *Vosem' mesiatsev plus* [Eight months plus] (Moscow, 2001), p. 93.

6. *Nezavisimoe voennoe obozrenie*, 1997, no. 6, p. 4.

7. *Rossiya (SSSR) v lokal'nih voynah* [Russia (USSR) in a local conflict] (Moscow: Kuchkovo pole; Poligrafresursy, 2000), p. 423.

8. G. Troshev, "Preludiya vtoroy chechenskoy voyny" [Prelude of the second Chechen war], *Nezavisimoe voennoe obozrenie*, August 24–30, 2001.
9. On the lessons of the Kosovo crisis, see A. Arbatov, *Transformation of the Russian Military Doctrine: The Lessons of Kosovo and Chechnya* (Garmisch-Partenkirchen: George C. Marshall Center for European Security Studies, 1999).
10. *Istoriya voennoy strategii Rossii* [The history of Russia's military strategy], V. A. Zolotariova, ed. (Moscow: Kuchkovo pole; Poligrafresursy, 2000), p. 497.
11. See P. Buwalda, J. Goodby, and D. Trenin, *Stable Peace* (Washington, D.C.: U.S. Institution of Peace, 2002).
12. As noted by Alexei Arbatov, the Kosovo conflict revived the discussion within the Russian government of a potential military conflict with NATO, which had died down in the 1980s.
13. *Voennaya doktrina Rossiyskoy Federatsii (2000 g.)* [The military doctrine of the Russian Federation (2000)].
14. A. F. Klimenko, "Osobennosti novoy voennoy doktriny" [The peculiarity of the new military doctrine], *Voennaya mysl'*, 2000, no. 3, p. 23.
15. This was also literally true. The Russian forces storming Grozny on New Year's Day 1995 had not been issued city plans.
16. S. Ivanov, "Voennaya reforma kak neobhodimaya chast' preobrazovaniy v Rossii" [The Military reform as a necessary part of Russia's transformations], *Krasnaya zvezda*, April 25, 2001.
17. Found at www.strana.ru/stories/01/08/29/1424/news.html.
18. Lieutenant General William Odom, until 1988 the head of the U.S. National Security Agency, has said no one had expected the Communist Party and the Soviet army generals simply to march toward the end of the Soviet Union. See W. E. Odom, *The Collapse of the Soviet Military* (New Haven: Yale University Press, 1998), p. ix.
19. B. Yeltsin, *Prezidentskii marafon* [Presidential marathon] (Moscow: AST, 2000), p. 369.
20. "The Defense Minister's New Year's Eve address," *Krasnaya zvezda*, December 30, 2000.
21. *Ot pervogo litsa: Razgovory s Vladimirom Putinym* [In the first person: Conversations with Vladimir Putin] (Moscow: Vagrius, 2000), p. 135.
22. V. A. Zolotariov, "Predislovie" [Foreword] in *Rossiya (SSSR) v lokal'nih voynah* [Russia (USSR) in a local conflict] (Moscow: Kuchkovo pole; Poligrafresursy, 2000), p. 10.
23. M. A. Gareyev, "Nekotorye problemy podgotovki Vooruzhennih Sil k lokal'nym voynam" [Some problems with the army's preparation for local conflicts], *Voennaya mysl'*, 2000, no. 1, p. 19.
24. V. A. Vahrushev, "Lokal'nye voyny i vooruzhennye konflikty: Kharakter i vliyanie na voennoe iskusstvo" [Local wars and armed conflicts: the char-

acter and the influence on the military art], *Voennaya mysl'*, 1999, no. 4, pp. 20–28.

25. Interview with M. Peshkov, *Krasnaya zvezda*, February 21, 2001.
26. *Rossiya (SSSR) v lokal'nih voynah* [Russia (USSR) in a local conflict], p. 320; *Gruppirovka Zavtra*, 1999, no. 1.
27. *Krasnaya zvezda*, August 7, 1996.
28. Ibid., February 6, 2001.
29. The Ministry of Defense put the number of rebel fighters in the fall of 2000 at 2,000; the FSB estimated the number in the beginning of 2001 at 5,000.
30. The lower range (300–600) was cited by the head of the border guards, General Konstantin Totskii; the higher range (2,000–7,000) to IDU's Tahir Yuldashev. See *Krasnaya zvezda*, March 3, 2001.
31. *Krasnaya zvezda*, September 14, 2000.
32. "Interview of the Ambassador A. Nanaev," *Nezavisimaya gazeta*, August 31, 2000.
33. M. Khodarenok, "Kto vladeet Groznym?" [Who controls Grozny?] *Nezavisimaya gazeta*, March 6, 2001.
34. See interview with Troshev, *Krasnaya zvezda*, January 10, 2001.
35. *Krasnaya zvezda*, September 14, 2000.
36. A. Tsyganov, "FSB gotova poymat' Maskhadova i Basaeva" [FSB is ready to catch Maskhadov and Basaev], *Kommersant*, April 19, 2001.
37. See for example, V. A. Vinogradov, "Kharakternye cherty sovremennyh obshevoyskovyh operatsiy" [The Features of the modern common to all arms operations], *Voennaya mysl'*, 2001, no. 1, pp. 23–26.
38. V. A. Zolotariov, "Krugly stol aontrterroristicheskaya operatsiya na Severnom Kavkaze: Osnovnye uroki i vyvody" [The round table antiterroristic operation in the North Caucasus: general lessons and conclusions], *Voennaya mysl'*, 2000, no. 3, p. 16.
39. *Nezavisimoe voennoe obozrenie*, November 18, 1995.
40. Y. D. Bukreev, "Krugly stol aontrterroristicheskaya operatsiya na Severnom Kavkaze: Osnovnye uroki i vyvody" [The round table antiterroristic operation in the North Caucasus: general lessons and conclusions], *Voennaya mysl'*, 2000, no. 3, pp. 5–10.
41. *Rossiya (SSSR) v lokal'nih voynah* [Russia (USSR) in a local conflict] (Moscow: Kuchkovo pole; Poligrafresursy, 2000), pp. 24–26.
42. I. N. Vorobyov, "Taktika boevyh grupp" [Battle groups tactics], *Voennaya mysl'*, 2001, no. 1, pp. 27–30.
43. A. B. Krasnov, "Nekotorye podhody k organizatsii I provedeniyu kontrterroristicheskih operatsiy" [Some approaches to the organization and conduction of the antiterroristic operations], *Voennaya mysl'*, 2000, no. 6, pp. 49–52.

44. See for example, E. Pain, "Vtoraya chechenskaya voyna i eyo posledstviya" [Second Chechen war and its consequences] in N. Petrov, ed., *Regiony Rossii v 1999 g.: ezhegodnoye prilozhenie k "politicheskomu almanahu Rossii"* [Annual application to "Russia's political almanac"] (Moscow: Carnegie Moscow Center, 2001), p. 280–294.

45. Sergei Rogov, director of the Institute for the USA and Canada Studies, for example.

46. The Chechens received 108 tanks, 51 aircraft, 153 artillery pieces, and 600 antitank missiles. Cf. Y. Primakov, p. 91.

47. *Nezavisimoe voennoe obozrenie*, 2001, no. 26, p. 2.

48. S. Mamayev, "Dve s polovinoy voyny" [Two and a half wars], *Expert*, April 23, no. 16, pp. 13–14.

49. *The Military Balance 2000–2001* (Oxford: Oxford University Press, 2000), p. 126.

50. *Rossiya (SSSR) v lokal'nih voynah* [Russia (USSR) in a local conflict], (Moscow: Kuchkovo pole; Poligrafresursy, 2000), p. 241.

51. M. Brill Olcott and N. Udalova, *Narkotrafik na velikom shelkovom puti: bezopasnost' v Centralnoy Azii* [Drug trafficking on the great silk road: the security environment in Central Asia] (Moscow: Carnegie Moscow Center, 2000), working paper #2, p. 5, available at www.carnegie.ru/en/pubs/workpapers/48568.htm.

52. N. Plotnikov, "Evropeyskiy voenniy desant na tajiksko-afganskoy granites" [European military landing on the Tajik-Afgan border], *Nezavisimaya gazeta*, April 27, 2001.

53. "Razgovor u 'zolotogo kostra'" [Conversation at the "golden bonfire"] *Krasnaya zvezda*, April 13, 2001.

54. *Voennaya doktrina Rossiyskoy Federatsii (2000 g.)* [The military doctrine of the Russian Federation (2000)].

55. *Rossiya (SSSR) v lokal'nih voynah* [Russia (USSR) in a local conflict], (Moscow: Kuchkovo pole; Poligrafresursy, 2000), p. 423.

56. Interview to NTV program "Segodnia," May 29, 2001.

57. General Troshev said that no new military hardware was received by the North Caucasus district in the 1990s. See *Krasnaya zvezda*, January 10, 2001.

58. Colonel General Zolotov, the commandant of the Land Forces Academy, noted that the rebels had far more effective small arms than had the federal forces. See *Military Thought*, 2000, no. 3, p. 17.

59. M. A. Gareyev, "Nekotorye problemy podgotovki Vooruzhennih Sil k lokal'nym voynam" [Some problems with the army's preparation for local conflicts], *Voennaya mysl'*, 2000, no. 1, p. 21.

60. General Sitnov put the military's requirements at 300–350 tanks, 400–450 armored infantry fighting vehicles (AIFVs), 250–300 SP artillery pieces, 1,500

other artillery pieces, 150–200 aircraft, 50–70 helicopters, and 5–7 air defense complexes. See *Krasnaya zvezda*, June 10, 2000.

61. *Krasnaya zvezda*, February 2, 2001.
62. Y. Gordin, "Kavkaz: zemlia i gory" [Caucasus: the land and the mountains], *Zvezda*, 2000, p. 142.
63. Y. Khristinin, "Finansovye granitsy" [Financial frontiers], *Severny Kavkaz*, November 2000, no. 41, p. 7.
64. O. D. Muliava and E. G. Vapilin, "Sotsialnye problemy voennogo obrazovaniya" [Social problems of the military education], *Voennaya mysl'*, 2001, no. 1, pp. 48–51.
65. T. Gantimurova, "'Kosoy' prizyv" ["Moved" draft] *Severny Kavkaz*, November 2000, no. 42.
66. A. Boroday, *Gruppirovka Zavtra*.
67. V. I. Lutovinov, "Patriotizm i ego formirovanie v obshestve i vooruzhennyh silah" [Patriotism and its forming in the society and armed forces], *Voennaya mysl'*, 1999, no. 4, pp. 62–70.
68. B. Yeltsin, *Prezidentskii marafon* [Presidential marathon] (Moscow: AST, 2000), p. 373.
69. Compare for example, the oral address by the Patriarch Alexy in Savior Cathedral to President Putin, who had just returned from Chechnya (Easter 2001).
70. M. Khodarenok, "Na grani razlozheniya" [On the edge of decay], *Nezavisimoe voennoe obozrenie*, 2001, no. 37, p. 8.
71. S. Mamayev, "Dve s polovinoy voyny" [Two and a half wars], *Expert*, April 23, no. 16.
72. "Stenogramma vstrechi rossiyskih 'silovikov' s glavnymi redaktorami gazet" [Shorthand record of the discussion of the Russian militants' meeting with the newspaper's editor-in-chiefs], *Komsomolskaya pravda*, May 17, 2001.
73. Interview with V. Kalamanov, *Segodnia*, 2001.
74. As reported by Serrgey Yastrzhembski, *Moscow Times*, January 4, 2001.
75. *Los Angeles Times*, December 31, 2000.
76. *Kommersant*, March 1, 2001.
77. G. Troshev, *Moya voyna* [My War: One General's Chechen Diary] (Moscow: Vagrius, 2001), p. 76.
78. See M. Fatullaev, "Dagestan: lhizn' vzaymy" [Dagestan: life in debt], *NG-regiony*, March 2001; and J. Daniszewski, "Grozny Digs for Oil in Backyards, Basements," *Moscow Times*, March 13, 2001.
79. M. Sokolov, "Bez vesti predannye" [Missing in loyalty], *Vne zakona*, April 16, 2001.
80. *Krasnaya zvezda*, June 6, 2001. Vladimir Lukin, vice speaker of the Duma, said that "1,500 men" represent just the tip of the iceberg.

81. T. Mikhailova, "Plennyh ne brat'" [Take no prisoners], *Severnyi Kavkaz*, January 2000, no. 2, p. 6.

82. S. Mamayev, "Dve s polovinoy voyny" [Two and a half wars], *Expert*, April 23, no. 16, p. 16.

83. Chechnya I sostoyanie rossiyskoy armii [Chechnya and the State of the Russian Army], available at www.mfit.ru/defensive/vestnik/vestnik6_1.html.

84. G. Troshev, *Moya voyna* [My War: One General's Chechen Diary] (Moscow: Vagrius, 2001), p. 331.

85. *Rossiya (SSSR) v lokal'nih voynah* [Russia (USSR) in a local conflict], (Moscow: Kuchkovo pole; Poligrafresursy, 2000), p. 321.

86. Ibid., p. 322.

87. Ibid.

88. V. Govorov, "Patriotizm: tsennost' neprehodiashiaya: Otkrytoe pis'mo Rossiyskogo komiteta veteranov voyny i voennoy sluzhby" [Patriotism: the lasting value: public letter of the Russian war and military service veterans' committee], *Krasnaya zvezda*, March 2, 2001.

89. Ibid.

90. Compare Putin's comments on Boris Nemtsov's peace plan and General Troshev's interview with ORT TV, September 8 and 9, 2001, respectively.

91. V. Manilov, "Army, Law, Humanism," *Krasnaya zvezda*, February 3, 2001.

92. The state program of patriotic upbringing, approved by the Russian government on February 16, 2001.

93. S. Saradzyan, "Teaching Russians to Be Patriots," *Moscow Times*, March 2001.

94. V. Azarov and V. Marustshenko, "Kavkaz v sostave Rossii" [Caucasus in the structure of Russia], *Krasnaya zvezda* (January 19, 2001).

95. Colonel General Boris Gromov, the last Soviet commander in Afghanistan, was subsequently deputy interior minister, a vice presidential candidate, Duma deputy, and since 2000 the governor of the Moscow region. Pavel Grachev, a division commander in Afghanistan, was promoted to commander of the airborne forces and then became the defense minister from 1992 to 1996. Alexander Rutskoi was the vice president of Russia from 1991 to 1993, the leader of a parliamentary revolt, a prisoner, and later the governor of the Kursk region (1996–2000). Alexander Lebed, the commander of the Fourteenth Army in the Trans-Dniester region, was a candidate for the presidency (1996), the secretary of the federation's Security Council (1996), and the governor of Krasnoyarsk (1997–2002).

96. B. Yeltsin, *Prezidentskii marafon* [Presidential marathon], (Moscow: AKT, 2000), p. 62.

97. G. Troshev, *Moya voyna* [My war: one general's Chechen diary] (Moscow: Vagrius, 2001), p. 67.

98. *Severnyl Kavkaz*, August 2000, no. 30, p. 8.

99. A. Golts, and D. Pinsker, "Voyna nevyuchennyh urokov" [The war of un-learned lessons], *Itogi*, October 19, 1999, p. 16.

100. B. Yeltsin, *Prezidentskii marafon* [Presidential marathon], (Moscow: AKT, 2000), p. 369.

101. As reported by VTsIOM in early 2001, 37 percent of Russians believed there was a threat of attack; 38 percent believed the threat was unlikely, and 8 percent did not believe it existed at all.

102. As reported by FOM, in February 1998, 43 percent of respondents believed the armed forces to be incapable of assuring national security. By May 2000 the proportion of skeptics decreased tenfold, and 31 percent believed that the military did offer protection, available at http://vvp.ru (accessed April 3, 2001).

103. From 29 percent to 49 percent and from 55 percent to 40 percent, respectively.

104. V. Markushin, "Vozvrashenie k evolutsii" [Return to evolution], *Krasnaya zvezda*, March 22, 2001.

105. "Kosovo I kontrol' nad Vooruzhennymi Silami" [Kosovo and the control under the Armed Forces], *Vestnik/Mezhregional'nyi fond informatsionnyh tehnologiy* [Bulletin/Interregional Foundation for Informational Technologies], 2000, no. 5.

106. *Rossiya (SSSR) v lokal'nih voynah* [Russia (USSR) in a local conflict], (Moscow: Kuchkovo pole; Poligrafresursy, 2000), p. 219.

107. N. N. Radaev, "Pokazateli riska i upravlenie bezopasnostyu voennosluzhashih" [Risk indices and servicemen's security management], *Voennaya mysl'*, 1999, no. 4, pp. 48–56.

108. "Govorit Maskhadov" [Maskhadov talk], *Kommersant*, November 1, 2000.

109. M. Kozyrev, "Togda schitat' my stali rany" [And then we counted up our wounds], *Kommersant*, August 4, 2000.

110. *Rossiya (SSSR) v lokal'nih voynah* [Russia (USSR) in a local conflict], (Moscow: Kuchkovo pole; Poligrafresursy, 2000), p. 401.

111. N. N. Radaev, "Tsena zhizni i sotsial'no ekonomicheskie kompensatsii" [Price of life and the socioeconomical compensations], *Voennaya mysl'*, 2001, no. 1, pp. 44–47.

112. L. Shevtsova, *Regim Borisa Yeltsina* [Boris Yeltsin's regime] (Moscow: Carnegie Moscow Center, 1999), p. 185.

113. *The Military Balance 1996–1997*, (Oxford: Oxford University Press, 2000), p. 109.

114. V. Mukomel, "Vooruzhennye mezhnatsional'nye i regional'nye konflikty: ludskie poteri, ekonomicheskiy usherb i sotsial'nie posledstviya" [International regional armed conflicts: human losses, economical damage and

social consequences], in : A. Malashenko, M. Brill Olcott, S. Statey, and V. Tishkova, eds., *Identichnost' i konflikt v postsovetskih gosudarstvah* (Moscow: Carnegie Moscow Center, 1997), p. 311.

115. I. Ivanyuk, "Budget 2001: na volne optimizma" [Budget 2001: on a wave of optimism], *Krasnaya zvezda*, February 2, 2001.

116. V. Georgiev, "330 mln. doll. na bor'bu s chechenskimi boevikami" [$330 million for the struggle against Chechen fighters], *Nezavisimoe voennoe obozrenie*, 2001, no. 26, p. 2.

117. A. Arbatov and P. Romashkin, "Kakie voyny Rossii po karmanu?" [What kind of wars Russia is able to pay for?], *Nezavisimoe voennoe obozrenie*, 2001, no. 15, p. 3.

118. V. Solovyov, "Vmeste protiv terrorizma" [Together against terrorism], *Nezavisimaya gazeta*, April 25, 2001.

119. "Putin's remarks at a meeting with CIS defense ministers," *Krasnaya zvezda*, November 23, 2001.

120. R. Stershnev, "Chuvstvo loktia" [Feeling of comradeship], *Krasnaya zvezda*, April 11, 2001.

121. V. V. Panfilova, "Ogne protivostoyaniya" [In a flame of resistance], *Sodruzhestvo NG*, February 28, 2001, no. 2.

122. *Krasnaya zvezda*, November 23, 2001.

123. Interview with S. Khayrulloyev, *Krasnaya zvezda*, February 22, 2001.

124. The Taliban reached the CIS border in early 2001 but made no attempt to cross it.

125. *Rossiya (SSSR) v lokal'nih voynah* [Russia (USSR) in a local conflict] (Moscow: Kuchkovo pole; Poligrafresursy, 2000), p. 220.

Chapter Six

1. Interview with M. Peshkov, "Chto nas dergit v tsentral'noy Azii" [What's holding us in Central Asia], *Krasnaya zvezda*, February 21, 2001.

2. I. Ivanov, Vneshniaya politika Rossii na sovremennom etape [Russia's foreign policy on a present phase], speech at the RAMI First Congress, April 20, 2001, doc. DIP MID RF #707-20-04-2001, p. 6.

3. Y. Primakov, *Vosem' mesiatsev plus* [Eight months plus] (Moscow, 2001), p. 107.

4. F. Stashevsky, "Tbilisi svoy vybor sdelal" [Tbilisi made its choice], *Nezavisimaya gazeta*, May 31, 2001.

5. About the situation on the Russia-Kazakhstan border, see D. Sokolov, "MitrichRubezh incognito"[Boundary incognito], *Izvestia*, July 11, 2001.

6. A. Nikolayev.

7. F. Stashevsky.
8. A. Malashenko, Postsovetskie gosudarstva Yuga i interesy Rossii" [Post-Soviet states of the south and Russia's interests], *Pro et Contra,* Summer 2000, vol. 5 (3), p. 43.
9. V. Tsereteli, "Rossiya i Gruziya: Post-sovetsky razvod" [Russia and Georgia: the post-Soviet divorce], *Central Asia and the Caucasus,* 2001, 3, p. 135–145.
10. See for example, the interview with Tengiz Kitowani, former defense minister of Georgia, *Nezavisimaya gazeta,* August 28, 2001.
11. *Krasnaya zvezda,* January 4, 2001.
12. A. Nikolayev.
13. Z. Mirzoev, "Paradoxy bezopasnosti" [Security paradoxes], *Biznes i politika* [Dushanbe], September 22, 2000; Z. Mirzoev, "Tezisy bezopasnosti" [The points on security], *Biznes i politika* [Dushanbe], February 9, 2000.
14. Constant U.S. dollars, SIPRI data.
15. Interview with M. Peshkov, *Krasnaya zvezda,* February 21, 2001.
16. D. Malysheva, "Konflikty u yuzhnyh rubezhey Rossii" [The conflicts on Russia's southern borders], *Pro & Contra,* Summer 2000, vol. 5(3), p. 17.
17. During the civil war, Tajikistan, subsidized by Moscow, was the only CIS state where old Soviet rubles continued to circulate.
18. Including the noted researcher and philosopher Sergei Panarin, writing in *Pro et Contra,* Summer 2000, vol. 5(3), pp. 118–140.
19. After an explosion in a Moscow underpass in August 2000, a top city official stated Moscow was the capital of a state at war. Later, it was proved the blast had nothing to do with the Chechens.
20. I. Kon, "Postignet li russkih sud'ba mogikan?" [Will Mohican's destiny comprehend Russians?], *Krasnaya zvezda,* February 21, 2001.
21. V. A. Zolotariov, "Predislovie" [Foreword] in *Rossiya (SSSR) v lokal'nih voynah* [Russia (USSR) in a local conflict] (Moscow: Kuchkovo pole; Poligrafresursy, 2000), p. 8.
22. *Kontseptsiya obespecheniya bezopasnosti i voennoy doktriny Rossiyskoy Federatsii (1992 g.)* [The concept of the security providing and the military doctrine of the Russian federation (1992)], project of Russian MFA, point VI.6.
23. A. Svaranets, "Neft' I gaz Kaspiya v geostrategii Soedinennyh Shtatov Ameriki" [Caspian oil and gas in the geostrategy of United States of America], *Nezavisimaya gazeta,* December 11, 1998.
24. O. Nikushkina and A. Sborov, "Terrorizm s chelovecheskim litsom" [Terrorism with a human face], *Kommersant,* April 24, 2001.
25. "Rossiya i antiterroristicheskaya operatsiya Soedinionnyh Shtatov Ameriki: Stenogramma interviju Prezidenta Putina shef-korrespondentam amerikanskih sredstv massovoy informatsii" [Russia and the antiterroristic

operation of the United States of America: shorthand record of the inter-view of the president Putin to the editor-in-chiefs of the American mass media], *Kommersant*, November 12, 2001.

26. E. Petrov, "Ankary konchilos' terpenie" [Ankara lost its patience], *Nezavisimaya gazeta*, November 29, 2001.

27. *Krasnaya zvezda*, December 28, 2001.

28. A. Nikolayev. See also O. Falichev, "Vostochniy vector prioritetov Rossii" [East vector of Russia's priorities], *Krasnaya zvezda*, January 4, 2001.

29. B. Shaffer, "Washington Cannot Stop Russian Nuclear Deal with Tehran," *International Herald Tribune*, December 28, 2000.

30. *Nezavisimaya gazeta*, September 2, 1997.

31. *Dipkur'er NG*, February 17, 2000.

32. "Moskva stanet musulmanskim gorodom" [Moscow becomes a Muslim's city: Abu Khamza's interview with Elena Suponina], *Vremya MN*, November 15, 1999.

33. There were suggestions that the Taliban was ready to stop aiding the Chechens if Russia stopped supporting Massoud.

34. "Poydet li vprok afganskiy urok?" [What will Afghan's lesson be for the future?] *Novoe delo (Makhachkala)*, January 1, 2000.

35. Primakov, p. 97.

36. E. Suponina, "Grazhdanin mira" [The cosmopolite], *Vremya MN*, September 2, 1999.

37. "Iranian foreign minister says no to mediation in Chechnya," BBC World-wide Monitoring, December 5, 1999.

38. A. Borisov, "Voyna v Chechne i islamskiy mir" [The Chechen war and the Muslim's world], *Blizhniy Vostok i sovremennost'*, 2001, no. 10, p. 65. Note that the estimates cited are much too high.

39. V. Putin's Interview to the U.S. mass media, *Kommersant*, November 12, 2001.

40. Y. Primakov, p. 107.

41. M. Fal'kov, "Na puti k moskovskomu khalifatu" [On a way toward the Moscow's khalifat], *Nezavisimoe voennoe obozrenie*, 2001, no. 16.

42. G. Troshev, pp. 348–349.

43. Fal'kov.

44. B. Yeltsin, *Prezidentskii marafon* [Presidential marathon] (Moscow: AKT, 2000), p. 377.

45. Ibid., p. 378.

46. *Rossiya (SSSR) v lokal'nih voynah* [Russia (USSR) in a local conflict], (Moscow: Kuchkovo pole; Poligrafresursy, 2000), p. 321.

47. N. Danilevskiy, *Rossiya i Evropa: Vzgliad na kul'turnye i politicheskie otnosheniya slavianskogo mira k romano-germanskomu*, [Russia and Europe: the look at the

cultural and political relations between Slavic and Romano-German world, 6th ed.], (St. Petersburg: Glagol, 1995), p. 37.

48. V. Denisov, "Ustanovit' sud'bu kazhdogo" [To adjust everyone's fate], *Krasnaya zvezda*, June 6, 2001.

49. *Kontseptsiya vneshney politiki Rossiyskoy Federatsii (2000 g.)* [The concept of the foreign policy of the Russian Federation (2000 ed.)], part 4.

50. Interview with V. Kalamanov, *Segodnia*, April 9, 2001.

51. Russian military officers privately expressed fears that Chechnya could be used by the United States as a pretext for launching a peace enforcement operation in the Caucasus.

52. Z. Brzezinski, p. 119.

53. M. Kurbanaliev, "Terrorizm: Eto sovsem blizko" [Terrorism: it is quite near], *Novoe delo* (Makhachkala), no. 40 (October 6, 2000).

54. I. Bulavinov, "Vtoroy front marshala Sergeeva" [The second front of marshal Sergeev], *Kommersant*, November 13, 1999.

55. M. Gafarly, "Ugroza bezopasnosti tsentral'no-aziatskih respublik i Rossii" [The threat for the security of the Central Asian republics and Russia], *Nezavisimaya gazeta*, February 5, 1999.

56. A. Dugin, "Evraziystvo: Ot filosofii k politike" [Eurasism: from the philosophy to the politics], *Nezavisimaya gazeta*, May 30, 2001.

57. A. Dugin, *Osnovy geopolitiki* [The principles of geopolicy] (Moscow: Arktogeya, 1997), pp. 238–242.

58. M. Shakkum, "Budet li Chechnya upravliat' Rossiey?" [Will Chechnya manage Russia?], *Nezavisimaya gazeta*, April 6, 1998.

59. M. Gareev, "Naprasno li srazhalis' geroi Afganskoy revolutsii?" [Was the Afghan revolution's heroes' fight in vain?], *Krasnaya zvezda,* January 11, 2001.

60. Z. Mirzoev, "Paradoxy bezopasnosti" [Security paradoxes], *Biznes i politika* [Dushanbe], September 22, 2000.

61. V. Mikhailov, "Kapriznye deti islamskoy revolutsii" [Capricious children of the Islamic revolution], *Vlast*, July 20, 1999, pp. 35–36.

62. General Tommy Franks's statement before the U.S. House of Representatives, March 28, 2001.

63. A. Nikolayev.

64. S. N. Konovalov, V. V. Yudin, "Traditsionniy smysl poniatiya "voyna" ustarel" [The traditional sense of the notion "the war" became obsolete], *Voennaya mysl'*, 2001, no. 1, pp. 53–57.

65. R. McFarlane, "Fueling a Revival," *Moscow Times,* April 11, 2001

66. R. Menon, "After Empire: Russia and the Southern 'Near Abroads,'" *The New Russian Foreign Policy*, (New York: 1998).

67. President Putin's televised address, September 24, 2001.

68. V. Putin's interview to the American mass media, *Kommersant*, November 12, 2001.

Chapter Seven

An earlier version of this chapter appeared in *East European Constitutional Review*, vol. 10, no.2/3 (spring/summer 2001).

1. *Human Rights Watch*, February 2002, vol. 14, no. 2.

Index

About the Authors

Dmitri V. Trenin is a senior associate and director of studies at the Carnegie Moscow Center. He retired from the Russian army after a military career that included participation in the Geneva strategic arms control negotiations and teaching at Russia's Military Institute. Trenin was the first Russian officer to be selected for the NATO Defense College and is a member of the International Institute of Strategic Studies. He holds a doctorate from the Institute for the U.S.A. and Canada Studies (1984), and he was a senior fellow at the Institute of Europe (1993–1997). He is the author of numerous articles and books on Russian security issues, including *The End of Eurasia: Russia on the Border Between Geopolitics and Globalization* (Carnegie Endowment, 2002).

Aleksei V. Malashenko cochairs Carnegie's Ethnicity and Nation-Building Project and is a leading expert on the role of Islam in Russia and the CIS. He is also a professor at the State Institute (University) for International Relations. He is a member of the editorial board of the journals *Central Asia and Caucasus* (Sweden), *Eurasian Studies* (Russia), and *Russia and Muslim Countries* (Russia). From 1986 to 1999 he was the head of religious studies at the Institute of Oriental Studies of the Russian Academy of Science.

Malashenko is the author of ten books and more than one hundred academic articles, as well as a frequent contributor to the Jamestown Foundation's reports on the Soviet Union. His articles are published in leading Russian newspapers. He received a doctorate from Moscow State University's Institute of Asian and African Countries.

Anatol Lieven is a senior associate for foreign and security policy at the Carnegie Endowment, currently studying the war against terrorism and underlying patterns in U.S. foreign and security policy. He previously worked at the International Institute for Strategic Studies in London.

Among his books are *Ambivalent Neighbors: The EU, NATO and the Price of Membership* (ed. with Dmitri Trenin); *Chechnya: Tombstone of Russian Power*; and *The Baltic Revolution: Estonia, Latvia, Lithuania, and the Path to Independence*. The last two are largely based on his work as a correspondent for the *Times* (London) in the former Soviet Union from 1990 to 1996. Before that, he was a correspondent for the *Times* in Pakistan, and covered the Afghan war from the side of the anti-Soviet mujahideen. He is also the author of Carnegie Endowment policy briefs *Fighting Terrorism: Lessons from the Cold War*, and *Rebuilding Afghanistan: Fantasy versus Reality*.